The Sex Lives of Saints

DIVINATIONS: REREADING LATE ANCIENT RELIGION

Series Editors

Daniel Boyarin
Virginia Burrus
Charlotte Fonrobert
Robert Gregg

A complete list of books in the series is available from the publisher.

The Sex Lives of Saints

An Erotics of Ancient Hagiography

Virginia Burrus

PENN

University of Pennsylvania Press
Philadelphia

Copyright © 2004 University of Pennsylvania Press
All rights reserved
Printed in the United States of America on acid-free paper

10 9 8 7 6 5 4 3 2 1

First paperback edition 2008

Published by
University of Pennsylvania Press
Philadelphia, Pennsylvania 19104-4011

Library of Congress Cataloging-in-Publication Data

Burrus, Virginia.
   The sex lives of saints : an erotics of ancient hagiography / Virginia Burrus.
     p. cm. (Divinations : Rereading Late Ancient Religion)
   ISBN-978-0-8122-2020-9 (pbk. : alk. paper)
   Includes bibliographical references (p.) and index.
   1. Sex—Religious aspects—Christianity—History of doctrines. 2. Christian hagiography—History. I. Title. II. Series
BT708 .B885   2004
261.8´357—dc21   2003053338

Contents

Introduction: Hagiography and the History of Sexuality   1

Chapter 1. Fancying Hermits: Sublimation and the Arts of Romance   19

    The Queer Life of Paul the Hermit   24
    The Queer Marriage of Malchus the Monk   33
    Hilarion's Last Laugh   39
    Prolongations: Fantasies of a Faun   46
    Reading (as) Another, Woman   49

Chapter 2. Dying for a Life: Martyrdom, Masochism, and Female (Auto)Biography   53

    Praising Paula   60
    Remembering Macrina   69
    Confessing Monica   76
    Testimony to (Woman's) Survival   86
    Fragments of an Autobiography   88

Chapter 3. Hybrid Desire: Empire, Sadism, and the Soldier Saint   91

    Domination and Submission in the Life of Martin   94
    Sulpicius's Passion   103
    The Hagiographer, the Ethnographer, and the Native   109
    Witnessing Ambivalence   122

Chapter 4. Secrets of Seduction: The Lives of Holy Harlots   128

    The Lamb, the Wolf, and the Fool: Mary, Niece of Abraham   132
    Seduction of the Eye: Pelagia of Antioch   137
    Sacrifice in the Desert: Mary of Egypt   147
    The Joy of Harlotry   155

Postscript (Catching My Breath)   160

Notes 163

Bibliography 199

Index 209

Acknowledgments 215

Introduction: Hagiography and the History of Sexuality

Erotic experience is possibly close to sanctity.
—Georges Bataille, Erotism: Death and Sensuality

The Sex Lives of Saints? What could such words possibly signify? Surely everyone knows that the repression of erotic desire is the hallmark of Christian sanctity: a "sex life" is precisely what a proper saint lacks. At most, ascetic eros—encoded as yearning for God—may be seen as the residue of an imperfectly sublimated sexuality. Better yet: it is a merely metaphorical expression for a purely desexualized love. Worse still: it reflects pleasure derived from practices of self-denial rooted in a pathological hatred of the body.

It is difficult simply to contradict such widespread and thus all too easily anticipated doubts. Nonetheless, I find myself moved to pursue a different path of interpretation. The wager is at once intellectual and spiritual: might it be possible to take *common knowledge* by surprise, to disarm its resigned certainties, to disturb it with the stirrings of a most *uncommon* love, and thereby to enable a *different knowing* of both "sex" and "sanctity"? My title, though lightly ironic, is not intended to be oxymoronic: ancient Lives of Saints, I suggest, are the site of an exuberant eroticism. Resistance to the pervasive *anti-erotic* interpretation of hagiography (and of asceticism more generally) is crucial to the excitement—or, more conventionally phrased, the "significance"—of this argument. That sanctity can be restyled as an erotic art, that the holy Life carries us to the extremities of human desire, that (conversely) "erotic experience is possibly close to sanctity"— these are admittedly queer notions, seductive insinuations, even downright perverse proposals, in relation to traditional readings of the Lives, whether popular or scholarly, literary-historical or doctrinal. I take the risk of transgressing more than a few cherished orthodoxies in the hope of thereby uncovering a theory and practice of eroticism that is responsively attuned to the hallowed texts of the Christian past while also remaining unapologetically attentive to an urgent need of the present moment—namely, to affirm the holiness of a love that is simultaneously embodied and transcendent, sensual and spiritual, painful and joyous; that may encompass but can by no means be limited to (indeed, may at points entail disciplined refusal of) the demands of either biological reproduction or institutionalized marriage; that furthermore resists the reductions of the modern cult of the orgasm. In the stories of saints who steadfastly reject both the comforts and the confinements of conventional roles and relationships (swapping and discarding "identities" like so many threadbare cloaks), we may discover not only evidence of the historic transformation of desire but also testimony to the transformative power of eros.

If the interests that impel this work are thus revealed to be broadly theoretical and theological, at once undeniably political and inescapably personal, the approach is first and foremost historical, betraying my own disciplinary orientation. The suggestion that hagiography conveys a sublime art of eroticism rather than a repressive morality of sexuality implicitly raises questions and disrupts assumptions about the position of Christianity in the "history of sexuality"—the by-now conventional label for a wide-reaching scholarly conversation flourishing in the wake of the publication of the first three volumes of Michel Foucault's ambitious (and unfinished) *History of Sexuality*.[1] Although the subsequent chapters will not cleave closely to an explicitly Foucaultian analysis, here at the outset I want to map the larger historical trajectory of my argument by offering a fresh reading of Foucault's own emplotment of Christianity in the history of desire. If Foucault's thought provides a promising point of departure, it will also draw me into a broader web of contemporary discourses of eroticism, within which I will subsequently situate readings of the hagiographical texts of late antiquity.

* * *

"The so-called Christian morality is nothing more than a piece of pagan ethics inserted into Christianity. Shall we say then that Christianity did not change the state of things?"[2] This is the question (following upon an assertion) that Foucault poses for himself in his oft-revised and teasingly unfinished attempt to insert Christianity into the history of sexuality.[3] It is also the question on which this present work turns. In respect to sexuality, how *did* Christianity *change the state of things*? What revisions and interruptions in ancient Mediterranean conceptions of erotic pleasure and sexual ethics were introduced with the rise of the church?

The "so-called Christian morality" to which Foucault refers crystallizes in a sacralized monogamy in which sexuality is a means legitimated by its reproductive end, while pleasure (a necessary evil at best) is shadowed by suspicion. Like Foucault in the cited passage, I am here less interested in the consolidation and transmission of such an incipiently heterosexist ethics—in which the christianization of Roman culture did, admittedly, play an enormously significant role—than in the simultaneous eruption of a powerful crosscurrent of asceticized eroticism.[4] This "countererotics," redolent with "counterpleasures,"[5] is arguably not only more innovative, historically speaking, but also more central to Christian thought and practice in the period of antiquity and well beyond. Indeed, in the wake of two decades of intensive scholarly focus on ancient Christian asceticism, the "so-called Christian" marital morality, characteristically prohibitive, begins to take on the appearance of a reluctant concession, an ambivalent by-product of a movement that, for all its immense diversity, was consistently and subversively antifamilial from its very beginnings.[6] As historian of Christianity Mark Jordan puts it, "We must recognize . . . that Christian marriage was justified against claims of virginity (rather than apart from them). It is not clear how far Christian marriage is an alternative ideal and how far it is a derivative ideal"—derivative, that is, not only in respect to Roman ethics but also in respect to Christian asceticism, due to its structurally dependent and secondary status.[7] Departing from Foucault's script—*perhaps*—I would go so far as to propose that there arises within Christianity a distinctive *ars erotica* that does not so much predate as effectively resist and evade the *scientia sexualis* that likewise emerges (derivatively) in late antiquity and eventually culminates in the production of a modern, western regime of "sexuality."[8] If it is scarcely an accident, it remains nonetheless also a paradox, that the authority of Christian tradition has come to be unquestioningly aligned with the interests of heterosexism and "family values."[9] One of the aims of this book is to make that paradox once again palpable, to explore its tensions, and thereby to begin to free a transformative theology of eros from the stifling grip of a repressive morality of sexuality.

I say that I am *perhaps* departing from Foucault's script, because Foucault himself is, I think, intriguingly ambivalent. For Foucault, ancient Christian asceticism constitutes both the matrix of modern "sexuality"—and thus the end of a still more ancient *ars erotica*—and, at the same time, an emergent strategy for escaping sexuality's disciplinary power. Christianity—as an ensemble of "techniques" that historically produces "the desiring subject"—is, in other words, at once the problem and the promise. The problem is perhaps easier to spot. Foucault locates the distinctiveness of Christianity in the rise of a "hermeneutics of the self" resting on practices of self-examination and confession in which "the problem is to discover what is hidden inside the self."[10] Intertwined are two sets of constraining obligations: "those regarding the faith, the book, the dogma, and the obligations regarding the self, the soul, the heart, are linked together."[11] The political context of such a doubly telling witness is no longer civic but "pastoral": self-examination and confession are structured around relations of total obedience, not to a code of law but to a divine *will*, and the goal is not the sacrifice of the citizens for the city but rather the mortification of the self ("a kind of everyday death") for the sake of "life in another world"—"a renunciation of this world and of oneself" that is at the same time "a kind of relation from oneself to oneself."[12] In this guise, ancient Christian practices of purifying self-relation are presented as the precursor to "the modern hermeneutics of the self."[13] The problem for Christianity is not (as it was in classical antiquity) penetration or domination but rather "erection," which is to say, desire itself.[14] (This uncompromisingly androcentric formulation succinctly conveys the persistent suppression of the feminine in the history of sexuality, amplified in Foucault's own *History*—a subject to which I shall return.) On Foucault's reading, ascetic Christianity—whether Augustine's or John Cassian's version[15]—initiates a trajectory of discursive ejaculation (a transformation of "sex into discourse") that eventually intersects, via the seventeenth-century confessional, with the modern practice of psychoanalysis.[16]

Having relentlessly exposed the circulation of knowledge, power, and pleasure that inheres in such a confessional sexuality, indeed having virtually equated (modern) sexuality with "power/knowledge," Foucault may appear—as Jean Baudrillard charges—to have rendered himself and his readers captive to a totalizing power of his own discursive fabrication.[17] Readers less skeptical of Foucault's argument than Baudrillard may be all the more prone to question whether it is after all possible to escape the iron grasp of this disciplinary regime on which, according to Foucault himself, our very sense of "self" depends. And if escape is not possible, from what vantage point can "sexuality" be critically engaged? This is the question raised by philosopher Judith Butler, in a sharp interrogation of Foucault's residual—and residually incoherent—emancipatory idealism.[18] "We are prisoners of the historical space of nineteenth-century psychiatry," notes philosopher and historian of science Arnold Davidson, in a more sympathetic glossing of Foucault's text. The gloss takes on a faint sheen of hope, as Davidson gives voice to the longing for liberation: "Perhaps there will come a time when we can think to ourselves, 'How do I love thee; let me count the ways,' and no longer fear our possible perversion."[19]

Foucault approaches such a possible time-to-come by a necessarily indirect route—"a long detour" into the past.[20] It is in the course of this detour, I would suggest, that the lingering opposition of "repression" and "liberation" critiqued by Butler begins to be more effectively deconstructed, giving way (however ambiguously) to a subversive reperformance of historical styles of self-formation that surface "the possibilities that emerge when the law turns against itself and spawns unexpected permutations of itself" (as Butler herself frames the desired outcome of a radically Foucaultian theory and practice).[21] Seeming both to concede and to question his own subjection to the modern discourse of sexuality that he explores in the first volume, Foucault describes his genealogical experiments in the later volumes of the *History of Sexuality* as a form of "ascesis," "an exercise of oneself in the activity of thought": "The object was to learn to what extent the effort to think one's own history can free thought from what it silently thinks, and so enable it to think differently." He acknowledges the "irony in those efforts one makes to alter one's way of looking at things," wondering aloud: "Did mine actually result in a different way of thinking?" Perhaps not; and yet something has shifted: "the journey rejuvenates things, and ages the relationship with oneself."[22]

Retracing the path of his own, already ancient thought, Foucault thus encounters himself from new angles. In his *History of Sexuality*, Christianity as an iterative technique of ascetic self-relation is not only the missing volume—tragically curtailed by the author's death—but also the receding frontier of a yet unthought difference. "What is expected" of ancient ascetics, Foucault reminds us in his lectures, "is humility and mortification, detachment with respect to oneself and the establishing of a relationship with oneself which tends toward a destruction of the form of the self."[23] Therein lies "the deep contradiction, or, if you want, the great richness, of Christian technologies of the self: no truth about the self without a sacrifice of the self," he proclaims. Therein lies also the "deep contradiction, or, if you want, the great richness" of Foucault's positioning of Christianity, and also of his positioning of himself in relation to Christianity, I would suggest. Far from leading *inevitably* to the modern subject of sexuality, the ancient Christian discourse of desire, Foucault insists (verging on inconsistency),[24] actively refuses the "positive self" on which the modern subject is grounded; in Christianity, sacrifice rather than positivism "was the condition for the opening of the self as a field of indefinite interpretation."[25] Thus, for Foucault, "the texts of the early church" become, surprisingly, "'a way out' of sexuality"[26]—a "way out," in other words, of the particular modern disciplinary regime that produces not only the concept of "sexual identity" but also the categories of "heterosexuality" and "homosexuality," which are grounded in a rigid binarism of "opposite sexes." Christian asceticism is, moreover, a "way out," he implies, not only or even primarily because it is "pre-modern" but rather because it was always already resisting closure, eluding essence.

Among Foucault's earliest "spiritual masters" (paving the way for his subsequent encounter with the ancient ascetics) are his more immediate philosophical predecessors, notable among them Georges Bataille and Maurice Blanchot: he acknowledges his specific debts to "the former's experience of eroticism and the latter's of language, understood as experiences of dissolution, disappearance, denial of the subject (of the speaking subject and the erotic subject)."[27] In an early essay honoring Bataille through an appreciative engagement of his magisterial tome *Erotism*, Foucault is already sketching a history of sexuality. Here he initially marks the difference between a "denatured" modern sexuality and "the Christian world of fallen bodies and of sin," which is linked to the "whole tradition of mysticism and spirituality" in which experiences "of desire, of rapture, of penetration, of ecstasy . . . seemed to lead, without interruption or limit, right to the heart of a divine love of which they were both the outpouring and the source returning upon itself."[28] At the same time, Foucault partly closes the gap between ancient traditions of Christian spirituality and the excessive reaches of modern philosophy: "The thought that relates to God and the thought that relates to sexuality are linked by a common form, since Sade to be sure, but never in our day with as much insistence and difficulty as in Bataille." In a rereading of Bataille's intertwined concepts of limit and transgression, Foucault locates "eroticism" at the transgressive edges of sexuality, in "an experience of sexuality which links, for its own ends, an overcoming of limits to the death of God."[29] For Foucault, the posited "death of God" draws close to a "negative theology" while also maintaining a critical distance.[30] "Transgression contains nothing negative, but affirms limited being—affirms the limitless into which it leaps as it opens this zone to existence for the first time," he states, continuing even more paradoxically: "But correspondingly, this affirmation contains nothing positive: no content can bind it, since, by definition, no limit can possibly restrict it."[31] Transgression, he notes, still following Bataille closely, was "originally linked to the divine, or rather, from this limit marked by the sacred it opens the space where the divine functions."[32]

In modernity, Foucault observes, sexuality has been absorbed by language. He thus finds particular promise in a philosophy that "experiences itself and its limits in language and in this transgression of language which carries it, as it did Bataille, to the faltering of the speaking subject."[33] ("I will go so far as to say that in my opinion, philosophy is also the death of language," writes Bataille, threatening—but also failing—to subside into silence. "It is also a sacrifice.")[34] In Foucault's early essay, the "philosophy" that is perched at the linguistic limits of the modern discourse of sexuality approaches the "religious eroticism" celebrated by Bataille; it also draws near to the "sacrifice of the self" that Foucault later discerns in the ancient Christian discourse of subjectivity. ("The deliberate loss of self in eroticism is manifest," intones Bataille. "No one can question it"—a posited limit to inquiry that seems to invite its own transgression.)[35] Is the "philosophy" here invoked by Foucault not even a kind of "theology" that anticipates his own faltering (unfinished) speaking about Christianity and also a style of "spiritual" self-formation that foreshadows his virtual appropriation of the techniques of ancient asceticism?

Foucault's asceticism has perhaps been nowhere more brilliantly illumined than in David Halperin's *Saint Foucault: Towards a Gay Hagiography*. Declaring that "the guy was a fucking saint," while at the same time testifying to the dynamics of desire and identification that infuse the authorial inscription of "sanctity" (*"Michel Foucault, c'est moi"*),[36] Halperin proceeds in his first essay to demonstrate, via the punctual style of anecdotal illustration, the coherence of thought and practice in the ascetic Life of Foucault. ("As was his speech, so was the manner of life" and "as his manner of life, so his speech": thus Eusebius recites what is already, by the end of the third century, familiar convention [*Church History* 6.3.6–7].) In a second essay, Halperin effectively refuses the temptations of narrative closure by enacting his resistance to prior biographical accounts (indeed, to the presumptions of "biography" itself) and thereby drafts an open-ended narrative of his own, a retelling of the Life avowedly fired by passion and therein locating its claim to a true witness.[37] In all these respects, Halperin follows the dictates—or perhaps rather emulates the highest ambitions—of the hagiographical tradition to which his title teasingly alludes. The Foucault whom he presents is finally not so much "gay" as "queer," proffering less an identity than a transformative strategy of resistance to the fixing of identity: "It is from the eccentric positionality occupied by the queer subject that it may become possible to envision a variety of possibilities for reordering the relations among sexual behaviors, erotic identities, constructions of gender, forms of knowledge, regimes of renunciation, logics of representation, modes of self-constitution, and practices of community."[38] Foucault's "queerness" is, on Halperin's reading, performed by a retrieval of Greek and Roman styles of self-cultivation. "To practice a stylistics of the self ultimately means to cultivate that part of oneself that leads beyond oneself, that transcends oneself: it is to elaborate the strategic possibilities of what is the most *impersonal* dimension of personal life—namely the capacity to 'realize oneself' by becoming other than what one is. This is what Foucault came to see himself as having done all his life."[39] Halperin's Foucault is thus, paradoxically, an ascetic *avant la lettre*, "before sexuality" and also before Christianity.

"It is significant that Halperin's work does not develop any of Foucault's reflections on Christian texts," as Mark Vernon notes.[40] Indeed, Halperin appears rather deliberately to *elide* Foucault's interest in Christianity, even as he represents him as an ascetic saint. Jeremy Carrette, in contrast, retraces Halperin's critical reading of Foucault's biographers, most notably James Miller, in an overt attempt to "rescue [Foucault's] silenced discussion of Christianity."[41] He suggests that "the stylization of Foucault in Miller's work, to which Halperin is so opposed, unwittingly rests on a particular religious distortion of Foucault."[42] Carrette deploys an alternate tactic, approaching Miller's work as "a negative from which to draw out the central theoretical issues underpinning Foucault's work on religion."[43] Arguing that Miller has viciously misconstrued Foucault not only as a sexual pervert (as Halperin amply demonstrates)[44] but also as a dangerous "mystic" courting a "limit-experience" in the erotic practices of sadomasochism, Carrette acknowledges nonetheless that there is insight to be extracted from the twisted strands of this account.[45] He affirms especially that "Foucault created a fascinating theological sub-text through the encounter with the avant-garde," above all Bataille (and, through Bataille, Sade).[46] However, "Foucault, like Bataille before him, suspends the mystical idea as soon as it is introduced. Foucault and Bataille are attempting to demarcate a new space in literature with inadequate old language."[47] Moreover, while "the pleasure from physical pain in martyrdom or religious suffering and S/M . . . may constitute a parallel event and hold a common denominator in the suffering body," sadomasochism and religious eroticism cannot be simply identified; nor, he implies, did Foucault make this mistake.[48]

Does Carrette protest a bit too much in his defense of Foucault, even as he also strains to "rescue" Miller's perversely "distorted" insights? Such complexly textualized ambivalence may be worth unpacking. To be sure, prior traditions of religious spirituality should not be *conflated* with more recent philosophies and practices of eroticism that similarly seek the sacred in the radical disruption of the subject through a violent traversal of the

Introduction 9

boundaries that separate self and other, sacred and profane, life and death, pleasure and pain. More importantly, neither of these should be *conflated* with oppressive acts of violence designed to "break" the psyche. At the same time, where modern discussions of Christian asceticism remain unavoidably haunted by the specter of a widely discredited "masochism" (associations both typically dismissive and difficult simply to dismiss), a more precise articulation of the relation between asceticism and sadomasochistic eroticism would seem to be called for. Foucault's work (pace Carrette) may indeed be read as initiating such an articulation, not least through its subtle attunement to the resonance, retrieved via "genealogy," between ancient Christian asceticism and ambiguously secularized modern discourses of desire, particularly at their most excessive, self-transgressive limits.[49] It is at this point, as Carrette acknowledges, that Foucault's work intersects powerfully with the prior texts of Bataille, who observes that the experiences of both eroticism and sanctity, traversing the boundaries of historical periods, "have an extreme intensity. . . . The saint is not after efficiency. He is prompted by desire and desire alone and in this resembles the erotic man."[50]

The call for a closer—and less skittishly apologetic—consideration of the relation between sadomasochistic and ascetic eroticisms has not, in fact, gone unheeded. Karmen MacKendrick's *Counterpleasures*, a work heavily influenced by both Bataille and Foucault, responds to just such a call, lending considerable philosophical nuance to the intuition that there are significant connections to be drawn between the lives of ancient and medieval saints and the modern pursuit of "counterpleasures," dramatically instantiated in s/m eroticism, an ensemble of practices that spans (and thus blurs the boundaries between) the most esoteric reaches of intellectual theory and the most inarticulate depths of bodily practice. The erotic pleasures that interest MacKendrick "are pleasures that queer our notion of pleasure, consisting in or coming through pain, frustration, refusal. They are pleasures of exceptional intensity, refusing to make *sense* while still demanding a philosophical unfolding. This unfolding takes odd forms; that of an infinite self-reflexion or a rupture of language in the very act of description."[51] Not unlike practitioners of sadomasochistic sex, "ascetics," MacKendrick suggests, "intensify both the Christian turn against the body and the incarnate and corporeal aspects of that 'same' tradition, revealing in their practice the seductive, defiant elements of religious practice that radically problematize its disembodiment, its hierarchicality, even its misogyny."[52] (MacKendrick, unlike Bataille, perceives the limits of "erotic *man*": she notes that gender is "another of the boundaries with which [s/m] delights in playing.")[53] Drawing attention to the inherent excessiveness of asceticism, as well as its paradoxical carnality, MacKendrick delineates the "movement of transgression by intensification" in which the (unachievable) aim is "the refusal of finitude, exhaustion, and limit—*all through the body.*"[54] In and through the extremes not only of self-denial but even of self-mutilation, the ascetic, however ambivalently, pursues both pleasure and desire. Citing the argument of literary critic Geoffrey Galt Harpham, she notes that "the ascetic in fact courts temptation": "the ascetic desire for desire, and for tempting objects of desire, is strong." Ascetic desire is paradoxical, taking pleasure "both in its increase . . . and in its own violent denial," to the point that satisfaction is "removed from the picture."[55] Thus eros thrives in the refusal of the telos of satisfaction; pleasure is perversely intensified through the prolongation of pain; and worldly power is undermined, even as God's grace is provoked "through a violent defiance," in the "subtle seductions" of asceticism, MacKendrick argues.[56] A transgressive eroticism has drawn close indeed to sanctity in this perversely reverent (indeed, surprisingly theological) philosophical unfolding of the "counterpleasures."

Harpham's *Ascetic Imperative in Culture and Criticism*, to which MacKendrick alludes, not only partly anticipates and affirms certain aspects of her argument, as we shall see, but also brings the study of ascetic eroticism onto a specifically literary terrain. Encompassing extended essays on Athanasius's fourth-century *Life of Antony* and Augustine's *Confessions*, Harpham's work closely aligns asceticism with textuality and, more especially, with narrativity. He locates both ascesis and narrative in the relational dynamic of temptation and resistance, which he understands as inherent in desire. "Narrative is an ascetical art of desire, an art of temptation—doubled, self-limiting, and self-resisting."[57] Here Harpham explicitly rejects the notion of desire as perpetual (limitless) motion or sheer transgression, underlining instead the dependence of desire on resistance and hence on temptation. Temptation is suspended in paradox: "in temptation, notions of transgression and limit are in force, but have not yet become identical or indivisible."[58] Narrative, as an ascetical art of desire, includes both the temptation of closure and the resistance to that temptation. "All the totalizing operations of narrative operate through resistance to de-totalizing operations; and so while narrative can organize a human life, it cannot do so simply or unequivocally, for all its coherence functions are implicated in their opposites."[59]

Narrative thus parallels, or includes, the "process of Christian self-formation" that Harpham has described earlier, which "differed from its pagan counterpart not only in being more extreme, to the point of self-deformation, but also in being complemented by an activity of self-unforming."[60] Hagiographical narrative can thus by no means be simply identified with the interests of a phallic subjectivity, for example: "For within its fascinated concentration on the masculine, hagiography focuses on the doubling and self-subversion of the subject, in which it ceaselessly discovers gaps or concentrations of desire. In other words, hagiography both establishes the masculine program and destabilizes it, 'feminizing' the subject by exposing its enigmas of desire and even the 'masochism' of its rigors." Narrative produces both orders of coherence and "incoherence and carnivalization."[61] In hagiography, the sexed subject—the subject itself—is continually deformed, unformed, and reformed in the dynamic of a desiring resistance, a resisting desire. Harpham caps his study with a hagiographical tribute to "Saint Foucault," highlighting the power of Foucault's theories and practices of resistance, most subtly articulated in his late—and, as Harpham notes, increasingly appreciative—reengagement with ancient Christian asceticism.[62]

Having returned, with Harpham, to my initial point of departure—Michel Foucault's evocatively ambiguous placement of Christianity in the history of sexuality—I am also carried to the brink of my own literary-historical reading of the counterpleasures suffusing the Lives of Saints.

* * *

Ancient hagiography—a practice of writing intriguingly revived in contemporary engagements with Foucault—provides a promising site for excavating the charred remains of those erotic theories and practices that once fired ancient Christian discourse and that continue to smolder and spark at the transgressed edge of western modernity, not least in Foucault's own life's work. Harpham follows time-hallowed tradition in beginning the history of hagiography with Athanasius's *Life of Antony*: "The master text of Western asceticism is the *Life of Anthony*."[63] Perversely, I will begin instead with Jerome's *Life of Paul*, written roughly fifteen years later. Perhaps I am thereby resisting the temptation to inscribe closure on the narrative of hagiography by fixing its point of "origin" too securely.[64] Undoubtedly I am also seduced by Jerome's own perversity. The point is not only that a Church Father notoriously accused of a unique level of obsession with sex seems a likely ally for a historian of ancient Christianity unusually preoccupied with eroticism. More importantly, Jerome, a supremely self-conscious writer, attracts an account of hagiographical "beginnings" by stridently insisting on his own initiative, refusing to be read as a mere follower of either Athanasius or his Latin translator Evagrius. (This is a gesture of refusal that other hagiographers will emulate: hagiography, constantly repeating itself, is always beginning again.) Jerome forces us to acknowledge the violence of creativity at work in those writerly acts of textual recycling—citation, iteration, imitation, mimicry, dislocation, translation, decomposition, fragmentation, and recombination—through which the Holy Life is produced and ever again reproduced, never quite the same as before. He refuses to conform to even a norm of his own making, authoring three remarkably different, yet (as I will show) equally "queer," Lives of male saints—Paul, Malchus, Hilarion, whose hagiographies are the focus of Chapter 1. The very aspects of these literary Lives that have most frequently irritated critics—overt inconsistency, excessive embellishment, and disjunctive narrativity—are here credited with the success of Jerome's literary-erotic project. Psychoanalytic-literary critic Leo Bersani's understanding of the "shattering of the self" aimed at in certain styles of interruptive and iterative narrativity (edgily positioned, as it happens, in relation to the theories of both Foucault and Harpham)[65] provides an illumining, if not unproblematic, theoretical intertext for such a reinterpretation of Jerome's hagiographical oeuvre. At the same time, Bersani's revision of Freud's theory of sexuality enables a rethinking of "sublimation" not as the defining characteristic of an ambiguously repressive asceticism but rather as the condition of *all* erotic desire.

Jerome also writes of women, and his encomium of his dear friend Paula will carry us into Chapter 2, where Gregory of Nyssa's fraternal *Life of Macrina* and Augustine's filial "confession" of Monica are likewise mined for traces of a distinctly "feminine" styling of sanctity. If the men's Lives considered in the first chapter can be read as resistant romances, the earliest women's Lives pivot on the eroticized death of a much-beloved subject and cleave closely to the traditions of both martyrology and letters of consolation, behind which lie funeral speeches of praise and lament. A "woman," it seems, must die in order to get a Life. The element of masochism (already conveyed in Bersani's theorizing) is here foregrounded, via the work of both MacKendrick and Lynda Hart: if psychoanalysis, as well as much popular culture, has tended to perceive women as (alas) merely *natural* masochists, hagiography radically denaturalizes the feminine as the unstable and queerly reversible site of a decidedly *perverse*, even effectively *feminist*, masochistic subjectivity that actively resists patriarchy from within the very structures of misogynistic discourse. Thus the repressed feminine returns, however ambivalently, to the history of sexuality. This chapter ends by opening a dialogue with Jacques Derrida and Shoshana Felman regarding the position of "woman" as subject of both death and survival in testimonial literature that straddles the boundary between (male) autobiography and (female) biography.

The gendering of the subject of hagiographical writings is not neutralized (as is frequently claimed) but rather intensified, on this reading. It is also rendered remarkably unstable and fluid, as the subsequent chapters further emphasize, repeating (with a difference) the alternation between male and female Lives. The soldier and the harlot, exotically eroticized figures of hypermasculinity and hyperfemininity respectively, take gender to its extremes of reversibility. Chapter 3, which considers Sulpicius Severus's repeatedly supplemented *Life of Martin*, picks up themes from the previous two chapters, suggesting that the soldier saint is not only virtually "queer" but also practically a "woman." The main emphasis, however, is on the disturbingly sadistic strain of violence in the Life, which simultaneously replicates and subverts the explosive pressures of empire, with its pervasive call to "dominate and submit"; the situation of desire within the complex hybridization of late antique Mediterranean culture is explored through engagement with (post)colonial critics Anne McClintock and Homi Bhabha.

Three Lives of "harlots"—Syrian Mary, Pelagia, and Mary of Egypt—are considered in Chapter 4. These somewhat later hagiographies are not only the least overtly martyrial but also the most explicitly "erotic" of the texts considered. (The *Life of Mary of Egypt*, in a pleasing symmetry, will return us not only to the desert but also to Jerome's *Life of Paul*.) Whereas the harlot saints have consistently been read as repenting of their transgressive sexuality, I will argue, in contrast, that their sanctity inheres in their unrepentant—if nonetheless transfigured—seductiveness. Jean Baudrillard's understanding of seduction here provides the major theoretical intervention, read explicitly against its antifeminist (as well as, implicitly, its anti-Foucaultian) grain.

The theoretical eclecticism of this approach will not, I hope, seem merely arbitrary. The "queer," the "sadomasochistic," and the "seductive" are overlapping (though by no means identical) concepts that collectively participate in a political and intellectual project that was also Foucault's—namely a reconceptualizing of eroticism that exceeds and thereby partly evades the constraints of modern "sexuality." Such an overlapped field of theorizing matches, as it has seemed to me, the similarly complex field of countererotics opened up within ancient hagiographical literature. Before addressing that literature directly, it remains for me to say a bit more about such a posited "countererotics"—loosening, without cutting loose from, the intertextual weave of contemporary scholarship in which I have already situated this work.

Saintly love begins with resistance to the temptations of "worldly" eroticism—resistance not merely to the transient pleasures of physical intercourse (opening onto a broader realm of tempting sensory delights) but also to perduring familial and political hierarchies, institutionalized relations of domination and submission that both structure, and are structured by, relations of sex and gender. Yet such resistance to cultural norms, aptly coded in contemporary terms as "queer,"[66] does not take an anti-erotic turn, proffering the sterile safety of a desexualized "agape" in exchange for the firm repression of sexual desire. Rather, it gives rise to an exuberant art of eroticism in which the negativity harbored within resistance is eclipsed by the radical affirmation of desire also conveyed in resistance. That resistance to desire should increase desire admittedly presents a perplexing paradox. "Whence the power of what seems to be a force of sheer negation, or the pleasure of what seems to be only pain and frustration?" queries MacKendrick. "Restraint . . . is a means of intensification: it disciplines the forces of desire so that their expression is both stylized and intensified. Desire is given time to *grow*; its quick release and undoing are prevented." In the process, she suggests, "the very nature of desire" is altered: it becomes a "desire beyond subjectivity."[67] The ongoing, iterative disruption of the subject within the movement of desire emphasized by MacKendrick is, for Bersani, the primary effect of all eroticism, revealing "*jouissance* as a mode of ascesis."[68]

Ancient hagiography, I am suggesting, participates in such a self-mortifying *jouissance*, such a divinely erotic joy, in which the performative "death" of the self becomes the sanctifying matrix of life's renewal—giving rise, in the field of literature, to ever-new Lives. The self that is sacrificed as desire extends "beyond subjectivity" is a self defined by its constructed isolation or boundedness, its approach toward the sterility of stasis.[69] In holy love, "transcendence" does not complete or fulfill the self; rather, as Jean-Luc Nancy puts it, "it cuts, it breaks, and it exposes."[70] Thus, erotic "self-shattering" differs dramatically from the "unmaking" of the self effected by techniques of torture that *intensify*—rather than *disrupt*—the isolation of the subject. As Elaine Scarry notes, in torture "the created world of thought and feeling, all the psychological and mental content that constitutes both one's self and one's world, and that gives rise to and is in turn made possible by language, ceases to exist."[71] The pain inflicted in totalizing acts of oppression, she argues, *shuts down* the generative processes of subjective transcendence by which humans continually create sharable, self-extending worlds. The agonizing pleasure pursued in eroticism, in contrast, *increases* transcendence to the point that the boundaries of individual subjectivity—the distinctions between the "internal" and the "external"—effectively dissolve. Such dissolution is partial and transient, though its effects may be enduring and even momentous. As Bataille observes (in an important qualification of his own pervasively, even hyperbolically, celebratory rhetoric of "sacrifice"): "Continuity is what we are after, but generally only if that continuity which the death of discontinuous beings can alone establish is not the victor in the long run. What we desire is to bring into a world founded on discontinuity all the continuity such a world can sustain."[72] However, if the processes of self-destruction enacted in political torture and eroticism are thus very nearly opposite, they are also, paradoxically, tightly linked. Indeed, eroticism may be seen to mimic and thereby subvert the "shattering" operations of torture, effecting not a destruction but rather a deconstruction (thus also a reconstruction) of subjectivity, through "dissonant displacements" that reconfigure the relations between power and resistance, life and death, body and spirit, by disrupting their oppositional inscription.[73] As Nancy puts it, the "break" in the subject conveyed in the movement of love "is nothing more than a touch, but the touch is not less deep than a wound."[74] When *jouissance* is understood as "a mode of ascesis," the ascetic emerges into view as an erotically *joyful* "body in pain," disclosing suffering as the vehicle of the ongoing unmaking and remaking of worlds.[75]

For the writers of holy Lives, it is God who measures the unfurling expanse of such a sublime erotic ambition. "You need to consider where God is in this, because God's position is a sexual option," quips theologian Marcella Althaus-Reid.[76] "God's position," we might say, is at the ever-receding point where the "object" of desire withdraws and eludes the subject, thereby temporarily disrupting the subject's self-certainty in the jolt of ecstatic dispossession—a disruption that lives on in the body's memory, as MacKendrick reminds us, enabling "the knowledge, impossible without a subject, of a possibility beyond subjectivity."[77] God inheres in the paradoxical act of self-sacrifice (a sacrifice at once "God's" and "ours") that is the gift of sanctity and the lure of a love that traverses all limits. The sacrifice—which is also a seduction—is mutual and reciprocal, inscribing the irreducible relationality of God and creation. As Baudrillard puts it, "One *seduces* God with faith, and He cannot but respond, for seduction, like the challenge, is a reversible form. And He responds a hundredfold by His grace to the challenge of faith."[78]

Is the God of the countererotic theology that I am retrieving not close kin to the God of mysticism's "negative theology," revived in the impersonal "sacred" of modern philosophers? Yes, but only insofar as there is a corresponding move within such a theology toward a "negative" or "impersonal" understanding of the human subject. Only, furthermore, insofar as the "negativity" of both God and human subjectivity marks an abysmal plenitude, and "impersonality" is seen as the effect not of the lack but of the extremity of passion, the active suffering of desire through which "personhood" is transcended and exceeded. God is encountered in the hagiographical texts in the moment when the beloved body traverses the boundary between life and death, in the saint's last, rejoicing breaths, in the disciple's lingering embrace of a corpse that already slips beyond the grasp of transient particularity—dissolving into finest dust, mingling with desert sand, participating again in the capacious potentiality of the cosmos. God is encountered in other such moments of violent traversal, transition, and reversibility, in the transvestite, the transgendered, the transfigured and disfigured subject, in the astonishing mobility and convertibility of the saint, the bottomless capacity for radical metamorphosis.[79] God appears (and also disappears) in the movement of love between and beyond persons, in the slide from the personal to the impersonal, from the self to the loss of self, from the discontinuous individual to the continuity of all existence. As Bataille puts it, the sacred or the divine—the God also glimpsed in a "negative theology founded on mystical experience"—arises in "the revelation of continuity through the death of a discontinuous being to those who watch it as a solemn rite." Sacredness, grounded in sacrifice, thus aligns closely with eroticism, which likewise inheres in the revelation of continuity through the dissolution of separative selves.[80] Indeed, argues Bataille, "all eroticism has a sacramental character."[81] "Flights of Christian religious experience and bursts of erotic impulses are seen to be part and parcel of the same movement."[82] Despite his strident critique of Christianity, Bataille understands his own work on eroticism as "nearer to 'theology' than to scientific or religious history."[83] (Thus it is that it can be so easily drawn into the citational weave of a work of "religious history" that itself draws near to "theology.")

The transpersonal God of negative theology continues, however, to yield intermittently to the shifting play of personifications within the Christian theological imaginary, in the context of a tradition that has remained, for the most part, not only productively "positive" in its metaphorical strategies but also persistently anthropocentric in its erotic fantasies. (Though we should not fail to note the fertile caves and springs, deserts, forests, and mountaintops, the fauns and centaurs, he-lions and she-wolves haunting the borders of the hagiographical texts.) In a recent theological act of self-proclaimed "indecency," Althaus-Reid does not negate but rather multiplies the "sexual option" of a personified "God's position," reciting a parodically perverse aretalogy: "God, the Faggot; God, the Drag Queen; God, the Lesbian; God, the heterosexual woman who does not accept the constructions of ideal heterosexuality; God, the ambivalent, not easily classified sexuality."[84] The theologian's tone is here both vividly ironic and deadly serious. In the inevitable interplay between life stories and theologies, she wonders, "can we keep carrying the burden of a theology which leaves us alone when having sex?"[85] The "we" whom Althaus-Reid invokes is a deliberately provocative (but not random or unconsidered) collectivity of transgressively desiring subjects, including lemon vendors without underwear, adulterers, sadomasochists, and transvestites. Her recounting of the "sexual stories" of everyday saints repeats the challenge of hagiography—to pursue God in the extremities of human striving.[86]

A divine sexual orientation courts transcendence through the risk of transgression; its sublimity far exceeds the bounds established by the concept of a de-eroticized "sublimation"; its goal is not the chastening of the sexual subject but rather the seduction of salvific grace through the sacrifice of a "self" reified—and thus entombed—in its very "sexuality"; its literary expression refuses the temptation of a reductive detachment of historical facts and carnal acts from the ethereal flights of fantasy upon which all desire is borne. In the Lives of Saints, we are able to perceive the crucial intersection of eroticism and theology. There we encounter no "safe sex" but only risks worth taking. (That the risks are *all too real* is evidenced by long histories not only of sexual repression but also of political oppression enacted in the name of God's desire.) There we encounter no "sexual orthodoxy" but only the continually reperformed trial of historical witnesses testifying passionately to the possibility of divine eros—which is to say, to the twinned (intertwined) possibilities of *God* and of *love*.

Such theoretical and theological reflections are conveyed by the historical argument that undergirds this book. The readings of ancient texts that follow adhere to a rough chronological order. They are not, however, intended to inscribe a narrative of internal development but rather to expose (albeit incompletely) the complex and shifting intertextual weave of a late ancient literary practice. To the extent that hagiography "tends toward a destruction of the form of the self," as Foucault describes Christian asceticism, the writing, and thus also the reading, of Holy Lives must be understood as an open, ever unfinished and unstable enterprise: an interpretive teleology should be courted, but also refused, at every turn.[87] In ancient hagiographical literature, sacrifice—here understood as the resistance of narrative closure—is "the condition for the opening of the self as a field of indefinite interpretation." What is true for the Lives themselves is also true for the history of Lives, which (I am suggesting) ought not surrender to the temptation to emplot the monolinear evolution of a definite "genre." Nonetheless, chronology—or rather, the specificity of context and the logic of temporality illumined by historical analysis—is not irrelevant to my broader interest in inserting the hagiographical texts into the history of sexuality. The (meta)historical account here introduced through a recapitulation of Foucault's genealogical project will continue to haunt the peripheral vision of the subsequent readings.

It is scarcely an accident that the incitement to hagiographical discourse arises within the charged and contested transculturalism of a late Roman empire perched at the edge of antiquity. Nor is it an accident that interest in a hagiographical erotics reemerges within our own similarly "multicultural," ambiguously "postcolonial," even possibly "postmodern" context.[88] We too are perched at a temporal edge (or so we imagine it), awash in an ocean of heteroglossia (in the academy and well beyond), sharply aware of the complex and mobile relations of power that infuse all of our practices (literary, erotic, and otherwise). Hagiography is a historical product, a queer, late version of the ancient novel, emerging at the intersections of romance with biography, historiography, panegyric, martyrology—a statement that does not so much define its genre as announce its persistent subversions of genre, its promiscuous borrowings, its polyphonous multiplication of contesting (and thus always compromised) voices, its subtle and ever-shifting resistances within power, its layered remappings of place and replottings of time, its repeated traversals of the boundaries of history and fiction, truth and lies, the realms of the sacred and the profane.[89] What will we late- or postmodern readers (re)discover in such texts? Will the encounter "result in a different way of thinking," as Foucault frames the question for himself?[90] Will it result, indeed, in a different way of *loving*? Such is the hopeful desire that infuses my own readerly detour through the ancient Lives of Saints.

Chapter 1
Fancying Hermits:
Sublimation and the Arts of Romance

Sublimation is coextensive with (rather than "beyond") sexuality.
—Leo Bersani, The Freudian Body: Psychoanalysis and Art

"How often, when I was living in the desert, in the vast solitude which gives to hermits a savage dwelling-place, parched by the flames of the sun, how often did I fancy myself among the pleasures of Rome (*putavi me Romanis interesse deliciis*)!" (Ep. 22.7). Thus begins Jerome's account of his own brief career as a hermit, intruded into a letter written to the Roman virgin Eustochium circa 384, some eight years after he had decisively fled the Syrian desert. In this passage, ascetic fantasy quickly overwhelms historical description. Still inventing himself in the present, Jerome's interest in his own past lies largely with the power of the imagination to shape—and reshape—a human life.[1] His autobiographical confession unfolds in a series of dreamily shifting scenes, as vibrant in emotional tone as they are rich in sensory detail. The remembered landscape conveys the tenor of the former life, even as the terrain of memory itself buckles and folds: in the desert he once fancied Roman allurements; in Rome he now fancies desert delights. Mobile displacements of pleasures thus make space for desire while transforming both topography and chronology.[2] Defined by mutual lack, desert and Rome, past and present, become (by mutual attraction) almost one topos, a savage habitation that is also the no-place where a sublime eros burns bright.[3]

As Jerome rewrites his past, he reinscribes the desert on his body, roughly effacing the soft pallor of Rome: "my skin from long neglect had become like Ethiopian flesh (*squalida cutis situm Aethiopicae carnis adduxerat*)." The scene bends back on itself, as his savagely "burning mind"—itself a desert product—in turn converts the almost intolerably bleak solitude of sandy wastes into a stage crowded with foregone delights: "I often found myself amidst bevies of girls (*choris . . . puellarum*)," he reminisces boldly (Ep. 22.7). In this fantastic desert that is also the site of Roman pleasures, Jerome appears virtually indistinguishable from the voluptuous bands of chorus girls, a confusion not repressed but intensified by the text. His skin weathered in the sun-scorched desert, the hermit has become as dark—and perhaps thereby as beautiful—as the sun-scorched bride of the Song of Songs (cf. Song 1.6),[4] whose naked desire he will, later in this same letter, commend to the girl Eustochium in terms exceeding even the Song's abundant eroticism (Ep. 22.25).[5] First, however, he abandons himself fleetingly to a still more exuberant identification with another sensuously, indeed sinfully, female biblical figure: "Helpless, I cast myself at the feet of Jesus, I watered them with my tears, I wiped them with my hair, and then I subdued my rebellious body with weeks of abstinence" (cf. Luke 7.38). Beating his breast and weeping copiously in the queerly feminized and darkly exoticized literary persona of his own construction,[6] Jerome quickly returns to the opening verses of the Song of Songs, now with an explicit citation, as he sings joyously to his Lord: "because of the scent of thy ointments we will run after thee" (Ep. 22.7; cf. Song 1.3). The words of the Song's lover and her maidens, directly voiced by Jerome, thus supplement the account of foot washing. The fragrant oils initially elided in his abstinent citation of the Lukan text mingle again with the foot washer's tears, and the mutely weeping woman is fractured, pluralized, and dispersed in dancing choruses of maidenly celebration—"bevies of girls" fit to accompany the Savior's bride, none other than Jerome himself, now more than ever one of the girls.[7] Authorial "fancy" is no longer worldly but rather densely biblical, as Jerome refashions his desire ascetically by rewriting the desert as a voluptuous scriptural text, thereby also reinscribing Scripture as a teeming desert of delights. Fact or fantasy? History or romance? *Sexuality or sublimation*? In the text of his own recollected life, Jerome dissolves such distinctions.

What of Jerome's *other* Lives—the holy biographies of Paul, Malchus, and Hilarion? "Are the Lives romances?" queried E. Coleiro in 1957, wondering aloud "whether Jerome meant the Lives to be considered as history or fiction." Skittishly, Coleiro concludes that, although Jerome certainly cannot have intended that his saintly biographies be read as novels, they do make for rather bad history while exuding considerable "romantic charm."[8] Coleiro stands in a tradition of scholarship that has attempted to discipline Jerome's disturbingly labile hagiographic compositions by giving them a respectable place within literary history, identifying them as variations on conventional genres of history, biography, or aretalogy and keeping the romance's troubling fictionality (not to mention its seemingly unmentionable eroticism) at arm's length wherever possible.[9] His sensitive reading of the Hieronymian Lives, however, partly subverts his own conclusion. In order to classify Jerome's Lives as "history"—or, more specifically, "biography"—he must demonstrate the (lamentable?) compatibility of "the more fanciful methods of Jerome" with contemporaneous historiography, which seemingly admitted "the possibility of non-historical additions," blurring the "line between reality and legend," introducing details that served a prurient curiosity more than a desire for accuracy, and frequently sacrificing narrative coherence for the vividness of swiftly shifting scenes that remain loosely linked, at best, not only with one another but also with the broader trajectory of "contemporary history."[10] "It is like the disconnected glimpses of a hidden sky that one would get if a cloud covering the whole length and breadth of it were to break up in parts and let one see a few patches of what is beyond," muses Coleiro.[11] Idealized "heroes" are dramatically depicted and "overstress is conspicuous," he continues.[12] Indeed, Jerome's Lives, with "their appeal to the imagination and their romantic associations," are (he admits) "delightful works of art." If not quite granting them the status of "romances," Coleiro is willing to catalogue their distinctly "romantic" aspects: "the use of the weird," the delight in presenting "the reader continually with unexpected situations," "the spirit of adventure," and above all the "taste for description."[13] Jerome is especially adept, as Coleiro reads him (reading him well), at using description to convey a particular *feeling*: "the reader sees the scene under the influence of that sentiment."[14] Nonetheless, "there is no doubt that [Jerome] intended the Lives to be considered as history." "Such considerations lead us to reject the opinion that the Lives are romances," intones Coleiro; "fundamentally, they represent historical truth."[15]

As a hagiographer, Jerome is, then, a master of romance but a lousy historian. All the same, we must read him for his history and resist the lure of his romance, eschewing "entertainment" in favor of "information," insists Coleiro. A dauntingly ascetic interpretive practice is here recommended. And perhaps we would do well to take the advice, even to take it to excess. Reading "romance" as "history" and writing "history" as "romance" may indeed be the genre-bending technique by which Jerome not merely blurs but effectively dissolves the distinction between "reality and legend" (or fantasy)—thereby rendering the concept of an extratextual "historical truth" virtually irrelevant. Ascetic "(in)formation," grounded in refusing the tempting reduction of "imagination and feeling" to a merely "entertaining" superficiality, may be exactly what Jerome intends for his readers.[16]

But what clues does Jerome himself offer us concerning his hagiographic intentions? As it happens, the three canonical Hieronymian Lives are all mentioned in the self-entry with which Jerome immodestly concludes his catalogue of Christian writers, entitled *On Famous Men*. Why not, then, begin there in re-posing the question of the hagiographer's generic purposes? Jerome's interest in this innovative literary-historical composition does not lie in correlating Christian writings with "Gentile" genres but rather in delineating the emerging corpus of distinctly Christian literature (*On Famous Men*, preface) and the rise of a new class of Christian men of letters—best represented by Jerome himself.[17] This overt authorial agenda, however, is not necessarily a problem. It may even offer valuable clues for students of Jerome's hagiography, inciting fresh interpretations of what is perhaps after all best read as a "new" kind of writing—created not ex nihilo but through inventive recyclings of materials borrowed from already overlapped traditions of historical, biographical, aretalogical, martyrological, and novelistic literature. Jerome's list of his own written works—presumably chronological—begins with the *Life of Paul the Hermit* and concludes (apart from a final, looser reference to his Bible translations, countless unpublished letters to Paula and Eustochium, and work-in-progress) with the works *On the Captive Monk* and *The Life of the Blessed Hilarion* (*On Famous Men* 135). Two of his conventionally identified hagiographies are, then, also designated by their author as Lives. Taking the form of a rhetorical *inclusio*, they neatly bracket the list of Jerome's polemical treatises, published letters, and historical, exegetical, and homiletic writings. If the Lives seem thus to claim a certain prominence in his own oeuvre, it is striking that Jerome credits only one among his Christian literary predecessors, namely, Athanasius of Alexandria, with authorship of a Life—the *Life of Antony the Hermit* (*On Famous Men* 87).[18] Does Jerome understand the ascetic Life as a distinctive Christian literary "genre," and, if so, where does this "genre" originate, what does it include, and how does he intend it to be read?

The hints supplied by *On Famous Men* draw us into the hagiographic texts themselves. In introducing the earliest of his Lives, the *Life of Paul* (written circa 374), Jerome acknowledges that it is "partly true" that Antony was the "originator" or "head" (*caput*) of eremitic asceticism. "Partly I say," he clarifies, "for the fact is not so much that Antony preceded the rest as that they all derived from him the necessary stimulus (*ab eo omnium incitata sunt studia*)." Jerome goes on to make it abundantly clear that Paul of Thebes, the hero of his own Life, did, in his view, precede Antony as the "leader" or "first" (*princeps*) in the eremitic venture (*Life of Paul* 1). In what sense, then, can Antony be understood as the "originator" or the "stimulus" for the ascetic endeavors of "all"? Jerome, I would suggest, has here deliberately confused the "Life" with the "life": his subtly displaced, but easily recognizable, claim is that it is the textual *Life of Antony* (transmitted by "both

Greek and Roman writers," as he goes on to note),[19] rather than the hermit Antony's living example, that provides the "stimulus" or "incitement" not to asceticism per se but, more importantly, to *hagiography*. We should not miss the payoff of this rhetorical sleight of hand. In the *Life of Paul*, Jerome implicitly inscribes the *Life of Antony* as a "source" (a reading that will prove extraordinarily influential)[20] only so that he—thus incited—may make himself the "first" author of holy Lives.[21] His seeming compliment to Athanasius, who remains unnamed here and elsewhere in Jerome's Lives (if not in his catalogue of Christian writers), is thus written with the left hand. If hagiography is a genre, from Jerome's perspective it is a genre of his own imaginative invention. Athanasius's work is merely the provocation—the pretext, one might say.[22]

Indeed, if Hieronymian hagiography is a genre, it is a genre always being invented. The Lives of Paul and Hilarion are intertextually linked through their common (if also strategically differentiated) construal of the *Life of Antony* as their literary point of departure—a linkage further strengthened by the explicit reference to the *Life of Paul* in the *Life of Hilarion*. The same is not true of *On the Captive Monk*. Yet this not-quite-*Life of Malchus* sidles up cozily enough to the *Life of Hilarion* in Jerome's *On Famous Men*, and indeed the oriental setting and overt historicism of *On the Captive Monk* (described by Jerome as a warm-up exercise for a future church-historical narrative) may be seen to anticipate the *Life of Hilarion*'s ambition to convey a broad history of eastern monasticism in which Syria-Palestine takes its rightful place. At the same time, *On the Captive Monk* is arguably the least metahistorical and most explicitly romantic of Jerome's three saintly biographies, reproducing the plot line and rhetorical style of the ancient novel with parodic near-exactitude. In these respects, it draws closer to the *Life of Paul*, while also sharply distancing itself from the latter's mythical flights of fancy, as well as from the focus on the miraculous characteristic of the *Life of Hilarion*. The point is that Jerome's hagiographic writings exceed and contradict even his own lightly insinuated generic definitions and refuse, collectively, to stabilize into a single literary form. Previous scholarly studies strongly suggest (not least where failing to achieve consensus) that the Lives are each generic hybrids, emerging in the interplay of already distinctly hybridized literary genres. Beyond that, I am suggesting, these ambiguously overlapped texts are also remarkably dissimilar to one another, to put it simply. Nor can their differences be easily smoothed away by plotting a linear development toward a single, culminating "end."[23] The reader of Jerome's three hagiographic compositions is, rather, left with the impression of an ongoing, even restless experimentation at work in these texts.

Hieronymian hagiography is, thus, a remarkably plastic genre. Possibly it is even a genre defined by its irreducible plasticity, which (by effectively refusing the contrast with "real life") exposes and exploits the promising fictiveness and malleability of *any* "life," remaining stubbornly resistant even to literary devices of normalization. Fact or fantasy? History or romance? What *is* a true story, who *is* a holy man? These are questions that Jerome's saintly Lives continue to incite, while successfully deferring conclusive answers. At this point, a "deferential" (which is also to say, a "differential") reading of Hieronymian hagiography may be just what is required, for would-be saints and other shifty subjects of phantasmatic desire. There is, there can be, no end to the incitement to write and read holiness, to discover new "queerings" of romance,[24] further intensifications of erotic longing within the operations of sublimation. From Jerome's perspective (as I here imagine it), there are always more Lives to be found and lost—multiplied, fractured, and destroyed—in the savage (dis)habitation, the prolific specula(riza)tions, of hagiography's fluid literary imaginary.

The Queer Life of Paul the Hermit

> Both art and criticism compensate for the surrender of physical sexuality by providing imaginative gratifications that have their own attractiveness. Freud argued that beauty . . . represented a sublimation of sexuality, a rerouting of transgressive energies along socially acceptable lines; and while this seems a decidedly modern view of the matter, I would argue that we can in fact locate the germ of sublimation, the beginnings of a modern understanding, in ascetic art and its cultural interpretation. As one among countless examples, I want to focus on a picture by Sasetta (c.1400–1450) . . . depicting . . . the meeting between Antony and Paul the Hermit. . . . The compensation I am hunting for does not withhold itself, for the meeting between the two saints represents a momentary relief from the intense solitude suffered by each; their holy embrace provides, in fact, not only an affirmation of the worthiness of the ascetic life, but an astonishing interval of sensation, an unrepeatable break amid the unrelieved decades of self, or rather the denial of self. . . .
>
> The dominant form of the painting is surely the arch; and it is replicated everywhere . . . as if their embrace replicated and brought into the human world not only a principle of affection, but also a principle of

> *natural form. . . . Still, one cannot help noticing that the position of the embrace itself is highly unnatural in the sense that it is clumsy, almost impossibly awkward, bad for aging backs. Why do they assume this queer posture?*
>
> —Geoffrey Harpham, "Asceticism and the Compensations of Art"

While setting the scene for the *Life of Paul the Hermit* (the "original" behind Sasetta's painting), Jerome reflects—with seeming inconsequentiality—on those techniques of torture designed "to destroy not bodies, but souls" (*Life of Paul* 2).[25] He supplies two exemplary anecdotes, each guaranteed to make the malice of Satan memorable. The first involves an already well-tested martyr whom "the devil ordered to be covered in honey and set out in the heat of the sun, with his hands tied behind his back," his cruel intent that "one who had survived fiery plates yield to the stinging bites of flies." The reader is left to wonder about the fate of the honey-dipped sufferer,[26] as Jerome rushes on to recount a still more titillating tale of diabolical torture and Christian witness. Although the second victim (described as being "in the flower of his manhood") is set in the shade of a lovely garden, this young man, we quickly learn, is destined to burn as well. "There, among the radiant lilies and blushing roses, next to a gently murmuring stream, while the wind softly whispered among the leaves of the trees, the youth was placed upon a bed of feathers and, so that he might not escape, bound with caressing garlands and then left alone." Attracted like a fly to honey, a beautiful prostitute soon arrives on the scene of Jerome's artful confabulation. Binding the youth more tightly than ever with her twining embraces, the *meretrix* goes so far as to stroke his virile member with her hands, explains Jerome (surrendering shudderingly to his own vulgarity, as he naughtily voices "what is wicked even to say"). Having palpably excited the young man's desire, the woman throws herself on top of him, and the "wanton *victrix*" is thereby on the verge of overthrowing his virtue. Not surprisingly, Jerome's martyr—Christ's soldier—"knows not what to do and where to turn." (Bound and mounted, he does not have much room to maneuver.) In the nick of time, divine inspiration strikes: the resourceful youth bites off his own tongue and spits it into the face of the woman as she kisses him. Pain surmounts lust, as Jerome remarks briefly, and thus we arrive at the bittersweet conclusion deferred in the first tale of bondage and biting—or so it seems (3). (It must be noted, however, that neither of these "martyrs" has managed to die.) Having diverted his readers long enough with such apparently digressive narratives, Jerome can now make a brisk transition to his main plot, explaining how the young Paul of Thebes—a contemporary of the two martyrs—came to invent asceticism while fleeing the temptations of persecution (4–5).[27]

It is a queer way to begin a saintly Life—more than that, a queer way to launch a competitive writing career, which is what Jerome is doing in this first, overt attempt to upstage the Athanasian *Life of Antony*.[28] The author is baiting his reader, but what kind of bait is he dangling, and what is to be delivered in its place? Jerome's *Life of Paul* is pervaded throughout by a bait-and-switch dynamic, and the deliciously teasing opening vignettes are, I would argue, more crucial to the text's constitutive mobilities than is commonly acknowledged by commentators apparently embarrassed to find themselves so easily seduced.[29] Despite the note of triumph on which he seems to conclude, Jerome's preliminary tales of torture are neither climactic nor anticlimactic but rather disturbingly open-ended and thus—having failed to demarcate their own limits—not, strictly speaking, "pre-liminary" at all. The first, incomplete narrative of martyrdom has already given way to the second, acquiring a supplement rather than coming to a conclusion; similarly, as the hard-bitten tongue of a mute renunciation is offered in place of manhood's more fluent ejaculations—as a painful pleasure is exchanged for a pleasurable pain—the ascetic life of Paul emerges as both a prolongation and a disruptive repetition of the martyr's tantalizingly arrested desire. In addition, Jerome has already warned that the account of Paul's career will itself be fragmentary, interrupted by a telling lacuna—the huge expanse of Paul's middle years, declared definitively inaccessible. Proceeding thus by fits and starts, shifting across gaps and intervals, and yet never really leaving anything behind, this nearly trackless narrative seems to consist solely in a series of switchbacks. In fact, I would go farther still: Jerome's *Life of Paul* is a purposefully torturous text that intends to "destroy souls," again and again; its interruptive and repetitive narrativity contributes to the (paradoxical) work of psychic deformation,[30] restlessly resisting the fixation of identity; it contributes thereby to the production of a queerly pure desire, whose end of self-dissolution turns out to be no end at all.

If we take the risk and read this Life, we must start by backtracking to the garden, for only when we have taken *that* bait can we make the switch to another fantastically paradisal scene, where we will eventually (and repeatedly) find (and lose) Paul. Lingering a bit longer with the enticing youth of Jerome's second martyrial exemplum, we might now note that he has, by the end, swapped tongues with the prostitute: Tertullian, for one, is familiar with the famous case of the "Athenian courtesan" convicted of conspiracy who, "subjected to torture by the tyrant," "still making no betrayal," "at last bit off her own tongue and spat it in the tyrant's face, that he might be convinced of the uselessness of his torments, however long they should be continued" (Tertullian, *To the Martyrs* 4).[31] The heroic tongue biting is thus not *merely* a euphemism for self-castration—a reading so teasingly available, so nearly literal, that it is almost thereby disabled, for the martyr does *not* after all give up his manly parts. Nor is the tongue-biting *merely* a reinscription of the seductress as the castrating agent, encased in a fantasy in which a man may take matters into his own teeth, thereby regaining a position of control. As the tale of the Athenian courtesan (not to mention the still more notorious case of Philomela) reminds us,[32] the youth's tongue-biting (upon which Jerome's readers hang with ba(i)ted breath) is crucially *also* an act of gender-switching, for only a female can truly lose her tongue, in the terms of cultural codes already ancient by Jerome's day.[33] A real man minds his tongue, able both to speak freely and to sustain a noble silence, whereas a woman, never in full possession of language (never fully possessed by language), can only finally control her tongue by destroying it, thereby attaining an almost absolute eloquence in perfect silence. If it is, then, a woman's tongue that sprouts in the youth's mouth in the ecstatic moment of its own leaping death, what of his *virilia*?[34] In Jerome's garden, the flowering member of manhood can, like its feminized lingual counterpart, be forced to betray truths better choked back—and therefore perhaps better bitten off and spit out once and for all, after all (after all is said and done). But what might that mean? From the youth to the prostitute, from the womanly tongue to the manly "tongue" and back again, along the series of switchbacks, we are invited to traverse the imagined scene. By the time we take the bait, by the time we *bite*, Jerome's martyr is neither intact in his manhood nor simply emasculated (the exchanges enacted in this text already result in something more complex than "feminization"); he is no longer either the bottom or the top; his triumph is also his surrender. This witness is located in the gaps, in the fragments, in the very mobility of his shifting desire. And if he has become mute, perhaps he is also, like Philomela, a weaver of a secret text, bearer of desire, carrying us . . . where? Well, for the moment, toward the young Paul.

It seems almost by accident that Paul—"proceeding step by step, sometimes advancing, sometimes retreating, sometimes retracing his steps" (5)—discovers the secret cave that was to become the permanent home of the man who thereby fashioned himself as "the first hermit" (1). "It is human desire to discover what is hidden," observes Jerome, as he describes Paul's removal of the stone and avid exploration of the cave's interior—which expands wondrously, as if to accommodate Paul's desire, opening to the sky, extending with the reaching branches of a palm tree, encircling a neatly contained stream. We are back in a garden, then. This time, it is a garden seemingly safely enclosed, the site of Paul's future self-sufficiency—and yet it also contains a few untidy nooks and crannies, littered with a strange debris of ancient parts and rusted tools. "Egyptian records report that this place was a clandestine mint dating from the time Antony was joined to Cleopatra," Jerome informs us authoritatively (5). What is intruded with this fragment of detailed "realism"?[35] By means of another narrative break and twist, the presence of "Antony" will soon be explained, but how are we to read the "Cleopatra" with whom he is, or will be, "joined"? Retreating, we discover the Egyptian prostitute who threatens to unman the martyr with the force of his own desire. Advancing, we encounter Paul, approached step by step, along the path of Antony's desire. Martyr and *meretrix*, Antony and Cleopatra,[36] Antony and Paul—so many switchbacks, both connective and disruptive, along the tortuous track of this tale.

Creating yet another small diversion by introducing comparative corroboration of Paul's miraculously restricted diet (consisting at this point solely of dates [6]), Jerome can then pretend to resume his account of Paul's life. In the meantime, he has opened and leaped yet another gap in his text. Now Paul—last sighted in adolescence—is 113 years old, and it is the relatively youthful Antony (a mere 90) who is roaming the sun-baked desert in pursuit of hidden things (7). Having been summoned by a dream to seek one who is a better monk than he, Jerome's Antony seems still, in his waking state, to traverse a dreamscape, "mother" of mythical figures that become literalized as signifiers while remaining oversaturated with sense—"hyper-icons,"[37] black holes of density in the text that threaten to suck the reader into their unplumbable depths, even as they also propel the narrative forward, luring us on, with Antony.

The first such figure that Antony encounters is a "human mixed with horse," to which "the fancy of poets assigns the name 'hippocentaur,'" notes Jerome (7). Patricia Cox Miller glosses the text further, pointing out that centaurs were "noted for two traits in particular: their hyper-masculine and violent sexuality, and their hostility to what the Greeks saw as foundational norms of culture."[38] Antedating not only marriage but also sexual difference itself, as Miller reminds us, the centaur belongs to an ancient, all-male realm of pure and undifferentiated "nature" while simultaneously functioning as the guardian of divinely transmitted arts of healing, music, and prophecy.[39]

With a gestured sign of his own sealed salvation, Antony protects himself from the portentous implications of such an alarming encounter. Addressing the beast sternly, he demands to know where the "servant of God" dwells. The hybrid creature is as mute as the tongueless martyr: "The beast gnashed its teeth and tried to speak clearly, but only ground out from a mouth shaking with bristles some kind of barbarous sounds rather than lucid speech." Before it vanishes from the text, however, it extends its right hand in a telling gesture of its own, thereby indicating unerringly to Antony "the sought-for route." Here Jerome pauses briefly to raise the question of "whether the devil himself took on the shape of this creature, thus to terrify Antony, or whether the desert, typically capable of engendering monsters (*monstruosorum animalium ferax*), also gave birth (*gignat*) to this beast." He concludes lightly: "we are uncertain" (7). Jerome's deceptively casual tone partly masks the shocking effects of his interjected "uncertainty":[40] insinuating indifference, he blurs the line between demonic perversion and desert fecundity; with a shrug of his writerly shoulders, he simultaneously creates an interval of difference between the disseminator of illusion and the matrix of myth (between lies and fiction)—even as he potentially narrows the gap between the maternalized earth and the father's cave.

At this point, Jerome's text—which is also to say, Jerome's expansively intertextual desert[41]—swiftly perpetuates itself by yet another inexact repetition. No sooner has Antony resumed his journey than he encounters a dwarf, a homunculus, "whose nostrils were joined together, with horns growing out of his forehead, and with the legs and feet of a goat" (8). As Miller points out, this figure—who confesses himself the member of a race commonly identified as "fauns, satyrs, and incubi"—"reduplicate[s] the centaur" in such a way as to highlight the "hybrid character of the inhabitants indigenous to the desert" while also underlining their hypermasculine sexuality, "by definition nonfamilial and wild."[42] "Stepping forward," Antony finds himself drawn a step closer to the uncanny creature, who offers him dates and identifies himself as a "mortal being"—that is, a virtual human—and also a fellow follower of Christ, leaving Antony both to weep with joy and to "marvel that he could comprehend the dwarf's speech." Do Antony and the homunculus, then, speak with the same tongue? Are they "brothers"? If the appearance of the stereotypically randy figure of the satyr in an ascetic text is itself sufficiently astonishing, the implications of this friendly exchange are almost unthinkable. Indeed, Jerome again expertly interrupts the narrative line before the thought can be completed: the satyr is gone in a flash, disappearing from sight as quickly as the centaur (8). Facing a flickeringly specular desert that has grown "vast" indeed, Antony—like the martyr overwhelmed by his wanton seducer—"knows not what he should do and in what direction he should turn" (9).

A third guide appears, "a she-wolf, panting with thirst," who crawls toward the foot of a mountain, where she enters a cave. Antony, perhaps panting too, follows her first with his eyes and then with his feet, his curiosity unsatisfied by his initial glimpse of the dim interior. "Truly, as the Scripture says, 'Perfect love drives out fear,'" comments Jerome: where pain displaced the martyr's lust, love now displaces the hermit's fear, and Antony advances "step by step" in the darkness, "sometimes standing still." He hears a sound, he perceives a light; stumbling, he creates a sound, and shy Paul (who, of course, waits at the heart of this cave), hearing a sound too, shuts and bolts his door. Performing his role flamingly in this almost parodically groping rite of courtship, Antony prays for hours on end for entrance, pronouncing himself "known" by Paul, acknowledging his unworthiness, and threatening nonetheless not to leave until he has seen his beloved. "You who receive wild beasts, why do you turn down a man?" he cries, and the distinction between man and beast, already doubly disrupted by centaur and satyr, dissolves further, even as Antony attempts flailingly to reassert his difference—now seemingly inscribed as a *sexual* difference (for it is presumably the she-wolf whom Paul has admitted). But if Antony is here (as Pierre Leclerc whimsically proposes) playing Romeo to Paul's Juliet, does his perversely ardent love—inverting the logic of pederasty—not make the younger man "a little more ridiculous"?[43] "I have sought and I have found; I knock that it may be opened," he proclaims.[44] "If I do not obtain my request, I shall die right here in front of your door. Then surely you will at least bury my corpse." Antony's final, nearly prophetic vow is, as we shall see, perhaps as much his desire as his threat. He begs Paul to open his cave, even if only to receive his death, to bury his corpse (9).[45]

Paul, teasing and laughing more like a courtesan than a hermit, finally opens. "Do you wonder that I do not let you in, when you threaten to die?" he quips merrily (9). The two embrace, call each other by name, and fervently offer thanks to God. Giving Antony a "sacred kiss," Paul displays his body—the body, as Miller suggests, of a desert "wild man,"[46] covered with unkempt hair, and also the body of a hybrid creature, straddling the boundary between life and death, nearly a corpse, shortly to be in need of burial. "You see before you a man soon to become dirt," he declares. Antony apparently likes what he sees. The two gossip sweetly. Unlike (and thus also like) the satyr, Paul serves no dates from his palm. Instead, a raven drops a fat loaf of bread into their laps and flies quickly away again—another fragment, or figment, in Jerome's prolific desert imaginary (10). Sitting by the spring, the two men argue for a full day over who will be the first to break the bread. Finally, in yet another comical moment, they determine to pull at the loaf simultaneously—neither will be first, neither will top—and then, after eating, they drink companionably from the spring.[47] Once again offering thanks to God, they spend the night together—"in watchful prayer," of course. The morning after, Paul delivers his painful news: the time of his death has arrived. "You have been sent by the Lord to cover my wretched body with soil, returning earth to earth," he informs his new friend (11). Antony—whose words at the cave's entrance have been returned to him in reverse, along another of the shifty switchbacks of Jerome's text—weeps and begs Paul not to leave him, "but to welcome him, Antony, as a companion for the great journey." In reply, Paul merely asks that Antony go back to fetch the cloak Athanasius has given him,[48] "to serve as a shroud for my body." Jerome explains Paul's real motivation: "he wanted Antony to leave him," so that he could "lighten the burden of grief Antony would bear at his death" (12). But perhaps Jerome's account is not as straight as it seems: the anticipated death and burial have the makings of a marriage, as we shall see, and Antony's temporary banishment will allow him to replicate the expectant motions of his journey; desire will once more be prolonged, while Paul, simultaneously coy and welcoming, prepares (again) to celebrate his meeting with Antony, in the desert that has become a queer kind of Paradise. ("Truly have I seen Paul in Paradise," Antony will explain to his brethren back at home [13].)

Driving his body to the limits of its strength, Antony returns quickly with the cloak. "He thirsted for Paul, he longed to see Paul, he concentrated his entire attention on Paul." (We recall the she-wolf, thirsting, crawling forward.) Just a few short hours from his goal, he receives a vision of Paul ascending to heaven. Grieving, Antony cries out in the unmistakable language of a lover, "Paul! Why do you abandon me? Why do you leave without saying good-bye? So late in my life I met you; so soon do you depart?" (14). Paul still has a surprise or two up his tattered sleeve, however. Antony reaches the cave to find the hermit's body erect, in prayer. Thinking him still alive, he attempts to join him in mutual devotions. But Paul is indeed dead, and Antony, now accepting that death, embraces and kisses a corpse that still knows the appropriate posture for thanksgiving (15). Wrapping Paul's body in the cloak and carrying it outside to the accompaniment of his own hymns and psalms (thereby taking on a traditionally feminine role in the rites for the dead—and perhaps also in the preparation of a bride for her marriage), Antony remembers that he does not have the necessary tool for digging a grave. Fresh grief at this lack gives way to wonder, as Jerome performs another breathtakingly mobile multiplication and shift between portentous signs. "From out of the deep desert came running two lions with their manes streaming back from their shoulders." Lion- (or lioness-) to-the-rescue is already a stock motif in Christian as well as non-Christian tales[49] (and this is not the last time Jerome himself will turn the trick)—but two such splendidly masculine creatures, racing together in such perfect coordination, thrashing their tails and roaring their lamentations in tandem, is almost more than a man could ask for. "Competing with each other to excavate the sand" (like Paul and Antony arguing and tugging at the bread), this odd couple neatly dig Paul's grave and then humbly gesture their desire to receive Antony's blessing, which he joyfully grants (16).

Alone again with Paul, Antony buries the corpse, covering it with desert sand, with which it will mingle, according to Paul's prediction: "You see before you a man soon to become dirt" (10). Having wrapped Paul in the cloak of Athanasius, Antony takes Paul's tunic, so that he may wrap his own body in the garment woven from the leaves of the paradisal palm—more shroud or wedding garment? "On the holy days of Easter and Pentecost, Antony always wore Paul's tunic" (16). Jerome, in closing the *Life of Paul*, makes his *own* desire clear, addressing his reader directly while naming himself (as so often in this text) in the third person: "If the Lord should give him the choice, he would rather have the tunic of Paul" (18). Shrouding Paul in the Athanasian text of Antony, Jerome (like *his* Antony) chooses the tunic of Paul for himself—the sign of Paul's always dissolving "presence," the veil of "death" that extends desire by thwarting possession. And what is the tunic if not the fabric of *this* text?

It is after all queer bait that Jerome has offered his readers, and his repeated switches are still more unsettlingly queer. My point is not merely that this highly innovative hagiographical romance draws us out of the compulsory regime of "civilized" desire and into a realm in which nature and culture collapse around shifting and shiftily gendered figures of male homoeroticism—though that must also be said.[50] Equally significant is the fact that the text will not, finally, *settle* at all, will not settle upon an *object of desire*. Resisting the temptation of objectification to the end by dissolving Paul into the desert sands (having already elided the narrative of the "life" of one represented as always already "soon to become dirt"), a literary discomposition that might be well renamed *The Corruption of Antony* thereby also gives tongue-tied witness to the perpetuation of a "pure" desire that "shatters" the subject, rendering it at once less continuous with itself and more open to the (ever receding) "other."[51] The constitutive textual practice of Jerome's hagiography is, to borrow Leo Bersani's phrasing, "the discursive exemplification of desire's mobile repetitions";[52] the disjunctions and iterations marking its apparent narrative failures (its proliferating resistances to closure) are the sources of its critical and critically erotic power. If "sublimation" here begins to seem "co-extensive with (rather than 'beyond') sexuality," it may also prove conceptually superfluous.[53] In other words, to describe ascetic love as "sublimated" is, paradoxically, merely to point to an *intensification* of the movements of displacement and deferral that are inherent in *all* desire.

The Queer Marriage of Malchus the Monk

> *Try to talk about friendship between the sexes, and the conversation always becomes about something else. The inevitable shift is part of what marks the topic as interesting—that it immediately summons a whole range of associations about the way people interact—and is also what defines it as an* idiomatic *problem: friendship between men and women, no matter how intensely it may be valued by how many people, is scarcely nameable as a thing unto itself. Contemporary phrasings, like their predecessors in earlier times, define male/female friendship according to what it is not. "Just friends," "only friends," "not lovers," and similar combinations all in effect describe friendship negatively; all insist that what friendship is not is sexual union or attraction; and all, in the process of making that negative declaration, invite the suspicion that what is being talked about is in fact not friendship but sex, whether unacknowledged, unrealized, or unrevealed.*
>
> —Victor Luftig, Seeing Together: Friendship Between the Sexes in English Writing, from Mill to Woolf

If the *Life of Paul the Hermit* experiments with a radical disruption of the genre of romance, Jerome's next—and much later—hagiography, *On the Captive Monk*, seems to follow a "straighter" course, eschewing the world of mythical beasts in favor of the plausibly realistic (even quasi-"historical") realm of novelistic discourse while also cleaving more closely to the conventional plot line of ancient fiction.[54] Indeed, although elsewhere a severe (and defensive) critic of the practice of "syneisaktism," or spiritual marriage,

Jerome (also famously the "friend" of the Roman lady Paula)[55] unexpectedly gives us a *married* monk in this almost parodically romantic Life. In the end, however, the particular emplotment of a captivatingly ascetic coupling puts "marriage" in question while refusing to offer sexual repression (or its kissing cousin, sublimation) as an easy answer, thereby opening up a strangely empty zone—a portentous "idiomatic" gap.

The tale is an old man's tale, related to Jerome in his inquisitive youth (or so he claims), and now retold via the device of reported speech in his own more settled senectitude. The beginning is familiar enough to readers of other christianized novels: a young man whose desire is all for God is pressured by his family to marry a mere girl. The youth flees and eventually—indeed, all too quickly and easily, given the voracious novelistic appetite for adventure—finds true love among the monks of the Syrian desert (*On the Captive Monk* 3).[56] This first miniplot is thus a failed romance, having neglected to defer its conclusion, and the narrator must begin again.[57]

Now the problem is framed in terms of the young monk's desire to visit his widowed mother and attend to his family estate. The old man recalls the thoughts that belonged to his own youth: "After her death, I would sell what little property there was, give part of the proceeds to the poor, erect a monastery with part, and—why do I blush to admit my infidelity?—put aside the remainder to pay for my own comfort." His abbot sees through the demonically inspired ruse and pleads with him to desist from his plans. "And when my abbot failed to persuade me, he fell on his knees and begged that I not desert him, that I not destroy myself." For a second time, the man—who is both our hero and our narrator, Malchus—resists paternal coercion and sets off (3). At this point, he will meet with the adventures he needs, and the story will become a real *story*. Traversing a barren wasteland with about seventy others banded together for protection against marauding Saracens, he and his party are beset by an exotic troop of "Ishmaelites," and Malchus—who had hoped to regain his home and inheritance—instead loses his very freedom. One other of his fellow travelers, a woman, is assigned as a slave to the same owner, and the two are carried by camels to their master's familial encampment in the heart of the harsh desert (4). Like a prisoner, as he comments, Malchus is stripped of his former identity: "I learned to go about naked, for the heat allowed no covering except of one's private parts." Dressed in only a loincloth, Malchus goes native—and thereby unexpectedly recovers the archaic purity of the desert shepherd. "It seemed to me that the holy Jacob and I had something in common; Moses also came to mind" (5). Fleeing the monastery, the slave Malchus is finally

Sublimation and the Arts of Romance 35

beginning to be a real monk by becoming a wild man. Captivity is now his desire and his pleasure.

But, of course, more trials await the hero. His master, pleased with the slave's performance, desires to reward him, so as further to secure his loyalty. The hitch is that Malchus is none too pleased with his prize. "He handed over to me a fellow-slave, the very woman taken captive with me." Malchus attempts to decline politely ("thanks, but no thanks") on the basis of religious values—invoking not, as we might expect, a monastic but a marital morality. "I . . . stated that I was a Christian and not permitted to accept as a wife a married woman whose husband was still alive." Why this subtle displacement of his resistance? Malchus, the narrator, fails to comment, and we are left to draw our own conclusions. At any rate, the strategy, if that is what it is, backfires. The master is not merely surprised but surprisingly enraged. "He lost his temper and started to chase me with sword drawn." Clearly, Malchus is expected to draw a "sword" of his own in self-defense. Does he? "Had I not immediately grabbed the woman and embraced her, he would have drained me of my blood on the spot," he declares (6). The defense seems a bit shaky for a monk well-practiced in daily martyrdom. But Malchus, as we shall see, prefers to perform his witness before a more private audience.

"Well, then," he continues, "night came, darker than usual and all too quickly, as far as I was concerned. I led my new wife, with misery our bridesmaid, into a half-collapsed cave." Malchus is just about "half-collapsed" himself by this point. Now, for the first time, he knows himself truly a captive. A prisoner in marriage, he resorts to playing the virgin. Throwing himself on the ground in lamentation, he waxes histrionic, bewailing the anticipated loss of his chastity, so long preserved. His concluding speech is that of any maidenly heroine—or martyr—worth her salt, ready to take matters into her own hands, if need be.[58] "Turn the sword against yourself: death of the soul is more to be feared than the body's demise," he proclaims, in self-address. "Sexual purity preserved also has its martyrdom. Let the witness for Christ lie unburied in the desert. I shall play both roles: persecutor and martyr." With these words, Malchus finally draws his sword, "which gleamed in the darkness." At this point, the woman finds her tongue and uses it to expose and explore a few gaps in Malchus's hysterically feminized discourse. Who is forcing him now, anyway? His "bride" may not be a virgin or even "single" (as Malchus has chosen to point out to his master), but this is *not* the opening scene of the *Life of Paul* and, thus, if the master has sheathed his sword without having violated Malchus's virginity, why is

Malchus now waving his own sword about? (And what is a slave doing with a sword? Or is it something else that gleams in the dark?) "Why should you die in order to avoid being joined to me?" queries the woman. (Or why not have died earlier, impaled on the master's sword, rather than grabbing me?) "I would die, if you intended to take me as wife," she proclaims, succinctly clarifying the situation. Having straightened out their roles, the woman—seeking an end to Malchus's alarmingly queer contradictions—makes a practical proposition. "Have me, then, as a partner in sexual purity and love the bond of the soul instead of that of the body. Our masters may presume that you are my husband; Christ will know that you are my brother. We shall easily convince them of our marriage when they see us act in a loving way." Malchus, not surprisingly, is "dumb-founded" (perhaps he has suddenly bitten his tongue). Impressed by the woman's strength, he suddenly "loved her as a wife all the more." More than what? More than when he first drew his sword, perhaps? At any rate, he now loves her "as a wife"—and that is *not* to imply that they are lovers (rather, "just friends"). "Never did I look upon her naked body. Never did I touch her flesh." The strategy is successful: the queer couple is happy, and so are their masters (6).

Malchus's contentment is short-lived, however. Observing a colony of ants, he finds himself missing life with the brethren. "I began to tire of my captivity, to yearn for the cells of the monastery, and to feel a need for the sense of purpose of those ants—where everyone works for the community," he recalls (7). Married, he again experiences himself as a captive in his less-than-monkish servitude. Longing restlessly for the monastery, he nonetheless still clings to his soul's mate: "I couldn't hide my melancholy; she asked why I was so troubled." Bound together in a pledge of secrecy, the two whisper intimately into their pillows, plotting their joint escape (8). But where will it end, for such a pair?

Fleeing by night, the couple hike ten miles to a river, hoping to put their masters off their trail by paddling across the water, supported on inflated sheep's bladders (supplied, with Odyssean effort, by Malchus). Losing most of their provisions in the crossing, they are now threatened by hunger and thirst as well as the dangers of overexposure to the sun, the bites of poisonous creatures that lurk in the sheltering shade of rocks, possible roaming bands of Saracens, and the wrath of their masters—who are certain to be soon in hot pursuit. "Even now, as I tell you this," recalls Malchus, "I begin to tremble in fear; even though I know in my mind I am safe, my whole body shudders" (8). (It is not hard to believe him.) On the third day, sure enough, they see two riders mounted on camels in the distance. They also see an underground cavern, extending to their right. Even more afraid of their master than of the possible dangers awaiting them in the shadows—"vipers, basilisks, scorpions"—they duck into a crevice just inside the cavern's entrance. There is good reason to think this might turn out to be their tomb, as Malchus tells it. Breathless with fear, they see their master and a slave appear at the entrance (9). A wondrously gruesome theater unfolds before their eyes. The master sends his slave into the cave. The slave enters, shouting to the runaways to give themselves up. "He was still crying out to us when lo! we watched in the darkness as a lioness attacked the man, ripped open his throat and dragged his bloody body into the cave." Torn between terror and joy, the two scarcely have time to recover before their master, impatient with the delay, bursts into the cave, sword drawn once again. "Before he reached our hiding place, he was caught by the wild beast. Who would ever believe that before our eyes a wild creature would fight for us!" enthuses Malchus. It is clear, however, that the lioness's defense of Malchus and his companion is understood as incidental to her own purposes, for Malchus is well aware that "death of a similar sort" is their likely fate. "We were armed solely with our knowledge that our chastity protected us as if by a wall," he adds. However, it is the lioness's own instinct for defense of herself and her cub to which he continues to attribute their safety, in the event. "When morning came, the lioness, fearing a trap and aware that she had been seen, picked up her cub by her teeth and carried it off, thus surrendering her refuge to us." Even then, the couple wait until evening before they dare move from their hiding place (9). Mounting the two camels conveniently positioned outside the cave and equally conveniently laden with provisions, Malchus and his woman slowly but steadily make their way back to civilization. Once safely home, they are even able to sell the camels (10).

Relating this story of salvation occurring "in the presence of violence, in the midst of the desert, and in the company of wild beasts"—as Jerome glosses it in his own notably concise (indeed, almost cautiously pat) conclusion (10)—Malchus takes us neither to the dreamlike desert of Paul nor to the demonic sandscape of the Athanasian Antony. His desert is uncompromisingly "natural"; the fierce lioness is no close kin of Paul's courtly gravediggers; the poison of vipers and scorpions needs no help from Satan; and miracles seem a matter of chance and interpretation.[59] But what of the final outcome? Here is Malchus's own report: "When I returned here, I handed myself over once again to the monks. . . . And as for this woman, whom I cherished as a sister, but did not commit myself to her as a sister,

I turned her over to the virgins" (10). *What*? "Did not commit"? That is all; again, we are left to draw our own conclusions. She: no longer a "wife." He: no longer answering to her call of "brother." He: once again brother to his brothers. She: . . . well, it is possible to hope that "the woman" fares better with her sisters—and why should she not?

Borrowing Malchus's voice, Jerome has here sustained a continuous plot and, in so doing, has risked running the romance into the ground. Closure is deadening without the shattering presence of a disintegrating corpse; desire withers without the deferrals of sublimation; freedom loses its sweetness when utterly released from constraint. Or perhaps the problem could be better stated otherwise: "the woman" who is here at the end so casually "turned over to the virgins" has a voice but never acquires a name. Could it be that Malchus, if he does not even remember what she is called, has long since ceased to hear her clearly, just as he refuses to look at her body or touch her flesh? Sleeping next to her night after night, has he eradicated even temptation? The first, truncated tale of true love in the monastery threatens to subsume and displace the second, more richly developed tale of a queer marriage: however promisingly they begin, this ascetic couple is, by Malchus's own account, an erotic failure, their story leached dry of desire.

Brought under the spell of Malchus's discourse, readers of this Life should not therefore cease to resist, here at the end: this is, after all, still *Jerome's romance*[60]—and thus crucially *not* a seamlessly woven text. Surely we may be expected to notice that the history that Malchus brings to such a calm conclusion not only fails to address the curious query that prompts its original telling[61] but furthermore subtly contradicts what Jerome himself claims to have *seen*—that is, an ancient and pious *couple* living companionably whom (but for their apparent childlessness) he might have mistaken for "Zacharias and Elizabeth of the Gospel" (2). (Manfred Fuhrman tucks his embarrassment at the contradiction into a squirming footnote: "One difficulty remains: according to chapter 2 Malchus lives with the *anus* in *contubernium*; in chapter 10 in contrast he affirms that 'I gave myself again to the monks and handed her over to the virgins.' One should thus assume that the two initiated the *contubernium* at an advanced age.")[62] In the gap between the young Jerome's initial, burning question concerning the character of this coupling—"what was the bond: matrimony, blood, or the Spirit?" (2)—and the elderly Malchus's elusively narrated answer, we can locate the "idiomatic problem" that is also a matrix of unmentionable desire. Perhaps it is the case (as the now-mature Jerome intones in closing) that "sexual purity is never a prisoner and that the person dedicated to Christ can die but cannot be overcome" (10). Nonetheless, the monk Malchus (so Jerome also insinuates) never ceases to be captivated by his queer wife, as long as he lives.

Hilarion's Last Laugh

> *What is peculiarly postmodern about these celebrity biographies is the way in which bisexuality, though it appears at first to be everywhere—on the jacket blurb, in the headlines, in the index—is ultimately, not nowhere, but elsewhere. Like postmodernism itself, it resists a stable referentiality. It performs.*
> —Marjorie Garber, "Bisexuality and Celebrity"

When Jerome takes to writing hagiography for the last time, he reverts once more to the affair of Paul, with which he had begun: "We despise voices of abuse of some who, as they once disparaged my Paul, will now perhaps disparage Hilarion." Soon to be companions in abuse (if not literal martyrdom), Paul and Hilarion are nonetheless positioned antithetically in the discourse of their detractors, as Jerome anticipates it: "Censuring the former for his solitude, they may find fault with the latter for his sociability; as the one who was always hidden did not exist, the other who was seen by many is deemed of no account." Rising to the rhetorical occasion with characteristic vigor, Jerome hurls his own voice of praise combatively at an audience determined (as he suggests, with heavy irony) neither to give nor to take any satisfaction. Paul's smilingly elusive solitude will be augmented by a more robust hilarity, his closeted lifestyle complemented by the exhibitionism of a holy man who is "out" to the world. If Paul was like John the Baptist, suggests Jerome, Hilarion is like Jesus, "in the busy throng, eating and drinking." In authoring the *Life of Hilarion*, Jerome is thus saucily turning the other cheek to the lashing tongues of his critics—whether real or fantasized. His muse is none less than the Holy Spirit, and once again inspiration propels him in startlingly new directions (*Life of Hilarion* 1).[63] Having recently, with *On the Captive Monk*, attempted a "straighter" romance, he now attempts a "straighter" hagiography,[64] sweeping the monsters from his closet and sorting out the dualisms of his desert according to (more or less) Athanasian standards of demonizing decency. But here, as in *On the Captive Monk*, it is precisely by playing at generic conventionality that Jerome achieves his queer results.

As in the *Life of Paul*, the emaciated figure of Antony is the pivot around which the tale of a holy man turns. If, in the bold rescripting of Jerome's first saintly Life, Antony's desire for Paul proves all-consuming, now it is the younger monk Hilarion who "is fired with a desire to see" Antony. In hot pursuit of a Desert Father, Hilarion repeats the journey of Jerome's Antony. He also, however, crucially replays the mimetic discipleship of *Athanasius*'s Antony—a doubled act of homage that places Antony in the role of master, even as Jerome allows himself (temporarily, as we shall see) to be mastered by the Athanasian hagiography. In the tactically citational *Life of Hilarion*, Jerome's eagerly imitative hero initially observes Antony as closely as Athanasius's Antony once observed the ascetics on the outskirts of his own village (cf. *Life of Antony* 4), "contemplating the method of his life and the gravity of his conduct, his assiduity in prayer, his humility in his dealings with the brethren, his severity in rebuke, his eagerness in exhortation." Where Jerome's Paul challenges Antony on the basis of seniority, his Hilarion—a younger man—seems determined to beat the Athanasian ascetic at his own game, matching him move for move. Although Athanasius's Antony has already made a city of the desert *(Life of Antony* 14), Hilarion, "deeming it a strange anomaly that he should have to bear in the desert the crowds of the cities," stubbornly retraces Antony's first, "precivilized" steps, backtracking to his own home to renounce his familial inheritance before plunging alone and defenseless into the perilous and still monastically pristine wilderness not of Egypt but of Palestine (cf. *Life of Antony* 2–3) (3).

There it is that the ostensibly sociable Hilarion accomplishes his foundationally eremitic self-refashioning. At 15, "stripped bare" of all but "the weapons of Christ" (3), he can be seen (through Jerome's ever-keen vision) to possess not only bright eyes and smooth cheeks but also a "body thin and delicate" (4). (Athanasius, perhaps a man of dim eyesight, never drops a hint concerning Antony's looks.)[65] Outfitted like the corpse of Paul in a rough cloak from Antony's swelling closet of monkish garments—and wearing no more than a regulation sackcloth shirt under that—Hilarion practices an asceticism so stringent that his physique grows yet more frail, premature aging prolonging and intensifying the appealing fragility of his youth: "he became so feeble and his frame so wasted that his bones scarcely held together" (5).[66] Like the Athanasian Antony, he finds himself in a bracingly hostile wilderness populated not by mythical guides but by malevolent demons (6–8), and he inhabits a distinctly nonparadisal cell, "more like a tomb than a house" (9).[67] When, at the end of twenty-two years of punishing solitude,[68] a woman suffering from sterility is "bold enough to break into the presence of the blessed Hilarion" (13), the holy man emerges ripe with the miracles demanded by visitors who beset him in ever greater numbers, when his fame begins to rival even Antony's—as the master himself acknowledges. ("And if ever the sick from Syria came to him, [Antony] would say to them, 'Why have you taken the trouble to come so far, when you have there my son, Hilarion?'" [24].)

If Jerome's renditions of Hilarion's demonic temptations and holy disciplines do not quite add up to the tale of ascetic progress that he pretends to offer (he confesses it "tedious to narrate singly the successive steps of his spiritual ascent" [10]), his representation of Hilarion's more mature Antonine career as miracle worker and semi-itinerant monastic leader is likewise marked by a strikingly disjunctive and oddly "distant"[69] style. The result is perhaps another kind of tedium,[70] at least for a reader seeking the satisfaction of a clearly drawn plot or sustained characterization, as Jerome loosely strings one miracle story after another, in a sequence that, however artfully constructed,[71] nonetheless builds toward no particular climax. Here we may sense him leaning (perhaps a bit lazily) on the prop of the Athanasian *Life*, whose progressions are clearly mapped across the terrain of the desert and punctuated by the well-rounded discourses of the ascetic sage. Here we may *also* observe Jerome beginning to explode the master text, in which he has initially planted his own deliberately "primitive" hagiography (with the help of the Holy Spirit): immodestly making himself over as Antony, Jerome's Hilarion has silently shed the Athanasian monk's cloak of restraint. Forgetting to mutter nervously that he derives all his power from God, Hilarion confidently cures illnesses (13–17, 19), engages in wrestling matches with demonically possessed strong men (18), and casts counterspells to protect the victories of charioteers (20) and the virtues of maidens (21). No wonder this holy man is easily taken for a magician (20).[72]

It is the death of Antony that releases the romance in the *Life of Hilarion*. It releases Hilarion first of all from the tedium of his placement "at the head of a grand monastery and a multitude of resident brethren," for it is shortly after apprehending Antony's passing (miraculously, of course [29]—and with reference not only to the Athanasian Antony's knowledge of Amun's death [*Life of Antony* 60] but also to the Hieronymian Antony's vision of Paul's death [*Life of Paul* 14]) that Hilarion makes his break for freedom. Unfortunately, his get-away ass is not quite quick enough: "ten thousand people of various ages and both sexes came together to prevent his departure." Literally made the captive of his devotees, Hilarion stages a seven-day hunger strike before he is finally liberated to undertake a journey in the company of forty hand-picked monks, eventually arriving (following a few teasingly tedious detours) at Antony's former desert abode. There he is determined to spend the night of the anniversary of his master's death "in vigil in the very place where the saint had died" (30). At this point, and perhaps for the first time, glimmers of a fertile Paradise known to Jerome's Paul and *his* Antony seem to shine through the text. "There is a high and rocky mountain extending for about a mile, with gushing springs amongst its spurs, the waters of which are partly absorbed by the sand, partly flow towards the plain and gradually form a stream shaded on either side by countless palms which lend much pleasantness and charm to the place," writes Jerome, once again at his descriptive best, as he expertly invokes the classical topos of the *locus amoenus*, painting a verbal picture of a "pleasant place." Pacing in Antony's footsteps, gazing on the garden of his design and planting, touching the hoe so often held by Antony's own hands, "Hilarion would lie upon the saint's bed and as though it were still warm would affectionately kiss it." Antony's cell cradles him as closely as a tomb (or rather a womb?), "its sides measuring no more than the length of a sleeping man." But there is more. "On the lofty mountain-top, the ascent of which was by a zig-zag path very difficult, were to be seen two cells of the same dimensions.... These were cut out of the live rock and were only furnished with doors." Why *two* cells, *two* living caves? Has Antony been awaiting his partner? Hilarion, who seems to sense that he has arrived very close to some destination, "further asked to be shown his burial place." Readers of the queer *Life of Paul*, perhaps beginning to feel at home in this text, should not be surprised by Jerome's next slippery switch: "but whether they showed him the tomb or not is unknown" (31).

For we are by no means at the end of this Life. Antony's death sets Hilarion in motion without giving him a clear orientation, it would seem; his restlessness, the counterpart of Malchus's, propels him not toward but away from his monastic brothers. The tale, with Hilarion, meanders farther and then nearly calms itself again on its own still waters, before first a persecution (33) and then the yet greater threat of recall to his monastery (34) gradually drive the reluctant hero away from both the Egyptian and the Palestinian cradles of asceticism. "The old man accompanied by Gazanus went on board a ship which was sailing to Sicily" (35). Again, the saint is at the mercy of his gift: working more wonders, he finds himself besieged by the crowds he ostensibly seeks to avoid, in a series of hyperbolic repetitions of the movement of social withdrawal and subsequent pursuit already established by the Athanasian *Life of Antony*.[73] But there is also a repetition of the more intimately coy withdrawal of Jerome's own Paul in the face of a lover's pursuit. Hilarion will have (and also be) his Antony both ways—and then some, as we shall see. "While this was going on in Sicily, Hesychius his disciple was searching the world over for the old man, traversing the coast, penetrating deserts, clinging all the while to the belief that wherever he was he could not long be hidden" (38). Hesychius, Jerome has informed his readers earlier, is a monk "to whom Hilarion is most powerfully attracted (*quo ille vehementissime delectabatur*)" (28). He also shares with Hilarion the nearly martyrial honor of having been singled out for imperial persecution during the reign of Julian (33). At some point, however, Hilarion has seemingly given his attractive friend the slip, sneaking away on a ship. The hapless Hesychius meets with no centaur or satyr, but after three years of searching he does encounter another queer guide: "a certain Jew, who dealt in old clothes"—perhaps used cloaks for would-be ascetic gents?—informs him of the presence in Sicily of "a Christian prophet" who "was working such miracles and signs one might think him one of the ancient saints." Hopping a ship, Hesychius closes in on his quarry. "And, to cut my story short, the holy man Hesychius fell down at his master's knees and bedewed his feet with tears; at length he was gently raised by him," reports Jerome. Hesychius arrives in the nick of time, as it happens. Although Hilarion remains mysteriously uncommunicative of his intentions with this purportedly delectable monk, his servant Gazanus informs Hesychius "that Hilarion no longer felt himself able to live in those parts, but wanted to go to certain barbarous races where his name and fame were unknown" (38). By now a wanderer of Odyssean (or perhaps rather Aenaean) proportions, Hilarion travels to Dalmatia and thence to Cyprus, working wonders and attracting troublesome crowds wherever he goes, always holding over their heads the magnificent threat of his imminent departure, upon which he acts just often enough (39–42). Hesychius, having been sent back to Palestine, returns to Cyprus to find his master not yet ascending to heaven but instead plotting his departure for Egypt. At this point, the disciple—seemingly unable to face another of Hilarion's sly slips—takes on the role of guide himself, cleverly locating a piece of nearly inaccessible Paradise for Hilarion in the mountainous interior of Cyprus.[74] As it turns out, it is Paradise with a serpentine twist that will finally outdo—and thus perhaps undo—even the demonically infested Athanasian *Life*. "It was indeed a lonely and terrible place; for though surrounded by trees on every side, with water streaming from the brow of the hill, a delightful bit of garden, and fruit-trees in abundance (of which, however, he never ate), yet it had close by the ruins of an ancient temple from which, as he himself was wont to relate and his disciples testify, the voices of such countless demons re-echoed night and day, that you might have thought there was an army of them." Hilarion is "highly pleased (*valde delectatus*)" with his new digs, and his spirits are revived by the frequent visits of Hesychius during his last years. Inevitably, a few others also manage to make the torturous climb to his lofty peak, their desire to seek out Hilarion only intensified by the seemingly well-founded rumor "that he could not stay long in the same place." ("This habit of his was not due to levity or childishness," notes Jerome somewhat defensively, "but to the fact that he shunned the worry of publicity and praise" [43]). One among the visitors is, evidently, worth naming: "There came also Constantia, a holy woman whose son-in-law and daughter he had anointed with oil and saved from death." Having written a will with his own hand leaving all that he owns—"that is to say, a copy of the gospels, and his sack-cloth tunic, cowl and cloak"—to the absent Hesychius, and having also instructed Constantia and his other visitors to bury him in his garden immediately, the aged saint draws his last breath (44–45).

Death does not, however, put an end either to Hilarion's restless travels or to his wondrously seductive appeal. Hesychius, having frustratingly failed to be present at the holy man's demise and burial, hastily returns to Cyprus and takes up residence on his master's mountaintop perch. If the tale seems here to double back on itself once more, with Hesychius playing Hilarion to Hilarion's Antonine corpse (and behind that, playing Antony to Hilarion's Pauline corpse), the repetition plotted by Jerome is (yet again) strategically inexact. Hesychius's mimesis turns out to be a clever ruse, and this time (it seems) the corpse will not elude its lover: "in the course of about ten months, though at great peril to his life, [Hesychius] stole the saint's body." And what a corpse it is, once triumphantly laid to rest in the Palestinian monastery that Hilarion has decisively and repeatedly (even tediously) fled: "His tunic, cowl and cloak, were uninjured; the whole body as perfect as if alive, and so fragrant with sweet odors that one might suppose it to have been embalmed" (46). The *tale* cannot, however, quite be laid to rest in Palestine. Jerome deems it inappropriate not to mention in closing "the devotion of the holy woman Constantia who, when a message was brought her that Hilarion's body was in Palestine, immediately died, proving even by death the sincerity of her love for the servant of God." He continues his brief account, apparently unperturbed by its tragic dimensions: "For she was accustomed to spend whole nights in vigil at his tomb and to converse with him as if he were present in order to stimulate her prayers" (47).

Leaving the jilted woman in the dust, Hesychius seems to have the fragrant object of his desire in his snuffling grasp at last. But does he really? Hilarion, after all, only intended to leave him his clothes and a self-inscribed volume of Scripture that he had once tried, without success, to give away to a ship's captain (having already memorized its contents). "Even at the present day one may see a strange dispute between the people of Palestine and the Cypriots, the one contending that they have the body, the other the spirit of Hilarion," remarks Jerome, sustaining the ambiguity introduced into his text at the penultimate moment. Where *is* Hilarion, anyway? the reader wonders. "In both places great miracles are wrought daily, but to a greater extent in the garden of Cyprus, perhaps because that spot was dearest to him," Jerome concludes (47). What? Dearer (more delectable) than the spot subsequently selected by the (also delectable) Hesychius?

Being both here and there, Jerome's Hilarion is, in the end, neither here nor there, as either subject or object of desire. (Yet he is "ultimately, not nowhere, but elsewhere.") And if this hilarious holy man has the last laugh,[75] proving as elusive in his publicized mobility as Paul in his concealed stability, does Jerome's closing statement not hint that Hesychius is the butt of Hilarion's best joke? Perhaps there are two holes carved out of living rock on a mountaintop not in Egypt *or* Palestine but rather in Cyprus, where a zig-zagging path dodges the devious misguidance of an overly literal-minded disciple. And what could be queerer, in the context of the incipient "homonormativity" of ascetic sociality, than to imagine that it is the holy *woman* who still holds ghostly converse with the monk Hilarion, in the garden of untasted fruit trees where he asked to be buried, near the haunted ruins of a temple—might it even be a temple of the Cyprian Venus?[76] (And might it even be Paula, Jerome's oh-so-"constant" companion, who disrupts the tedium of a desert of renunciation with her juicy hilarity?) Ah, but perhaps Jerome has let more out of the closet, here at the end of this last Life, than he quite intended.

"In the beginning, there can be only dying, the abyss, the first laugh. After that, you don't know. It's life that decides. Its terrible power of invention, which surpasses us. . . . Write! What? Take to the wind, take to writing, form one body with the letters. Live!"[77] Jerome is always beginning his Life, writing, writing all the beginnings.

Prolongations: Fantasies of a Faun

> But, enough. such a secret chose for confident
> The vast and twin reed on which one plays under the blue sky:
> Which, diverting to itself the cheek's disturbance,
> Dreams, in a long solo, that we are beguiling
> The surrounding beauty by fictive
> Confusions between itself and our credulous song;
> And (dreams) of making—as high as love modulates—
> Vanish from the everyday dream of a back
> Or of a pure side followed by my closed eyes,
> A sonorous, illusory and monotonous line.
> —Stéphane Mallarmé, "The Afternoon of a Faun"

This passage from a poem about an artfully dreamy faun engages Leo Bersani's revisionary reading of Freudian theories of "artistic sublimation"—a reading that may in turn illumine the artistry of Jerome's sublime eroticism. In the cited verses Bersani finds "the suggestion that sublimation is not a transcendence of desire, but rather a kind of extending of desire which has taken the form of a productive receding of consciousness."[78] The faun's physicalized sensuality—"the cheek's disturbance"—is "diverted to," replicated, supplemented, and modulated by the reed. The reed's song is not, however, "the esthetic distillation of his sensual fantasies of a nymph's back or thigh,"[79] which would, in translating the body's lines into an equivalent line of music, disguise or repress the sensual impulse. Rather, it is an anticipatory dream of such a translation, a dream that effectively extends and suspends desire by an ironically dismissive deferral that finally eludes the "sonorous, illusory, and monotonous line" and thereby retrieves the "songe ordinaire" as free-floating "reverie" (played on an instrument "vast and twin"). The faun wonders if he has really seen the nymphs or merely imagined them, seduced by his own art. And yet what is reality if (as he dreams it) nature itself is "beguiled" by the confusions between itself and his song? Balancing a "credulous" fiction against a nature imagined as equally credulous, the faun's self-irony unsettles the "real." "To remember [the nymphs] is to wonder if he really saw them. Yet to doubt their reality is to wish to paint them, and to paint them is to return to his desires, and to confuse, once again, what he desires with what may really be there." Thus, the faun moves from "an art of entrapped realism to an art of happily mobile ironies."[80] On Bersani's reading, the poem "encourages us to view sublimation not as a mechanism by which desire is denied, but rather as a self-reflexive activity by which desire multiplies and diversifies its representations." He adds, "There is, to be sure, a certain purification of the desiring impulse, but purification should be understood here as an abstracting process which is not necessarily desexualizing."[81] In fact, Bersani suggests that sublimation—understood as the mechanism of desire's prolongation—is "coextensive with" sexuality. Its effect, exemplified by Mallarmé's poem, is to make "the objects of desire productively unlocatable"[82] and thereby also to dislocate, even very nearly annihilate, the subject. "In his willful recreation of scenes which may never have taken place"—that is, the faun's subsequent (fantasized?) sexual assault on the nymphs—"the faun narcissistically indulges a self already burned away. Desire purifies the faun of his identity."[83]

Reading Mallarmé's textual faun over Bersani's shoulder, I am not only interrupting but also thereby prolonging my own reading of Jerome. Slipping and sliding between fantasies of fauns, returning once again to Jerome's improbable homunculus, I privilege certain aspects of the *Life of Paul* for the purpose of proposing an interpretation of Hieronymian sublimation, the movements of which are replicated, supplemented, and modulated in his subsequent hagiographies. In the already delicately ironized persona of Antony, Jerome "dreams" a centaur, a faun, a she-wolf, a raven, twinned he-lions—and thereby also dreams a holy man in the desert. Are these demonic illusions or the offspring of the desert itself? he queries. (Is the author himself mastered by his own fantasy? Is the desert—that "surrounding beauty" so frequently and artfully depicted in Hieronymian ekphrasis—itself "beguiled," seduced by his "credulous song"?) "We are uncertain" is his own answer. Indeed, as readers we are destined to remain uncertain. The objects of desire and identification, already phantasmatically multiplied and diversified within the *Life of Paul*, are "productively unlocatable." "To remember is to wonder if he really saw them. Yet to doubt their reality is to wish to paint them, and to paint them is to return to his desires, and to confuse, once again, what he desires with what may really be there." Is it possible that the quintessentially elusive, ever dissolving Paul himself, "one who was always hidden," "did not exist" (as the Life's detractors claimed [*Life of Hilarion* 1])? We remain uncertain. And thus, as the anticipated "sonorous, illusory, and monotonous line" of the song eludes us (as we elude it), through the artful interruptions and inexact repetitions by which Jerome's narrative is left ever incomplete, our own desire is purified, made sublime, reaching "as high as love modulates." In the process, we readers are purified of fixed identity: where the object of desire is infinitely dispersed, so too is the subject. Jerome's "edifying" hagiography does not so much fashion an ascetic self by suppressing desire as intensify desire to the point that the self itself is fragmented, multiplied, rendered "productively unlocatable."

But the peculiar purity of the *Life of Paul*, marking the beginning of Jerome's sublimely sensual writing career, gives way to further genre-shattering repetitions. Conceived much later (and in practically the same breath), the strikingly different accounts of Malchus and Hilarion significantly supplement not only the *Life of Paul* but also each other. In *On the Captive Monk*, strategic gaps between the first-person accounts of "Jerome" and "Malchus"—both represented in the act of recollecting their past—crucially disrupt the narrative line of the not-quite-Life. Malchus seems to wish to be seen from the perspective of his desire for his faceless "brethren," configuring "captivity" as that which alienates him from the male monastic collective. And yet his own account already produces a fracturing of both the subject and the object of desire. It is his virtual "wife," partner of his captivity, who acquires a "face"—who attains a nearly recognizable persona—in Malchus's narrative; yet she remains not only nameless but also seemingly unmentionable as an object of desire in the inconclusive moment of her studiedly casual dismissal. Malchus's imperfectly sublimated love for the woman who threatens (or promises) to captivate him is gapingly unresolved, the incompleteness of his narrative intensified by its unacknowledged inconsistency with Jerome's own narrative of a cohabiting "couple" who had survived captivity through the liberative power of their collusive virginity. In the same stroke, Malchus's love for his shadowy monastic brothers is also rendered tantalizingly incomplete—a barely imaginable figment in the text. One who attempts to identify Malchus's desire—to identify *with* Malchus's desire—is thwarted. This seemingly satisfying romance is finally profoundly unsettling. Painfully suspended in the fracturing moment of interruption, the reader is pushed into "a self-reflexive activity" in which the self itself recedes in the face of the abysmal uncertainty regarding desire's proper object.

With the *Life of Hilarion*, Jerome's "happily mobile ironies" are in full play. Indeed, his laughing holy man is an icon of the mobility of desire itself. Constantly on the run, Hilarion is always thereby prolonging his longing; the goal of his journey is ever-shifting, frequently indeterminate. Miracles proliferate as so many replicating signs of excess, saturating nature's credulity with holy power while propelling him onward. A slippery subject, he is also a frustratingly unlocatable object of desire, as his devoted follower Hesychius discovers repeatedly. Ironically represented as Hilarion's beloved, Hesychius takes the part of the active lover, incited to imitate his master's mobility in his vigorous pursuit of Hilarion. But does he become a worthy disciple? Does he master the supple arts of sublimation under Hilarion's sly tutelage? We are uncertain. Now a trickster himself, Hesychius thwarts Hilarion's return to Egypt—site of Antony's holy mount—by replicating the Antonine Paradise in Cyprus. Subsequently, he steals away with Hilarion's relics, restoring them to their proper place, so as to restore to Palestine its proper holy man. Hesychius's doubled duplicities produce unexpected and ambiguous results. The Cypriot garden, perhaps still haunted by the goddess of love (and clearly marked by a holy woman's constancy of desire), continues to divert the holy man, exceeding and thereby escaping Hesychius's (mis)direction. A third place, of productive indeterminacy, neither Egypt nor Palestine (and thus "off the map" of established ascetic practice and pilgrimage), Cyprus effectively disturbs, without decisively canceling, Palestine's claims on Hilarion. A contested object of desire, Hilarion, "who was seen by many," is in the end quite literally unlocatable, and thus he reclaims the trickster's role for himself, giving the final slip that makes this endpoint of Hieronymian hagiography another beginning for ascetic dissolution. Disrupting (yet again) the "sonorous, illusory, and monotonous line," withdrawing even the disintegrating not-quite-presence of a corpse, Jerome shatters his readers with the purity of sublime desire.

Reading (as) Another, Woman

> *One must assume the feminine role deliberately. Which means already to convert a form of subordination into an affirmation, and thus to begin to thwart it. . . . To play with mimesis is thus, for a woman, to try to recover the place of her exploitation by discourse, without allowing herself to be simply reduced to it. It means to resubmit herself—inasmuch as she is on the side of the "perceptible," of "matter"—to "ideas," in particular to ideas about herself, that are elaborated in/by a masculine logic, but so as to make "visible," by an effect of playful repetition, what was supposed to remain invisible; the cover-up of a possible operation of the feminine in language. It also means "to unveil" the fact that, if women are such good mimics, it is because they are not simply resorbed in this function. They also remain elsewhere: another case of the persistence of "matter," but also of "sexual pleasure."*
>
> —Luce Irigaray, This Sex Which Is Not One

The "hom(m)o-sexuality" (re)produced by the *Life of Paul*[84]—differently, partially, and ambiguously disrupted by both *On the Captive Monk* and the

Life of Hilarion—raises particular challenges and creates distinctive opportunities for one who would read for the "woman" in Jerome's hagiographies—for one who would read *as* a "woman," even if also to lose "her(self)" in the process. Bersani has suggested that male homoeroticism may serve as a potent figure for the disruptive potentialities of sexuality, in the context of the long and violent discursive reign of a phallic subjectivity. Writing boldly into the storm of the AIDS crisis, he proposes that, "if the rectum is the grave in which the masculine ideal (an ideal shared—differently—by men *and* women) of proud subjectivity is buried, then it should be celebrated for its very potential for death." He continues: "If sexuality is socially dysfunctional in that it brings people together only to plunge them into a self-shattering and solipsistic *jouissance* that drives them apart, it could also be thought of as our primary hygienic practice of nonviolence. . . . Male homosexuality advertises the risk of the sexual itself as the risk of self-dismissal, of *losing sight* of the self, and in so doing it proposes and dangerously represents *jouissance* as a mode of ascesis."[85] At this point, my reading of Bersani must become explicitly supplementary, extending consideration of the sexual difference that is so swiftly marked as to be partly elided in his (awkwardly positioned parenthetical) text. If the "ideal of proud subjectivity" is undeniably "shared . . . by men *and* women," what are the limits to the commonality so forcefully underlined by the conjunctive "*and*," limits nonetheless signaled by the acknowledgment that the ideal, and thus presumably also its erotic shattering, is "shared—differently"? Does the death of "man" still leave "woman" "elsewhere" in relation to even a distinctly queered discourse? Is our theory of sexuality queer enough, is it sufficiently ascetic, if it does not also unveil "the cover-up of a possible operation of the feminine in language"?[86]

Reading the *Life of Paul* yet again, assuming the feminine role deliberately through mimetic play, it is my desire to begin with (to begin as) the garlanded subject in the garden of delight, surrendering to the torture of stream's murmur, wind's whisper, feathers' softness, petals' caress, and (finally!) of a lover's rousing fondling of nakedly bared skin—and then (when I can bear it no longer) to find myself just barely restored to power, by the skin of my teeth. (But, one might object, teeth have no skin, no softness, and, yes, the bite of my skin *is* my womanly hardness.) Reading as a woman, am I not, however, also the seducer and the torturer in this text? At the same time, am I not the one tormented by my own desire, my own tantalizingly thwarted desire, spit back chokingly into my kisses, like a disavowed tongue? The tongue, however, was mine to start with, its disavowal stolen from me: now I claim it again. But what do I claim, the tongue's integrity or its articulate dismemberment? Where does the biting frustration of bodily longing lead, what is lost, what is gained (what is prolonged), in the conversion desired in the *Life of Paul*, produced by the desire of this text, provoked by my desire to read this text, from within, and also from elsewhere?

Having temporarily lost my tongue (along with my bearings), I find myself again where Jerome would have me, wandering through the desert, tracking my bitter-sweet, hard-bitten longing. I am Antony. (But how can this be? Where is the place for a woman in Antony's desert, in his city of men,[87] and is Paul's desert any different? Is she a *mother*?) Ah: there it is, the monstrous mute signifier, horse-man, so excessively male as to be almost something more . . . , something *less* . . ., than a man. Tracking the signs, dreamily traversing the signs, slipping from one to the next, centaur—satyr—*she*-wolf, I am drawn into another Paradise. The gain (following upon the huge loss) is another garden (with a single, spreading tree), another spring of well-contained wetness, other shadows and other light, another cave (but whose?), other delights in a cave. Banished again (for my lover is stern and commanding), I will again be restored: I am now purposefully in pursuit of my desire. Recovering the lover finally, embracing, kissing once more, in my arms I find . . . a corpse. The lover has eluded me; the lover is mine. Yes, we are twinned like the long-maned lions who help me dig this grave. I give the lover my cloak; I take the lover's tunic for my own (I will never take it off again!); we wear one another's clothes. Covering the body with dirt, I know my own corruptibility: I am the dirt that clothes my lover; the decaying corpse is my threadbare garment. We mingle and are dissolved in one another, like the desert sand. Tasting Paradise in the grit on my tongue, I no longer know myself as woman, or man.

Sliding into the tale of a captive monk, I have indeed found my tongue again, now a woman's tongue unambiguously interpellated into the text, a sharp tongue of direct address, hailing a hesitant desire, attempting to give rise to a man who can only speak of swords and wives, who can only perceive his own captivity when confronted (in a cave) by my unvirginal singularity. Malchus! I call him. He mumbles my name inaudibly, but I imagine I can hear it, even if no one else can. Together we face the master's sword; together we elude the sword; together we are saved from its violence by a mother's incidental intervention. Emerging from the lioness's cave, we are like twinned cubs. And yet, where the path leads from there, I cannot say. I see only the doublings of duplicity, a multiplication of possibilities, which may or may not cancel each other. A sister who is not a sister, a wife who is not a wife, I tease at the cords of my constraint and my freedom; my tongue teases this text, explores its potential worlds—life with the sisters, life with the brother, life with the brethren. Shattered by so much freedom, so much constraint, I am swallowed up by a text that can scarcely hold a place for me, can scarcely hold me in place. It is from elsewhere that I will return, again and again.

Hailed now by name, by the name of Constance, I assume a role once more, extending myself into the *Life of Hilarion*. Easily recognizable are the holy man's laugh, his constant motion, the felicitous ironies that provide for a provisional constancy of desire, that make provisionality the only basis for desire's mobile constancy. But I, Constantia, am the true trickster in this tale, Hilarion my happy conspirator—or so I fancy it. Playing at my womanly devotions, I find myself haunted by this garden, at home in this haunted garden, where Venus's gloriously terrifying fruits delight most when not consumed. I know how to taste without devouring, and I desire to be tasted but not devoured (not put to the sword). I live alongside the fruits of the garden, I am among its fruits. Indeed, there is no God who will banish me. With veils of tears, I cover up my juicy laughter. Playing at tragedy, it is I who give the last slip in this comedy of Hesychian error (and if Hilarion wants to slip back into this grave with me, dying another death, let him come). Ha! Dying to desire, dying of desire, dying for desire, we are only beginning to unwrite—and thus to rewrite—our lives.

Already fractured, disappearing from (her own) sight, is it not (also, differently) another, "woman," who "proposes and dangerously represents *jouissance* as a mode of ascesis"? Is it not "woman" who knows that the "shattering" of the self is not an end in itself but rather the beginning of a subjectivity that is ever coming to be?[88] Does Jerome himself not hint at this very possibility?

Chapter 2
Dying for a Life: Martyrdom, Masochism, and Female (Auto)Biography

Masochism is proscribed for women even as it is understood, indeed precisely because it is understood, as the ontological condition of femininity. Despite the numerous testimonials of women who describe their masochistic experience as performative, the presumption remains, among many theorists, that masochism can only be performed by men.
—Lynda Hart, Between the Body and the Flesh: Performing Sadomasochism

Against all appearances, the pleasure of pain and restraint is the joyful triumph of the body.
—Karmen MacKendrick, Counterpleasures

Loosing her tongue, Ambrose's Agnes gives shameless witness to her desire for the executioner's sword: by such violent proxy is she made Christ's bride (Ambrose, *On Virgins* 2).[1] In contrast, Jerome's unnamed youth (subjected to a still stranger persecution) bites his tongue, thereby excising his shameful desire for the torturess who has him bound and mounted: thus he becomes a hermit (*Life of Paul* 3). The virgin martyr surges toward an erotic consummation, joyfully impaling herself on the steely blade that may be exchanged for a heavenly husband. (She is something of a literalist as well as a sensualist.) The masochistic boy practices a different art of deferral, sublimating the witness of death by transposing it into a (way of) Life. His story, which introduces the *Life of Paul*, is the harbinger of Hieronymian hagiography. But is the genre thereby gendered? Will the woman *also* get a Life?

Many years after penning the tale of the tongue-biting youth, Jerome addresses Eustochium on the occasion of her mother's death: "If all the members of my body were to be converted into tongues, and if each of my limbs were to be gifted with a human voice, I could still do no justice to the virtues of the holy and venerable Paula" (Ep. 108). Having made a career of hard-bitten renunciation (as well as biting critique), Jerome now imagines himself *all tongue*. Yet even this does not satisfy his desire, which must be ever again multiplied, displaced, and diffused within the witnessing body of Jerome's ascetic invention. Indeed, however skilled in the arts of sublimation, the mature monk seems strangely at a loss, replaying a youthful fantasy of lingual excess and inadequacy when faced with the task of *praising a woman*. How many tongues would it take to do justice to a female Life? he wonders (perhaps licking his *own* lips nervously).

Credited with authorship of three canonical Vitae—those of Paul, Malchus, and Hilarion—Jerome appears to have remained tongue-tied after all, when it comes to female subjects. Then again, the canon of Hieronymian hagiography should not be closed too swiftly: it may yet be possible to supplement it so as to accommodate a sexual difference. "I think first of all that it would be necessary to link another writing, 'hagiographical' in certain respects, with these three *Vitae*," muses Yves-Marie Duval. The work he has in mind is not the epistolary encomium of Paula (for which Jerome initially fears himself linguistically inadequate) but rather "Jerome's first letter, about the woman of Vercellae."[2] This letter, written circa 370, concludes with an admiring reference to Evagrius (Ep. 1.15), author of the Latin translation of the Antonine Life with which Jerome's *Life of Paul*, written shortly thereafter, directly competes. The woman of Vercellae is thus not only the subject of Jerome's earliest surviving text—a work, as Jacques Fontaine puts it, of "youthful romanticism."[3] She is also the pretext for his entry into the game of literary one-upmanship that soon results in his first "proper" hagiography.

The heroine of this initial epistolary romance has been brought to trial for the crime of adultery. Cruelly tortured in the hope that she will confess her guilt, she insists steadfastly that she has been falsely accused. When she invokes Jesus as witness to the injustice of her threatened execution, her suffering and anticipated death become, in turn, a witness to Christ. (It is difficult to remember that this is not, strictly speaking, an account of persecution.) Echoing the language of the virgin martyrs who eschew earthly marriage in order to remain faithful brides of Christ,[4] the woman proclaims: "I desire to put off this hated body, but not as an adulteress. I offer my neck; I welcome the shining sword without fear; yet I will take my innocence with me. The one who is slain in order to live does not die" (Ep. 1.3).

Indeed, it begins to seem as if this viraginous pseudomartyr cannot be killed at all. Jerome elaborates the titillating torments meted out by a "cruel judge ... overcome with passion." "She is bound by the hair to a stake, her whole body is fixed more firmly than ever on the rack; fire is brought and applied to her feet; her sides quiver beneath the executioner's probe; even her breasts do not escape." In response, the tortured woman merely rolls her eyes. "She has but one thing to say," Jerome reports admiringly: "'Beat me, burn me, tear me, if you will; I have not done it'" (Ep. 1.6). The torturers are finally worn out by the repetitive labor of beating, burning, and tearing.[5] Now the judge and his staff press on hurriedly toward the climactic act of execution. At this point, the victim appears gratifyingly helpless: "she knelt down upon the ground and the shining sword was lifted over her quivering neck." However, the executioner is not up to the task of enforcing the judge's penalty, any more than of persuading the woman to confess her guilt. His first blow grazes her skin, barely drawing blood. Alarmed by his "drooping sword," he raises the blade for a second stroke, but again the steel fails to penetrate. Poised to deliver a third blow, he is interrupted by the woman, who politely informs him that his jeweled brooch has dropped to the ground: not surprisingly, this stroke also proves ineffectual (Ep. 1.7). Now the stalwart swordsman attempts to provide manual support for his unreliable tool: "no longer trusting the blade, [he] proceeded to apply the point to her throat, in the idea that though it might not cut, the pressure of his hand might plunge it into her flesh." When even this desperate effort to reassert his manhood fails, the executioner's humiliation is complete: "the sword bent back to the hilt, and in its defeat looked to its master, as if confessing its inability to slay" (Ep. 1.8). (Brent Shaw offers a helpful hint for the potentially perplexed reader: "Jerome's words and images all have strong sexual connotations.")[6]

A second soldier must be summoned before the woman can be killed—but it appears that he succeeds only because she now *desires* death. Indeed, here as in other ancient Christian accounts of torture and resistance, the plot pivots on the subject's consent: the perverse extravagance of her passivity is the source of her power. Martyrdom is thereby construed as an ascetic practice, and submission is converted to defiance, subverting the fraudulent script of "self-betrayal" insinuated by the ritual of forced confession and further underwritten by the body's betrayal in pain. Reclaiming her voice (not least through the eloquent performance of the "noble silence" of bodily endurance by which pain itself is betrayed), the woman gives witness not only to her own faith but also to the injustice of the torturer's tyranny.[7] "The victim takes her place, protected only by the favor of Christ.... Previously she had received four strokes without injury: now for a little while she seemed to die" (Ep. 1.11).

"*Seemed* to die"? At this point, Jerome's already notably ironic (very nearly parodic) account of a woman's virtual martyrdom takes a distinctly novelistic turn, prolonging a narrative that may seem to have attained its end. The tale extends and elaborates the conventional Christian scripting of a witnessing death, in a narrative literalization of the prior theological claim that "one who is slain in order to live does not die" (Ep. 1.3). "Suddenly the woman's bosom heaves, her eyes seek the light, her body is quickened into new life," reports Jerome wonderingly (Ep. 1.12). Heroines of ancient romances are notorious for their improbable acts of resuscitation, and Jerome's accused adulteress is, seemingly, not to be outdone by her pagan sisters.[8] Even as death gives birth to life, with the woman's "resurrection," martyrdom's public performance makes way for the paradoxically private witness of asceticism: "they cut her hair short and send her in the company of some virgins to a sequestered country house" (Ep. 1.14) With a little help from romance, might not a martyrology already subtly shifted out of the context of the persecution of Christians now also be transmuted into a literary Life for a woman? Duval's tentative classification of the letter as "'hagiographical,' in certain respects," hints that the process is here under way.

And yet we should not fail to note that when Jerome actually pens his first Life, he must begin again. Reinscribing his pre-text by way of introducing Paul, he is now careful to make the "martyr" male—one whose death, moreover, is not crudely reversed in the event but rather artfully elided in the telling. As we have seen, Jerome's *Life of Paul* symbolically inscribes a youth's sexual encounter as torment and death (the "little death" of a tongue), where his first letter has, conversely, sexualized a woman's torture and execution. Martyrdom is thus a metaphorical affair for the man, whose Life is thereby prolonged, extended through the repetitions of sublimation into a truly lengthy hagiographic text. Life for the woman, on the other hand, must emerge through (the recounting of) her actual death, if it is to exist at all. Indeed, she becomes visible in the marks of death, as her history is incised in her flesh. "There she changes her dress for that of a man, and scars form over her wounds," Jerome concludes the tale of the miraculously revived woman of Vercellae (Ep. 1.14). Hers is, then, a marked life, a marred gender. But it is also, it seems, the matrix of Hieronymian hagiography—even if the genre must be born again in order to make itself properly male.

Jerome's first letter promises a Life after death for the woman, but does Jerome himself actually produce such a Life? The answer to this question turns on the assessment of the relation of hagiography not only to martyrology but also to the letter of consolation. Of the nine consolatory letters written by Jerome between 384 and 412—Epistles 23, 39, 60, 66, 75, 77, 79, 108, and 127—six lament the deaths, celebrate the lives, and comfort the friends or relatives of *women*. Two of them minimize the element of consolation, which draws these letters closer to the praise-centered genre of the funeral oration—Epistle 108, written to Eustochium in memory of Paula, and Epistle 127, to Principia in memory of Marcella. Epistle 108 in particular appears to be bursting the seams of the consolatory genre, rather literally: it is one of the longest of all Jerome's letters. "Its avowed purpose is to console Eustochium on Paula's death (108.2.2)," notes J. H. D. Scourfield, "but Jerome's main concern is to celebrate the praises of her distinguished mother; the result is rather a memoir, or an obituary, with considerable biographical content, than anything else."[9] Thus, the flexible letter of consolation, stretched as far as possible to contain "considerable biographical content," results in something not quite identifiable but perhaps "'hagiographical,' in certain respects" ("rather a" Life "than anything else"?). Appropriately enough, many readers of female hagiography simply refer to Epistle 108 as "The Life of Paula."[10] But perhaps it is also worth pausing to notice the particular literary sleight of hand by which the female "Life" is actually produced. In Jerome's writing, martyrology gives birth to hagiography along two rather distinctly gendered paths—and the umbilical cord is more decisively severed in the making of the male saint. The female Life remains wedded to death, but it is now a death that re-members.

Is Jerome's hagiography a special case? No doubt it is, but it is also an especially revealing case—possibly even typical. "From the heading of this work, you might think that it is a letter, but it has extended itself into a rather lengthy monograph (ἐις συγγραφικὴν μακρηγορίαν),." This line comes not from one of Jerome's consolatory epistles but from Gregory of Nyssa's *Life of Macrina*, written circa 380 and generally acknowledged to be the "first" female Vita[11]—not only because it predates Jerome's letters of consolation (if not his tale of female martyrdom) but also because it appears to exceed them in conformity to the biographical genre. Gregory, for his part, seems aware not of his conformity but of his generic transgression, explaining that the subject on which his addressee Olympius has requested that he write "goes beyond the scope of a letter." "We spoke of a woman.... You suggested that a history (ἱστορία) of her good deeds ought to be written," he recalls. Obedient to the request, Gregory has set out "to write her life story (ἱστορῆσαι)"—making it as brief as possible, as he assures the reader of this admittedly "rather long" text—"in an artless and simple narrative (ἐν ... διηγήματι)." It is striking that Gregory is not sure what to call his overextended epistle—monograph, history, narrative? His vocabulary is as imprecise as it is varied.[12] Similarly, he is not sure how to name his subject. "We spoke of a woman, if indeed she was a woman; for I do not know if it is proper to name by her nature one who went beyond nature" (*Life of Macrina* 1).

Implicit is Gregory's acknowledgment that if Macrina had *not* exceeded her female nature it might have been improper to "name" her at all; it is as a "philosopher," and thus an honorary male, that she can be made the subject of even a biography ambiguously packaged as a letter.[13] Commentators have emphasized the point, and not without reason: Gregory's Macrina is a "male woman," and this is how she—first of all women in antiquity—comes to have a full-length Life. Considering the question of genre, Pierre Maraval states emphatically that Gregory's *Life of Macrina* is a philosophical biography—*not* a funeral oration, he adds firmly. Yet Maraval also acknowledges the work's generic unorthodoxy, evidenced not least in the amount of space devoted to the account of Macrina's last days, her death, "la toilette funèbre," and the funeral itself, as well as in the emphasis on her martyrial role.[14] Anthony Meredith notes similarities between Macrina's Life and contemporaneous philosopher-biographies of Plotinus and Pythagoras—but he also wonders why "this highly philosophical lady, who has so much in common with her spiritual ancestor Diotima in the Symposium, should on Gregory's showing in the VSM have been ... employed [in philosophical reflection] so rarely."[15] Elena Giannarelli places the Macrinan Life at the end of a gradual development of the literary figure of the female philosopher that makes the philosophical woman available, if still problematic, as a subject of biography. Or rather, as a subject of *hagiography*: for the somewhat perplexing fact remains that female biography appears to be *a distinctly Christian product*. Giannarelli also, however, pauses to acknowledge the limits of her own monolinear history, highlighting (by way of example) the significant but relatively unexplored territory of "the relation that takes shape between the protagonist and her body, and the theme of beauty, negated in life and recovered as ἱερὸν κάλλος in death."[16]

Her body: her beauty: her death. Giannarelli's closing remark opens up a new view that may begin to accommodate the distinctly Christian cast of the female Life. What the philosophic biography cannot quite contain—what the generic identification cannot quite account for—is *Macrina's alluring corpse.*[17] (Here we circle back to the not-quite-martyr of Vercellae, whose body, like Macrina's, is marked by a scar.) As for Jerome, so also for Gregory, the possibility of writing a female Life turns rather more on the subject's eroticized death than on her desexualizing virilization.

Indeed, holy women—like virgin martyrs—only really become representable in the moment of their dying, the moment when they meet their Bridegroom. Subjects of lament, their "romances" are narrated from death's vantage point, their Lives are memorialized in the rituals of mourning.[18] Correspondingly, women's Lives can only be written by those who can be seen to grieve. As Giannarelli points out, the authors of early female Lives are inevitably men, and, more than that, they are men who represent themselves as standing in a privileged relationship with their subjects. The same is not the case for the writers of male saints' Lives.[19] The disclosure of the woman's story is a delicately public performance of an ostentatiously private grief, as intimate (and transgressive) as the pushing aside of a cloak to unveil a telltale breast, as intimate (and transgressive) as the fingering of an almost-forgotten scar. A visible but also a mute, even subtly secretive witness, the female Life thus distinguishes itself sharply from the publicly declaimed funeral oration, that tearless celebration of the quintessentially masculine dead[20]—although at the same time (and paradoxically), where lament inevitably gives way to praise, the Life of the woman is partially virilized in its publication.[21] (Nor should we forget that the Macrinan Vita is preceded not only by Jerome's protohagiographical account of the woman of Vercellae but also by Gregory of Nazianzus's gender-bending funeral oration in praise of his sister Gorgonia, also written circa 370.)[22] The hagiographer himself seems to play the role of the bridegroom—or even the executioner—in relation to the holy woman, and he does so with the awareness of his transgression, awed equally by her power and his own violence. Intruding under the cover of his grief into a private and distinctly feminine world, in which the primary bonds are between women, most typically between mothers and daughters,[23] he opens space for a heteroeroticism of an uncommon order. Making a woman of her, he makes a man of himself—but what kind of sex is this?

The female Life may appear to be an afterthought, an add-on, a late and unnecessary supplement to the essentially masculine genre of biography (even a second chapter!). Yet the passionate death of the woman is also the genesis of hagiography, the matrix of biography's afterlife in Christian literature, I am suggesting (after the fact). Her story is the *first letter* in the textual corpus, her corpse the beginning of a new style of Life. *But is the genre thereby gendered?* "We spoke of a woman . . ." (Is every hagiography in the beginning a female Vita, born out of the martyrdom of desire, conceived from a woman's "natural" masochism?) ". . . if indeed she was a woman." (Is every hagiography in the end made male, erected on the altar of female sacrifice? Does every female Life give way to the *confession* of a masculine autobiography?) Perhaps it is possible to postpone conclusions, to linger with the body, to let the letter of love and lamentation grow a little bit longer: perhaps it is possible, in the interval produced by deferral, to read the Life of a *woman*.

Or rather, to read the Lives of *three* women—Paula, Macrina, Monica. These texts do not reduce to a single "woman's Life"; they do not construct a monolithic female essence. They also do not simply demarcate three "types" of ascetic femininity—say, widow, virgin, mother.[24] Seemingly independently produced, if also intriguingly resonant, the biographies of Paula, Macrina, and Monica open onto an expansive field of broadly shared, yet infinitely differentiating, intertextuality. Writing the death of an intimate other, Jerome, Gregory, and Augustine—similarly, differently—also write their own desire and grief. In mourning, the Life of a woman can be written and rewritten. Indeed, hagiography first writes "woman" as a lamentable subject, even as a lamentably "masochistic" subject. Might what appears at first glance as cause for fresh grief be reclaimed, "against all appearances," as a distinctly feminine performance of "the joyful triumph of the body"?[25]

Praising Paula

> *Gain your freedom: get rid of everything, vomit up everything, give up everything. Give up absolutely everything, do you hear me? All of it! Give up your goods. Done? Don't keep anything; whatever you value, give it up: are you with me? Search yourself, seek out the shattered, the multiple I, that you will be still further on, and emerge from one self, shed the old body, shake off the Law. Let it fall with all its weight and you, take off, don't turn back.*
>
> —Hélène Cixous, "Coming to Writing"

Addressing a grieving daughter, Jerome laments his lingual inadequacy: with only one tongue, he is incapable of describing the many virtues of the recently deceased Paula, Eustochium's mother and his own longtime companion in ascetic life. Attempting nonetheless to rise to the occasion, he highlights the dramatic reversals in fortune entailed in Paula's radical (and radically economic) asceticism, a theme that is threaded throughout the lengthy letter: the lady's material wealth, through its conversion into poverty, buys heavenly riches, we are told. Thus, recalls Jerome, the unconverted remainder of materiality represented by corporeal existence itself regularly caused Paula to burst into tears, "for as long as she was in the body she was absent from the Lord" (Ep. 108.1).[26] If Jerome himself seems surprisingly dry-eyed as he eschews mourning in order to sing Paula's praises, Paula, in contrast, is immediately distinguished by her capacity for grief, as well as her desire for the Lord.

Jerome's narrative is rather elaborately mapped onto place, here even more than in his other Lives. It was in Rome, through the union of Paula's parents, Blaesilla and Rogatus, that the bloodlines of the Gracchi and the Scipios converged with the still more ancient ancestry of the Greek king Agamemnon, as Jerome recounts it (3). Paula's husband's heritage matches her own: "Paula married Toxotius in whose veins ran the noble blood of Aeneas and the Julii." To this propitious couple are born four daughters and one son. Representing the culmination of so much history (of so many roads leading to Rome), Paula ought to have remained rooted in the spot and bathed in the limelight. After all, as Jerome puts it, "the whole city" approved of her (4). The drama of Jerome's narrative is largely gathered in the startling event of Paula's departure from Rome and her choice instead to live in Bethlehem. If from a Roman perspective she may have seemed to be "hiding," Jerome knows better. "One who while she lived at Rome was known by no one outside it has by hiding herself at Bethlehem become the admiration of all lands Roman and barbarian." He adds, "She was hidden and yet she was not hidden" (3). With Paula, history has been diverted and maps have been redrawn, as Bethlehem supersedes and displaces Rome. But "where" is Bethlehem?

Jerome tells us that Paula's "eyes were dry" as she left her children behind on the shores of Italy. He thereby focuses attention on Paula's (unshed) tears. Her family members, gathering at her departure, were "eager by their demonstrations of affection to overcome their loving mother"; Paula, for her part, "overcame her love for her children by her love of God." In the end, however, she was almost undone by the battle of loves. "Her heart was rent within her, and she wrestled with her grief, as though she were being forcibly separated from parts of herself." Her grim resistance is to the very "laws of nature," we are told. As the ship pulls away, she cannot look back to the shore "without agony." "No mother, it must be confessed, ever loved her children so dearly," Jerome proclaims grandly (6). Earlier he has recalled Paula's sorrow at the deaths of Blaesilla, Paulina, and Rufina ("whose untimely end overcame the affectionate heart of her mother"), as well as her husband ("when he died, her grief was so great that she nearly died herself") (4–5). Such passages may or may not be evidence of Jerome's coldheartedness (as some have claimed); certainly they demonstrate his attempt to represent Paula as distinctly hot-blooded. Jerome's Paula is a woman of excess, defined by her love and her nearly coterminous grief. Immensely wealthy, her voluntary poverty is thus of highest value. An unparalleled lover of her children and husband, her love for Christ—measured competitively—is off the scales. It is almost obscene.

Setting sail from Italy, Paula's mobility rivals Hilarion's—revealing a passion even less passive. Where Hilarion is ever withdrawing from yet another crowd, Paula is ever rushing on to yet another site. "In visiting the holy places so great was the passion and the enthusiasm she exhibited for each, that she could never have torn herself away from one had she not been eager to visit the rest" (9). The place of Christ's passion arouses her own: "before the Cross she threw herself down in adoration as though she beheld the Lord hanging upon it"; "she kissed the stone which the angel had rolled away from the door of the sepulcher"; "ardent" and "athirst," "she even licked with her mouth the very spot on which the Lord's body had lain." (One recalls Hilarion at Antony's cell: "Hilarion would lie upon the saint's bed and as though it were still warm would affectionately kiss it" [*Life of Hilarion* 31].) "What tears she shed there, what groans she uttered, and what grief she poured forth, all Jerusalem knows," summarizes Jerome. If here he almost seems to be suppressing a sigh of exasperation (what *will* the neighbors think?), he swiftly adds, on a more pious note, that "the Lord also to whom she prayed knows" (9). At Bethlehem, Paula's propensity for biblically inspired (and strikingly empathetic) visions, anticipated at Golgotha, comes to the fore. "She protested in my hearing," reports Jerome, "that she could behold with the eyes of faith the infant Lord wrapped in swaddling clothes and crying in the manger.... She declared that she could see the slaughtered innocents, the raging Herod, Joseph and Mary fleeing into Egypt" and cried out "with a mixture of tears and joy" (10).[27]

Bethlehem is, however, not yet the end of Paula's journey—far from it. A tireless traveler, she traverses the Holy Land, finally reaching Egypt, where she tours the ascetic settlements at Nitria. Again, Jerome emphasizes Paula's (almost excessive) passion. "Was there any cell that she did not enter?" he queries rhetorically. "Or any man at whose feet she did not throw herself?" Seeing the ascetics, "she believed that she saw Christ Himself." "Forgetful of her sex," as Jerome puts it, she even entertains thoughts of living more permanently among these colonies of male hermits. (It might, after all, take "thousands of monks" to satisfy Paula's desire for Christ.) But feeling drawn by a "still greater passion for the holy places," she returns to Palestine by sea. Soon thereafter, Jerome reports with surprising brevity, she decides to dwell permanently in Bethlehem, establishing monastic communities (14). Here Jerome concludes the "narrative" portion of his account of Paula.

In Paula we have learned to encounter a pilgrim. But what does this mean?[28] Again, we recall Hilarion, whose lover's pursuit of Antony extended into a lifelong habit of wandering (which Jerome claims to find slightly embarrassing); we recall Hilarion, whose restless travels—continuing even after death—positioned him as the elusive object of both male and female desire, neither "here" nor "there." Paula's is a different mobility, her passion (in Jerome's eyes) perhaps still more perverse, but no more than Hilarion does she "settle." Propelled by a love even greater than her already excessive love for her children, she is set in motion, released from Rome; and in a sense she *remains* in motion, not because her love is too slight to bind her in place (on the contrary) but because still greater loves intervene. The narrative is a "narrative of the journeys," as Jerome frames it, and only briefly in closing that narrative does he mention Paula's arrival at what *might* have been construed as the final destination, the climax of the account (14). The point is not just that her path from Rome to Bethlehem does not run straight but that her searching for the incarnate Lord knows no end.[29]

Having thus "narrated" less in order to bring Paula to her goal than to set her loose on the power of her passion, Jerome can now pause, ostensibly to describe her virtue. In fact, he thematizes an excessiveness that threatens to place her beyond virtue: "her self-restraint was so great as to be almost immoderate" (17). At the same time, Jerome protests tellingly, "I am no flatterer; I add nothing; I exaggerate nothing; on the contrary I tone down much" (15). (He thereby invites us to imagine the virtually unimaginable— what a *not*-toned-down portrait might look like.) Paula's regime is quickly sketched: she dressed like a servant, never ate with a man, rarely bathed, and slept on the ground—to the extent that she slept at all. She prayed constantly, and prayer for her was lamentation: "Her tears welled forth as it were from fountains, and she lamented her slightest faults as if they were sins of the deepest dye." If there is a hint of irony in Jerome's mountains-out-of-molehills depiction of Paula's tearful self-flagellations, he nonetheless represents himself (without detectable irony) as solicitous of her health: "Constantly did I warn her to spare her eyes and to keep them for the reading of the gospel." Sparing herself, however, is hardly what Paula has in mind, and Jerome himself comes off looking a bit foolish. Her response: "I must disfigure that face which contrary to God's commandment I have painted with rouge, white lead, and antimony. I must mortify that body which has been given up to many pleasures. I must make up for my long laughter by constant weeping. I must exchange my soft linen and costly silks for rough goat's hair. I who have pleased my husband and the world in the past, desire now to please Christ" (15). What Lynda Coon has dubbed "the patristic theology of the cosmetic"[30] is more than a matter of simple inversion. Resisting Jerome, Paula claims her ascetic practice as her own. Seeming to swap beauty for ugliness and pleasure for pain, she is making herself over as the bride of Christ. Her fasts are heroic (17), her illnesses frequent (19). Face furrowed by grief, body practically a corpse, her mortal flesh betrays an immense desire. Good looks disordered, her power to please is out of this world.

Overwhelmed, Jerome finds it necessary to protest on behalf of Paula's chastity while going on to praise her charity. "Her liberality alone knew no bounds." But perhaps boundlessness has its limits as a virtue.[31] Citing Scripture, Jerome questions Paula's creative financing: "so anxious was she to turn no needy person away that she borrowed money at interest and often contracted new loans to pay off old ones." Paula overrules his objections, and Jerome admits he "was wrong"—and yet he cannot quite seem to let go of his doubts. "My prayer is that I may die a beggar not leaving a penny to my daughter and indebted to strangers for my winding sheet," proclaims the stubborn saint. We are not told whether she went to her Bridegroom naked, but Jerome does not tire of exclaiming over the size of the debt with which Paula's death eventually left Eustochium "overwhelmed" (15).

"I am aware that a talebearer—a class of persons who do a great deal of harm—once told her as a kindness that owing to her great fervor in virtue some people thought her mad and declared that something should be done for her head" (19). By the time Jerome conveys this tale of talebearing—out of "kindness"?—his readers are well prepared to wonder whether Paula's sanctity did not come at least partially at the expense of her sanity. Seeming to shift topics, as he turns to describe "the order of her monastery" whereby Paula converted carnal goods to spiritual, in fact Jerome is still pursuing the question of whether it is possible to make a virtue of excess. Whereas previously he has represented himself as "admitting" to Paula that he was wrong to criticize her extreme generosity, now he confides in the reader: "I admit that in this [her dietary regime] she was too determined, refusing to spare herself or to listen to advice." He attributes

Paula's uncompromising severity to "the passion of her mind and the yearning of her believing soul, both of which made her sing in David's words, 'My soul thirsteth for thee, my flesh longeth after thee.'" Against Paula's biblicism, however, he arrays the wisdom of the philosophers, remarking primly that they "are quite right in their opinion that virtue is a mean and vice an excess." Viciousness at least temporarily wins the day in Jerome's rhetoric, as Paula is shown to veer from one extreme to another. "While thus unyielding in her contempt for food Paula was easily moved to sorrow and felt crushed by the deaths of her kinsfolk, especially those of her children," Jerome notes, seeming to detect an inconsistency in the midst of excess. Having revived the theme of Paula's maternal grief, he now specifically associates it with both her emotional intensity and her physical weakness, thus restoring consistency to Paula's portrait without clearly contributing to her credit.

Jerome indeed seems lacking in tongues to sing Paula's praises, as he himself acknowledges: "the careful reader may say that my words are an invective rather than an eulogy." Forced to reflect on his own position as writer, he addresses the question of his text's genre. "So far from unduly eulogizing her or depreciating her I tell the truth about her as one Christian writing of another; . . . I am writing a memoir and not a panegyric." If not quite a eulogy, this overlong letter is also not quite a hagiography, but rather a memoir, an act of remembering. Is Jerome too close to his subject to give her a saintly Life after all? Speaking of Paula's faults, he suggests, is a necessary response to his own sense of loss (21). Having (almost) invoked his own grief, Jerome can (almost) acknowledge Paula's death. "O blessed change! Once she wept but now laughs for evermore. Once she despised the broken cisterns of which the prophet speaks; but now she has found in the Lord a fountain of life" (22). As Jerome trembles on the brink of tears, Paula seems to attain hilarity.

At this point, under the pretense of lauding Paula's orthodoxy, Jerome makes a rather sudden and unexpected detour. Welling tears of grief are swiftly dried in the heat of his anti-Origenist polemic, as an apparently self-indulgent digression interrupts the account of Paula's life. A second glance, however, suggests that the vehement theological exchange, far from being irrelevant to the rest of the text, may contain some of Jerome's most pertinent insights—and reveal some of his deepest convictions—regarding the sexed life of which he writes. His disagreement is with "a certain cunning knave" who preached to Paula a "spiritual" resurrection in which all naturalized social distinctions—all physical marks of difference—would be elided. Jerome, in contrast, insists that it is the difference between present and eschatological identities that must be refused; asserting the continuity of the self, he defends the irreducibility of difference among selves. He represents himself interrogating the teacher who had attempted to lead Paula astray: "Will the bodies that rise again be the same or different?" The man answers that they will be the same. Then Jerome demands: "What of their sex? Will that remain unaltered or will it be changed?" The answer appears to Jerome self-evident. He continues: "If the woman shall not rise again as a woman nor the man as a man, there will be no resurrection of the dead. For the body is made up of sex and members. But if there shall be no sex and no members what will become of the resurrection of the body, which cannot exist without sex and members?" (23).

The resurrected body is thus a sexed body. It is no accident that this theological point is articulated just as Jerome is about to recount Paula's death, to encounter his own grief, and therein—retrospectively—to discover her Life, the life-after-death, irreducibly female. The "theology of the cosmetic" is unforgiving in its demands for radical physical transformation (rather than transcendence of the physical), not merely preserving but also intensifying difference. But there are compensations, as ever, for the disciplining of the flesh. If Paula's is a sexed body, so evidently is her Groom's. "If He stood, He must certainly have had feet. If He pointed to His wounded side He must have also had chest and belly for to these the sides are attached and without them they cannot be," Jerome continues with relentless logic. Tongue, hands, arms—What else? "Since therefore it is admitted that He had all the members which go to make up the body, He must have also had the whole body formed of them, and that not a woman's but a man's; that is to say, He rose again in the sex in which He died." Here Jerome has virtually stripped Jesus of his well-known loincloth. And yet it is not his male member so much as the gash in his side to which Jerome's eyes and hands are drawn, with Thomas, in this exploration of the Lord's sexed carnality. "How do you explain the fact that Thomas felt the hands of the risen Lord and beheld His side pierced by the spear?" "I wonder that you can display such effrontery when the Lord Himself said, 'reach hither thy finger, and behold my hands; and reach hither thy hand and thrust it into my side . . . ,' 'handle me and see . . .'" (24). Our Lord's sex is here rendered queerly penetrable. (We recall, perhaps, that Paula's Holy Land is a place of caves, she the intrepid explorer of its hidden interiors as well as its exposed surfaces.) As for Paula's own sex, however much Jerome pays lip service to her intellectual "docility" and receptive nature, the woman cannot seem to stop talking back to her teacher, and he brags that her facility with tongues exceeds his own (27). The sexed body has many members. Difference, not eradicable, is nonetheless fluid, even reversible.

In the face of this all-too-carnal theologizing, Jerome's grief, so long delayed, overtakes him. "What ails thee, my soul? Why dost thou shudder to approach her death? I have made my letter longer than it should be already, dreading to come to the end and vainly supposing that by saying nothing of it and by occupying myself with her praises I could postpone the evil day." If praise is possible only while grief is deferred, the deferral of grief makes the letter long, longer than it should be—it is almost a Life. And yet grief cannot be postponed indefinitely: the praise of a woman must claim its price. "For who could tell the tale of Paula's dying with dry eyes?" Now it is Jerome who weeps. (Like little Toxotius on the shore of Italy, we seem to see him stretching "forth his hands in entreaty" [6].) Paula, dry-eyed, sets sail. (Perhaps she is already anticipating her well-earned eternity of laughter [22].) Weeping, Jerome nonetheless remains an outsider in relation to his own grief: Paula's impending death enfolds mother and daughter in a single embrace, and Jerome—now writing to the daughter—is an awkward intruder on this stage of female intimacy (28). "Why do I still linger and prolong my suffering by postponing it?" he asks again, as if unable to release Paula's already cooling body, caught up by his own narrative performance of (sexed) re-membering. It is Paula who helps him over the edge, as he tells it. "As soon as Paula heard the bridegroom saying: 'Rise up my love my fair one, my dove, and come away: for, lo, the winter is past, the rain is over and gone,' she answered joyfully 'the flowers appear on the earth; the time to cut them has come' and 'I believe that I shall see the good things of the Lord in the land of the living'" (29).

Paula's funeral drew throngs of bishops, the entire urban population of Palestine, and every single monk and virgin; it lasted for days, as Jerome tells it. As her body lay on a bier in the center of the Bethlehem church, "the paleness of death had not altered her expression; only a certain solemnity and seriousness had overspread her features." Jerome adds (gazing with the eyes of a bridegroom?), "You would have thought her not dead but asleep." He insists that "no weeping or lamentation followed her death," but only the chanting of psalms. Vying with this touted decorum, however, "the destitute cried aloud that they had lost in her a mother and a nurse" (29) and—naming his addressee, Eustochium, in the third person—Jerome reports further that "Paula's daughter . . . , 'as a child that is weaned of his mother,' could not be torn away from her parent." Elaborating the scene, he adds,

"She kissed her eyes, pressed her lips upon her brow, embraced her frame, and wished for nothing better than to be buried with her" (30).

In the end, Jerome acknowledges quite explicitly that he has borrowed Eustochium's grief in order to sing Paula's praises, writing of her death as a "martyr" in order to articulate the passion that could scarcely be contained by a "Life" (32). "I have spent the labor of two nights in dictating for you this treatise; and in doing so I have felt a grief as deep as your own," he addresses the daughter who desired only to be buried with her mother. Jerome grieves with (and as) the woman, here at the end. Through Eustochium, he makes Paula's grief his own. "I say in 'dictating,'" he continues, "for I have not been able to write it myself. As often as I have taken up my pen and have tried to fulfill my promise; my fingers have stiffened, my hand has fallen, and my power over it has vanished." Grieving Paula, Jerome is unmanned (not unlike the executioner of his first letter). But grief also gives rise to a new Life, for both woman and author. "In this letter, 'I have built' to your memory 'a monument more lasting than bronze,'" Jerome quotes triumphantly, "which no lapse of time will be able to destroy." The metaphor is almost literalized, in the last, hardening lines of appended text: "I have cut an inscription on your tomb, which I here subjoin." Jerome's "hand" is now steady and forceful; he is carving his words into rock, erecting an edifice of memory.

Indeed, the woman has a near-Life experience in Jerome's overlong letter. She is remembered in her death: "she leaves her traces, . . . she lives on."[32] Grief, the shadow of desire, gives rise to her afterlife as a subject—an event taking place not only in the marks of Jerome's monumental mourning but also in that which is produced as both prior and anterior (very nearly shattering the monument), namely, Paula's own bottomless suffering, the scars of her converted desire for children and husband, the searingly pleasurable pain of her love's deferral. In Jerome's (perhaps not after all monumental) text, material wealth funds an ambitious erotic economy that defies all balance sheets, peregrinations extend desire beyond any destination, and the severity of physical disciplines pushes mortal flesh toward the divine perfection worthy of a lover of Christ whose (anti-Origenistic) anticipations of the afterlife are sublimely carnal.

It is nearly impossible to write about the woman; and yet it seems she is also already inscribed. As he traces the not quite legible wounds of Paula's sex, Jerome weeps in joy and frustration, his vision blurs—is he or is he not the author of this marked flesh? Where are the signs of his authority? (Firmly dismissing his scribe, he tightens his own grasp on his pen.) There could never be enough tongues to praise Paula sufficiently! This is itself the true subject of lament and laudation. The hagiographer's thematized inability to come to terms with the object of his praise, to subject her to his own writerly will (his vir-tue, his vir-ility), produces the surplus that allows her to exceed his frame—and that thereby leaves him partly outside it as well. Jerome's writing remains autobiographical (and thus also autoerotic), but it does not end there. Something else emerges between the sheets of his memoir: another subject, an exchange between subjects, and even a slipping beyond subjectivity—a communion of painful pleasure, an extravagance of love, an "economy of joy."[33]

Remembering Macrina

> *What do we want from each other*
> *after we have told our stories*
> *do we want*
> *to be healed do we want*
> *mossy quiet stealing over our scars . . .*
> *the all-powerful unfrightening sister*
> *who will make the pain go away*
> *. . . . .*
> *mother's voice in the hallway*
>
> —Audre Lorde, "There Are No Honest Poems About Dead Women"

At first glance, Gregory of Nyssa's *Life of Macrina* seems to deliver a far more *proper* biography than Jerome's emotionally overwrought encomium of Paula, simultaneously excessive and ambivalent. Decorously reviewing Macrina's ancestors and the course of her life up to her final illness, the first fourteen chapters of the Vita are arguably unconventional in only one significant respect—namely, the gender of their subject. Gregory is scarcely unaware of that singular anomaly; on the contrary, he actively thematizes it, beginning, as we have seen, by simultaneously emphasizing and erasing the mark of sexual difference: "*we spoke of a woman, if one may refer to her as that*" (*Life of Macrina* 1).[34] His written narrative repeats the double gesture of the remembered word. Initially, he *writes of a woman* in terms reassuringly recognizable (albeit subtly out of place in a philosophical biography, if that is indeed what this is): the young Macrina, as we initially encounter her in his text, is well-bred, chaste, exceedingly beautiful, delightfully demure (3, 4). She is also quite capable of defying her father's wishes, when it comes to affairs of the heart. Such defiance is typical of romantic heroines (if not of philosophical heroes); taking it to almost tricksterish extremes, however, Gregory lures us into seeing this attractive woman—*if one may refer to her as that*—in a rather different light (as rather more masculine, perhaps?). Having become a widow before her time (indeed, before her marriage), Macrina—like a perversely precocious Penelope[35]—protests undying fidelity to her dead fiancé in order to evade the clutches of her all-too-live suitors, with whose desires her father seems inclined to collude. With just a bit of hindsight, we may wonder if the husband whom *she* intends is not Christ himself (who, like Odysseus, is only *presumed* dead). With still more hindsight, we may wonder if her intended is a proper husband at all. For the moment, we note that the girl, cleverly evading marriage with a mere *man*, remains queerly devoted to her *mother*, who protests that this firstborn child, alone of all her ten children, has never left her womb.

No ordinary daughter after all, Macrina (as Gregory tells it) quickly replaces her father as the man of the house. (Conveniently for the narrative, if not also for Macrina herself, the patriarch has died [5].) At the same time, she makes that house over as a matriarchal monastery. Metaphorically cross-dressed in a philosopher's cloak (6, 11), accessorized with an athlete's laurel wreath (14, 19), by the end of Gregory's opening narrative, which brings us to the brink of her death, the virginal Macrina may seem indeed as sexless and dispassionate as the angels to whom her brother so frequently compares her (11, 12, 15, 22). Her ethereal androgyny—which is also to say her transcendent virility—manifests itself first and foremost in her capacity to rise above grief. Sternly guiding her mother back to the path of "reason" after the death of a much-beloved son has left her "like a noble athlete felled by an unforeseen blow," Macrina herself bears the pain of multiple losses— including the death of her beloved mother—with an uncanny Stoic calm: "she remained like an undefeated athlete, in no way overcome by the onslaught of misfortunes" (14).[36] Has Gregory—in marked contrast to Jerome—placed his unfeeling sister not only beyond criticism but also beyond desire?[37]

Such a judgment, while not invalid, is nonetheless premature, for the text is not yet at an end. Jerome tells a tale of a lady's unexpected journeys, Gregory of a woman's surprising insistence on staying in place (Jerome of excessive passion, Gregory of hyperbolic self-control), but in both cases the "narrative" is only the beginning—a forecourt perhaps. Reaching the inner spaces of the Life, the reader suddenly comes face to face not only with the woman but also with the author himself, boldly trumpeting an autobiographical voice even as he daringly intrudes onto female terrain—ostensibly in order to testify to the woman's ascetic virtue, in fact, to give firsthand witness to her erotic death (which may, I am suggesting, amount to much the same thing). In the cloister of Gregory's Life, the funeral liturgy eventually echoes and displaces the daily rites of evening prayer and eucharistic offering; these are in turn gathered and repeated in Gregory's act of hagiographical composition, as Derek Krueger has shown.[38] On the cusp of death, Macrina holds it all together, recalling her own life and thereby offering thanks: she shows Gregory how to perform the sacrifice after she has gone. His own autobiography thus conveys her initiating self-commemoration, whereas the initial biographical narrative of chapters 1 through 14 appears, after the fact, both secondary and in need of a second reading. In the cloister, we encounter sexual difference after all, even (indeed, *especially*) among "angels," and we also confront the extreme instability and reversibility of that difference: the other, woman, appears simultaneously dauntingly remote and frighteningly intimate (*At any moment, "I" may be becoming "her"*). Macrina's "feminine" passion melts the ice of her initial memorialization; she lends her brother her memory so that he may learn how to convert numbing grief into the extremity of a love that is also a letting go of self.

But let us back up and make the approach with Gregory. Suffering "trials," he has been gone for eight years. As he sets his face toward what used to be home, three times he dreams the same dream: "I seemed to be carrying the relics of martyrs in my hand and a light seemed to come from them, as happens when the sun is reflected on a bright mirror so that the eye is dazzled by the brilliance of the beam." Reaching the outskirts of Macrina's estate, he learns from one of the laborers that his sister, their Superior, is ill, a report that only increases his sense of urgency (15). Arriving at the monastic community itself, he is greeted by groups of both men and women. When the women subsequently all withdraw, notes Gregory, "I correctly surmised that their Superior was not among them" (16). Here we catch him in an interesting piece of guesswork. Previously he has given us his sister's literary portrait while protesting that her beauty is too great to be captured by a painter (4); now we realize that recognizing the saint will not be easy without the help of an artist's sketch. (What *does* a conventionally feminine, yet also decisively butch, middle-aged angel look like, after all? Does she, perhaps, look like her brother?) After eight years, even the brother is searching for clues, drawing inferences from gestures, scanning faces for marks of identity, like Odysseus returning home from the wars. (The tale will, however, turn on the recognizability of Odysseus himself—and Gregory is not the only Odysseus in the text.)

Gregory is brought to his sister's chamber, a "sacred place" (16). Artfully controlling the scene, she asks questions, delivers monologues, recounts memories, and prays, in a closeted encounter that Gregory will attempt to make public in at least one other place, namely, the dialogue *On the Soul and Resurrection*. From the start, it is Macrina's physical pain and the power manifested in her conversion of pain into joy that draws Gregory's attention (17–18). ("Self-mastery can itself be transcended in a self-defiance that overcomes the self in the discipline of restraint and the delight of pain.")[39] Gregory himself is caught up in Macrina's ecstasy: "my soul almost seemed to be lifted up out of its human sphere by what she said and, under the direction of her discourse, take its stand in the heavenly sanctuaries" (18). Dismissed to take his rest in a garden, he realizes (somewhat later than the reader) that the martyrial relics of his dream point to his sister, whose fragile limbs already shine with the power of the spirit. "Thus the dream not only predicted her death but also showed her translation to heavenly status in a transformed body, fragmentary though it was," comments Patricia Cox Miller.[40] Recalling his earlier, static comparison of Macrina to an undefeated athlete, Gregory is now able to recognize the e/motion in the figure: "For just as a runner who has outrun his rival and comes to the end of the course when he nears the judges' stand and sees the victor's crown," so too Macrina rejoices in her anticipated victory, seeming to echo the words of "the apostle": "I have fought the good fight, finished the race, kept the faith" (cf. 2 Tim. 4.7, 8) (19). Soon she resumes the thread of her tireless discourse: "she took up the story of her life from infancy as if she were putting it all into a monograph" (20).[41]

When the next day dawns, Gregory realizes it will be Macrina's last. Her philosophizing already pushes her almost beyond the bounds of mortal existence: angelic, she straddles the chasm between body and spirit, life and death, grief and desire. "For this reason, she seemed to me to be making clear to those present the divine and pure love of the unseen Bridegroom which she had secretly nourished in the depths of her soul, and she seemed to be communicating the disposition in her heart to go to the One she was longing for, so that, once loosed from the chains of the body, she might quickly be with him." Erotic imagery merges with athletic tropes to emphasize the pressing urgency of Macrina's joyful desire. "Truly, her race was towards the Beloved and nothing of the pleasure of life diverted her attention" (22). (Here she is both like and unlike the virginal runner Atalanta, who pursues her lover like so many golden apples along purposeful paths of indirection.) As the day draws to an end, Macrina does not so much fade with the sun as become yet more luminous and fiery in her passion. "Indeed as she neared her end and saw the beauty of the Bridegroom more clearly, she rushed with greater impulse towards the One she desired, no longer speaking to those of us who were present, but to that very One toward whom she looked with steadfast eyes" (23). From that point on, Gregory's sister has words for no one but her Lord, and her words are fierce and uncompromising in their embrace of a God of absolute power. This God—her Bridegroom—crushes the head of the serpent, breaks down the gates of hell, destroys the adversary, shatters the flaming sword, meeting the utter submission of his martyrial bride, who willingly—thrillingly—offers him her suffering, her very life. "For I, too, have been crucified with You, having nailed my flesh through fear of You and having feared Your judgments," the woman cries with her last breaths (24).

While Macrina seems to have reached the summit of her ascent, Gregory has not. It is in the intensely erotic, lamp-lit encounter with her corpse that Gregory finally sees his sister clearly (and thus is able to show her to us). Initially, he is overwhelmed by a grief that is marked by its feminine excess. "My soul was disquieted for two reasons, because of what I saw"—namely, the eerily serene beauty of his sister's body, which appears to be not dead but sleeping—"and because I heard the weeping of the virgins." Macrina, as the living incarnation of Reason (as Wisdom herself),[42] has withdrawn, and thus Passion can no longer be held back. "Suddenly, a bitter, unrestrained cry broke forth, so that my reason no longer maintained itself, but, like a mountain stream overflowing, it was overwhelmed below the surface by my suffering and, disregarding the tasks at hand, I gave myself over wholly to lamentation." In this remarkable line of prose, Gregory makes the virgins' voice his own. (We recall Jerome's revoicing of Eustochium's grief.) In counterpoint to Macrina's own prayer, they (the virgins, but also Gregory) bewail the withdrawal of their formidable protector and lover: "the lamp of our life has been extinguished; . . . the safety of our lives has been destroyed; the seal of our incorruptibility has been removed; the bond of our union has been demolished." Gregory adds that "the ones who called her mother and nurse were more seriously distraught than the rest" (26).[43]

It is the memory of Macrina that calls them (temporarily) to their senses (27). And in that space of intervening calm, Gregory finally approaches the body of his sister, having been assured by one of her nuns that "she ordered her body to be prepared by your hands" (29). (Why, we might wonder, is her body to be touched by a *man's* hands? And if the duty is to fall to a brother, why not Peter, Macrina's monastic colleague, who has been sent off in misdirected pursuit of Gregory in the opening scene? But Gregory insists upon his election.) Though the saint possesses nothing but the simple clothes she is wearing at her death, Gregory, having solemnly accepted his charge, determines to dress her in fine linen (29)—like a bride (32). He is assisted by the noble widow Vetiana, to whom he gives the pendant around Macrina's neck, Gregory taking her ring for himself (30). As he is about to robe his sister, Vetiana stops him, with portentous words: "Do not pass over the greatest of the miracles of the saint." That miracle, it seems, is quite literally written on her body. Unveiling the marked corpse, Vetiana is not only inexplicably transgressing Macrina's soon-to-be-vaunted modesty ("Macrina considered worse than the disease laying bare part of the body to another's eyes") but also, as Georgia Frank has shown, replaying a charged Odyssean scene of recognition, upon which Gregory's text will pivot.[44] Odysseus is known by the scar on his thigh, revealed to the touch of his nurse (*Odyssey* 19.385–475). Macrina's "scar" has been touched by her mother; now it is being gazed on by her brother, in the presence of her female attendant, who lays bare a part of her—a part of her breast. (The brother sees what Penelope, by divine device, could not yet see [*Odyssey* 19.476–479].) The scar is not easy to spot: Gregory can scarcely make it out. (We, too, strain for a peek.) It looks, he remarks, "like a mark made by a small needle." But that is precisely what it is not, for Macrina—out of modesty—has refused surgical removal of the cancerous sore with which she was formerly afflicted. Instead, she has treated herself with mud from her own tears shed in supplication to God, over which her mother has (at her urging) made the sign of the cross. The tears of the dry-eyed woman and the faith of an overly anxious mother have, then, healed her. In place of her disease there remains only the mark, "a reminder . . . of the divine consideration, a cause and reason for unceasing thanksgiving to God," as Vetiana names it (31). A reminder, a site of grateful recollection, for Macrina, and now—in the Life—for Gregory and his readers too. As Frank puts it, "Macrina's scar becomes the site of a *locational memory*, a place from which to remember the departed Macrina. . . . Gregory provided a scar where the story demanded none so that readers could have a 'gathering place' at which to assemble and cue their memory of Macrina, . . . to fix Macrina's shifting identities."[45] The scar made visible, then, is a metonym both for Macrina's body—her insistent corporeality[46]—and for the text itself. Repeating Macrina's own act of grateful and sacrificial commemoration, Gregory also reinscribes her already-marked body, writes her body as an already marked text.

If Macrina has become Odysseus in this scene of recognition, she is a flamboyantly feminine, as well as philosophic, Odysseus. (But, then, Odysseus was known for his versatility and even for his femininity—a man famous for his wiles and his tears). Playing her epic role, Macrina finally returns "home" to her wise and well-matched spouse. (Perhaps it is not only Macrina herself but also the spouse who is played by Lady Wisdom. It is, after all, Gregory who insists on a *Groom*.) Meanwhile her earthly sisters are as bereft as those alluring women whom Odysseus left behind on his journey. And where does this leave *Gregory*? Weaving and reweaving the shroud of her Life, reveiling her body, cloaking her bright dress in a dark mantle, he cannot postpone the wedding any longer: "even in the dark, the body glowed, the divine power adding such grace to her body that, as in the vision of my dream, rays seemed to be shining forth from her loveliness," Gregory reports. (He is, we also note, still viewing her martyrial body through the eyes of his dream.)[47]

Nothing can subdue the glow of the bride's body, and nothing can quite suppress the mournful wails that once again interject the reasonable discourse of praise—the masculine performance of funeral oratory—with the passionate cries of lamentation. God knows, Gregory tries. "The maidens' psalm-singing, mingled with lamentation, resounded throughout the place," drawing huge crowds from the surrounding area, as he describes it. Out of the virgins' hybrid voice of song and lamentation, now swollen with the wails of the country folk (and troubled as well by his consciousness of his own distress), he eventually achieves a "suitable" effect by "separating the flow of people according to sex": "I arranged for the singing to come rhythmically and harmoniously from the group, blended well as in choral singing with the common responses of all" (33). But control by sexual segregation is tenuous at best. During the burial, as Gregory reports it, one virgin cried out, and "the rest of the maidens joined her in her outburst and confusion drowned out the orderly and sacred singing." Soon everyone was weeping. As the habitual prayers were intoned by the persistent clergy, the people only gradually returned their attention to the liturgy (34). Following the burial, we find Gregory himself crying again (36). Even as the smooth surface of Macrina's Stoic calm has been dissolved by tears, cut by pain, branded by desire for a divine lover, so too Gregory's voice, Odysseus-like, conjoins passionate grief to philosophic contemplation in re-membering the Life of his sister, part by part. "Recognition" is not, finally, a singular event in this mobile and multifaceted text in which subjects are continually dispersed and regathered, positions identified, split, and swapped, in the kaleidoscopic reflections of biographical and autobiographical recollection.

Gregory's *Life of Macrina* does not so much posit an "inversion" of gender as perform the fundamental reversibility of gender, where gender itself is made visible in the charged and constantly shifting field of erotic play. As Frank notes of Gregory, "Just as he could cast himself as returning Odysseus and then unwitting Penelope, so could Macrina function as steadfast Penelope and disguised Odysseus."[48] (Similarly, in the literary doublet to this work, Gregory's dialogue *On the Soul and the Resurrection*, Gregory can play the weeping virgin to Macrina's Socrates or Socrates to her Diotima.)[49] Such reversibility is not incidental—far less a sign of sexual indifference— but rather is crucial to a text that relocates, or rather persistently dislocates, eroticism in the continual inscription and reinscription of a difference that resists the fixity of identities and is most lively in the passages in between. (In this sense, Gregory is after all the trickster Penelope, unraveling the text as soon as it threatens to become complete.) As Shoshana Felman remarks, in a reading of a differently incestuous tale of a brother, a sister, and another, which likewise hinges on (mis)recognition, "The substitutions of woman for man and of man for woman, the interchangeability and the reversibility of masculine and feminine manifests a discord that subverts the limits and compromises the coherence of each of the two principles. . . . The signifier 'femininity' no longer fits in the code of male representation or in any representative unequivocal code. . . . It is precisely constituted in *ambiguity*, it signifies itself in the uncanny space *between two signs, between* the institutions of masculinity and femininity."[50] Gregory's Life "moves from field to field of testimony, recording how the wounded teach each other," as the poet Adrienne Rich has it.[51] The scar bears witness, in vain defiance of flesh's corruptibility, focusing the gaze on what is already disappearing, what can only be fixed— what is also always shifting—in the performative act of remembrance.

Confessing Monica

> The tears I shed at night! The waters of the world flow from my eyes, I wash my peoples in my despair, I bathe them, I lick them with my love, I go to the banks of the Nile to gather back the peoples abandoned in cradles of reeds, for the fate of the living I have the untiring love of a mother, that is why I am everywhere, my cosmic womb, I work on my worldwide unconscious, I throw death out, it comes back, we begin again, I am pregnant with beginnings.
>
> —Hélène Cixous, "Coming to Writing"

Confessions is a woman's Life. Is that so strange a claim? The womb of the Life—cradled in the center of the text—is, once again, the account of the woman's *death*. It is in grieving his mother, Monica, that Augustine discovers his point of departure, just when we might have thought he was finished with his account. He departs, he begins again, then, in the middle—*in medias res*. Grieving Monica, remembering his mother, delivering her eulogy to God in the pseudoprivacy of his ancient prayer closet, Augustine learns to read; he begins to write in earnest. *In principio Deus creavit*, runs the text. "In the beginning you made heaven and earth," he addresses the author of both Scripture and cosmos wonderingly (*Confessions* 11.3).[52] Augustine creates too, he is also a writer: *he makes his confession* brashly "in this book before the many who will read it" (10.1). But perhaps *we make too much* of his sheer originality, his autogenerativity.[53] We forget—or fail to notice—that it is his mother who provides him the narrative material out of which to conceive time and space, to frame the very cosmos. Monica's Life (centered on her death) gives him his opening, keeps his story of conversion open. Monica is Augustine's eternally unfinished business; she is present in all his beginnings.[54]

A beginning that is in the middle of the thing, an irruptive potentiality that resists narrative closure, Monica plots and is emplotted, simultaneously generates and disrupts storylines. Less an item than a happening, she *takes place* in the argument of Augustine's *Confessions*, and thus we must strive to understand *what that place is*. Present from the beginning (1.11), she meets her end (and in a sense also makes her formal debut) in book 9, where the narrative portion of the *Confessions* likewise concludes. There is a certain substitutionary logic to the mother's dying the death impossible for the author of an autobiography. The existence of book 9 nonetheless presents a dilemma, for book 8 already contains all the makings of another kind of ending, having staged the intense struggle of will that culminates in Augustine's dramatic "conversion" (the liberating death of his formerly enslaved self).[55] For the first-time reader, it must come as something of a surprise when Augustine extends his story into a ninth book that relates, first, his ascetic withdrawal and baptism and, second, his memories of the life of his mother. The centerpiece of these memories is a shared mystical experience occurring shortly before Monica's death and Augustine's oddly unexplained and open-ended departure for Africa at the portentous age of 33. (We recall Gregory's similar experience in the company of Macrina.) Such a dizzying spiritual encounter, following the dramatic experience of divine intervention in book 8's scene of conversion, seems excessive—more than the story demands, almost more than it can accommodate.

Yet, perversely, having scripted such a dubious *double climax*, Augustine may seem to add narrative insult to injury by going on to write a distinctly *anticlimactic* tenth tome. Previously swept along on the waves of the author's passionate recounting of the misadventures of his youth and the struggles of his conversion, tossed high by the unexpected thrill of his maternally mediated heavenly ascent, now as readers we find ourselves stalled on the vast, midlife calm of his mental abstraction. We may share Pelagius's outrage that Augustine is killing the tale in more ways than one:[56] when viewed from the sober perspective of the morning after, conversion loses its sharp edge, the bloom of optimism fades, and old habits reassert their sway even in the life of a would-be saint. (Who wants to read about *that*?) But books 9 and 10 are only the beginning of Augustine's refusal to allow his *Confessions* their proper end: three more seemingly superfluous books follow, as he makes yet another fresh start, now posing as biblical commentator, resituating his account in the beginning, in *Genesis*, in the generation of world and written word. At this late point in the text, Augustine's snail's-pace advance through the first slim chapter of the capacious Book of books seems to make not only a mess but a mockery of the search for an end to the story of his life. Sucked into the ever-receding depths of Scripture's polyvalence, almost parodically prolific in his interpretive reinscriptions, Augustine the reader has, by any strictly linear measure of progress, come to a virtual standstill. Has the text, drained of desire, simply petered out?[57] Rather, as Augustine would have us understand it, his own restless curiosity—tracked over time—has been converted into eternal rest in the performative reading of the scriptural Sabbath.

The question is: Why *does* Augustine keep writing so far past his famous conversion? What—if anything—links the autobiographical books 1–9 of *Confessions*, which the Life of Monica finally *overtakes*, with the exegetical books 10–13, in turn *overtaken* by silent repose? (A repose that represents not, Augustine would urge, the stasis of death but instead yet another opening door [13.38]).

We can begin by observing that the reader's quest for the structured coherence of *Confessions* is inextricably intertwined with Augustine's narrated quest for Wisdom: "to love Wisdom herself, whoever she might be, and to search for her, pursue her, hold her, and embrace her firmly—these were the words that excited me and set me burning with fire" (3.4). As Danuta Shanzer interprets him, the author of *Confessions* constructs a deliberately enigmatic and suspenseful text by combining a Proverbial "choice motif"—*Folly versus Wisdom*—with a "search motif"—*where is Wisdom to be found?* At least as early as book 3, when Augustine explicitly represents himself as seduced by Folly (3.6), "we are detectives with a Scriptural clue (Stultitia presupposes her opposite), and a Scriptural description or identikit picture of Sapientia, if we are prepared to use it to find or recognize her," Shanzer suggests.[58] Shanzer's reference to the "Scriptural clue" of book 3—namely, the allegorical figures of Folly and Wisdom in Proverbs 9—is itself a further clue but one that we, like the Augustine of book 3, have trouble putting to good use. Searching for the hidden Sapientia, we may not notice that she is there alongside Stultitia from the start: "And behold I saw something—or someone—neither disclosed to the proud nor laid bare to children, but humble in gait, sublime in accomplishment, and veiled in mysteries. And I was not the type who would be able to enter into her or to bend my neck to her guidance" (3.5). It is difficult to say at what point most readers realize that the Holy Scripture—for that is "who" is here described—does not merely offer clues but is also itself (herself) the answer to the riddle posed by the work: the Augustine of books 11–13, lost in silent contemplation of the biblical writings, absorbed in their depths, has indeed reached the end of the quest delineated in books 1–9. It is difficult to say at what point readers *also* realize that the end is always only beginning: there is no limit to knowing the beloved, to loving Wisdom, to interpreting a text. Perhaps we only recognize that *Scripture is Augustine's Lady Wisdom* when we too have become her lovers—readers sufficiently skilled as to be able to perceive the unity in a complex and open-ended work. Some of us may have to read the *Confessions* again and again before we see the Lady at all.[59]

Shanzer suggests that "Scripture's many faces, when she is seen as a woman, prefigure her many interpretations, when she is seen as a text."[60] *One face that Shanzer fails to mention is the face of Augustine's mother.* Indeed, Shanzer's framing of the autobiographical allegory of Folly and Wisdom developed in books 3–7 and culminating in the Herculean "choice" of book 8 seems to leave the minibiography of Monica in book 9 awkwardly caught, along with the rest of book 9 and book 10, in the liminal zone between the narrative quest and its exegetical consummation. Yet I would suggest that the "Life of Monica" is the crux of the narrativized enigma (*where is Wisdom?*), a riddle that is not so much solved as displaced—repeated and reframed—by the later exegetical performance (*she is [in] Scripture*).

"Behold, moved by your prayers, I come to you, natural mother of all things. . . whose single divinity is venerated over the whole earth under many faces, varying rites, and changing names." Thus speaks the goddess in

Apuleius's *Golden Ass*—a text that may be of special importance for understanding the structural significance of the figure of Monica in Augustine's *Confessions*. As John Winkler has argued, the eleventh and final book of Apuleius's novel, which contains the solemn epiphany of the many-named and many-faced goddess Isis, comes as a shock to a first-time reader of this witty and sophisticated text (*Metamorphoses* 11.5). It also dramatically destabilizes the familiar parodic quest tale that is seemingly Apuleius's point of departure—namely Pseudo-Lucian's *Lucius, or the Ass*. "For if the ass-tale is a take-off on 'I went in quest of wisdom' narratives, then Apuleius has translated the parody, with all its ridicule of the quester intact, but has added at the end the very sort of epiphany and revelation that the *parodied* works contained."[61] Winkler emphasizes the uncertainty introduced by the supplemental Isiac book, which reinstates divine revelation in (relatively) "straight" terms at the conclusion, and outside the frame, of an (ambiguously) parodic narrative. The Apuleian novel, he argues, thereby refuses to adjudicate between competing truth claims and thus shifts the burden of decision to the reader while at the same time making it clear that the decision lies outside the domain of rationally negotiable propositions. "The *Golden Ass* is an evocation of a religious experience bracketed in such a way that the reader must, but cannot, decide the question of its truth," Winkler suggests. "The implicit argument of the novel is that belief in Isis or in any integrating cosmic hypothesis is a radically individual act that cannot be shared."[62]

Augustine follows Apuleius's example, constructing a quest narrative that begins falsely with carnal curiosity and ends felicitously with divine disclosure.[63] Here—in contrast to his treatment of Virgil's *Aeneid*, for example—he lets a significant literary predecessor go utterly unnamed. This may be a necessary exercise of tact, where allusion so dangerously combines admiration with aggression. The Apuleian novel is quite possibly already making a mockery of Christianity,[64] and if Augustine subtly turns the tables in countermimicry he cannot deny that there is also genuine flattery in his imitation. Apuleius seems to have a written his novel less to propagandize the Isiac cult than to question the totalizing claims of all such cults, and Augustine arguably replays Apuleius's plot less to unseat a false goddess—Isis—and replace her with a true one—Wisdom—than to undermine an ironic agnosticism so as to assert the authority of divine revelation, not least by sternly imposing his "converted" perspective on the account of his earlier life. But how successful is he? As Winkler describes Augustine's *Confessions*, noting the contrast with Apuleius, "The present narrator invades his past as an enemy territory, using his god as a powerful ally to destroy the lingering vestiges of the pleasure he originally felt" (141). The contrast is real; nonetheless, we should not exaggerate the differences between these two literary works, the one a novel narrated in the first person and frequently read as autobiography (indeed, so read by Augustine himself), the other a novelistic autobiography occasionally labeled (as Augustine labeled Apuleius's work) a lying fiction.[65] Each pivots around a surprise ending that calls upon us to reassess the text retrospectively, thereby thematizing the necessity for artful interpretation—underlining the indispensability, and also the indeterminacy, of exegesis.

Winkler warns readers of Apuleius not to impose monologic and moralizing readings on a fundamentally complex and deliberately ambiguous text. Such a warning would likewise be well heeded by readers of the later North African. *Confessions* is seductive and hermeneutically challenging precisely where it is most powerfully empathetic—and most surprisingly noncommittal—in its replaying of the emotions of the author's earlier selves. Augustine sustains a remarkable level of ambivalence throughout the narrative books of his work—though unlike Apuleius he (narrowly) avoids parody. To cite merely a well-known example: his recollection of a boyhood theft of pears, frequently viewed as evidence of excessive critique of past behavior, skillfully introduces and interlaces moral judgment with vivid evocations of the fundamentally "good" pleasures that motivated the paltry crime—sensory gratification, social esteem, and above all "the delightful bond" of friendship (2.5). Much as Apuleius's narrator delivers a harrowing rendition of a "murder" that turns out to be no more than a slashing of wineskins (*Metamorphoses* 2.32–3.10), here Augustine deliberately makes much ado about almost nothing. His purpose, it seems, is to cut moral transgressions down to their ordinary, nonheroic size while at the same time restoring a sense of their modest complexities. Likewise, Augustine's tender accounts of his various (with the exception of his concubine, homoerotic) "lovers" (e.g., 4.8, 6.15) appear no more regretful than Lucius's enthusiastic recountings of his luscious nights with Fotis (e.g., *Metamorphoses* 2.16–17). (In fact, if we take Lucius's later recriminations of Fotis seriously, Augustine may be the less regretful.)

Perhaps even more surprising (and even more often repressed) than the relatively forgiving, almost Apuleian eye that Augustine casts on his own past is the negativity that he introduces into the supplementary "book of the mother." As we shall see, he thereby sustains a positive ambivalence where we might expect (indeed, have been led by his interpreters to expect) a more reductively idealizing portrait to emerge. In this respect, book 9 of *Confessions* is as much a counterpart to the portrait of Venus in Apuleius's centrally embedded tale of Psyche and Cupid *(Metamorphoses* 6) as it is an evocation of the final epiphany of Isis (*Metamorphoses* 11). (Like Monica's, Venus's opinion of what—or who—is best for her son initially differs from his own but is subsequently revised.)[66] The "ultimate" surprise ending of *Confessions*—showcasing an unambivalently positive representation of the divine female figure Sapientia/Scriptura that more closely matches Apuleius's Isis—is deferred to the last three books, which thus supplement the supplement. As in Apuleius's novel, the extended revelation—itself taking unexpected form—includes the equally unexpected message that no revelation is conclusive. Texts continue to give rise to interpretation.

It appears, then, that Augustine's *Confessions* only pretends to imagine itself the one and only, first and unique, thereby slyly challenging us to notice its deep dependency and intricate intertextuality. Augustine writes over the lines of other texts, both biblical and secular. He has precursors, but he *also* has contemporaries, as we have seen. Others of the time—other Christians—are writing female biographies, inscribing the Lives of women even as they write their autobiographies. Like Jerome and Gregory, Augustine writes from the perspective of a man grieving; like these others, he mourns a much-loved woman, grieves like a woman—reluctantly, and also excessively, with ambivalence. "The tears dried in my eyes. . . . It did not bring me to tears. . . . I did not weep." So he begins, only to reverse himself quickly. "The tears which I had been holding back streamed down, and I et them flow as freely as they would," Augustine next confesses, pleading that his reader not despise such womanish behavior but rather imitate it. "Let him not mock at me but weep himself, if his charity is great" (9.12).

Like Jerome, Augustine writes with tearful ambivalence of a woman, and he inscribes his ambivalence into the Life. He writes with two hands, giving praise with one and taking it away with the other. The Lives of women are not quite hagiographies, no matter who writes them. Monica, Augustine makes painfully clear, was no saint.[67] She had bad habits, perverse desires. "I cannot presume to say that from the time when she was reborn in baptism no word contrary to your commands ever fell from her lips," notes the son in the midst of his mourning. Since he is stating the obvious, why does he say it? "I will lay aside for a while all the good deeds which my mother did. For them I thank you, but now I pray to you for her sins" (9.13).

Indeed, Monica the well-intentioned sinner never quite gets it right, according to her son. Her life is always in need of revision; she is always in need of our prayers. We see this most clearly from the vantage point of her death, where Augustine, who has just promised to "omit not a word that my mind can bring to birth concerning my mother, your servant," now seems to have an oddly selective memory, zeroing in first on an account of childhood alcoholism framed by class conflict, on the one hand, and spousal abuse interlaced with intergenerational conflict, on the other, positioning his mother as a dubious pupil in a school of very hard knocks indeed. "Each day she added a few more drops to her daily sip of wine. 'But little things despise and little by little you shall come to ruin.' It soon became a habit, and she would drink her wine at a draught, almost by the cupful" (9.8).

Peter Brown notes that, in book 9's portrayal, "Monica, the idealized figure that had haunted Augustine's youth like an oracle of God, is subtly transformed, by Augustine's analysis of his present feelings upon remembering her death, into an ordinary human being, an object of concern, a sinner like himself, equally in need of mercy."[68] There have also, however, been earlier signs of Monica's flawed character in the text—leading little by little toward her "ruin" in book 9. Remember? As a young mother, she shuns the "better course" of an early baptism for her son and instead defers the rite, preferring that "the great tides of temptation . . . beat upon the as yet unmolded clay rather than upon the finished image which had received the stamp of baptism" (1.12; cf. 5.9). When, after a visit to the public baths, her husband proudly reports "the signs of active virility coming to life" in their son, Monica again responds inadequately, worrying too little about Augustine's desires and too much about his career. "She was afraid that the bonds of marriage might be a hindrance to my hopes for the future, . . . my hopes of success at my studies." (Here Augustine's subsequent attempt to christianize Monica's motive—because such an overt rationalization—merely calls attention to his mother's queer worldliness: "Both my parents were unduly eager for me to learn," he recalls, "my mother because she thought that the usual course of study would certainly not hinder me, but would even help me, in my approach to you" [2.3].) Having left the tides of temptation to engulf her son, Monica unleashes a flood of her own into the text, worrying and weeping ceaselessly. "It cannot be that the son of those tears should be lost," a weary bishop finally snaps, a statement that she is pleased to accept as prophetic (3.12). If, as a mother, she is now metonymically defined by her tears, her sorrow begins to seem a bit much. A reader can easily imagine why Augustine sneaks away in the night, "leaving her alone to her tears and her prayers," boarding a ship for Rome—like Virgil's Aeneas giving Dido the slip.[69] As Augustine represents it, even God's patience with the woman has grown thin by this point: Monica's excessive grief at Augustine's departure, "her too jealous love for her son," is identified as a divine punishment that fits the female crime of passion. Indeed, her maternal sorrow is itself the mark of sin, "proof that she had inherited the legacy of Eve" (5.8).

Crying is not all that is left to Monica, however. She still has scope to mismanage Augustine's life. Astonishingly, she has followed him all the way to Milan (6.1)—no Dido, she, after all.[70] Now, when it is too late, she finds her son a wife (6.13). Too late for Augustine, who has a longtime, devoted lover and a son. Too soon by at least two years for the prepubescent wife. Into the gap, a stopgap mistress steps. (For, in preparation for his socially advantageous marriage, Augustine's common-law wife has been "torn from his side" and sent back to Africa; there, grieving like a widow and vowing chastity, *she* now plays Dido to his Aeneas while his mother stands staunchly *at his side*, like Adam's rib. The unnamed concubine also plays an unsuccessful Psyche to his Cupid, with Monica in the role of Venus, most difficult of mothers-in-law.) Bereft of his soulmate and cleaving to alien flesh, Augustine suddenly finds his own sinfulness nakedly revealed. He cannot imitate the woman—his former lover—for whom his heart still bleeds. He cannot even wait for his new wife. The waves of longing for erotic intimacy with a woman beat upon him with the relentless force of an addiction, "an uninterrupted habit" (6.15). Little by little, he's been hooked, like Monica in the cellar with her sips of wine.

Augustine is not original, but he *is* creative. Writing the Life of a woman, he gives birth to his own Life. His *Confessions* is a "great book" but (like the Life of a woman) not quite a hagiography. The Saint's Life is in his field of vision, but it is not his point of departure. When "a book containing the life of Antony" is read by another, Augustine leaves it lying just barely outside the frame of his text, a found object in another man's story of a stranger's conversion (8.6; cf. 8.12). His own Life thereby also escapes the frame of holiness. It is—necessarily—unfinished. It is unfinished business, always beginning again. It is perpetually in the process of revision.

Augustine never quite gets it right. (This theologically weighty self-presentation—conveying the stubborn imprint of "original sin"—is, after all, the root of his famous disagreement with Pelagius.) For one thing, he keeps picking the wrong woman. First there was the Folly of Cicero, and then that of Mani. Now, so close to a proper catholic orthodoxy, in his final nightmarish staging of Proverbs 9, he finds himself of two minds, struggling to decide between the austere beauty of Lady Continence (looking suspiciously like his virtuous African concubine) and the more local comforts of Mistress Habit, who beckons him to do "this thing or that"—"things so sordid and so shameful that I beg you in your mercy to keep the soul of your servant free from them!" the poor man cries (8.11). When Augustine eventually makes his choice for Continence, his mother, he tells us, is "overjoyed." "For she saw that you had granted her far more than she used to ask in her tearful prayers and plaintive lamentations" (8.12).

Is the reader surprised by Monica's spontaneous delight? We should not fail to note that, if the mother's sorrow has been exchanged for joy, it has entailed a complex conversion. Monica's tears have not been rewarded but chastened by gladness, her dream for the son of those tears not fulfilled but, little by little, revised. Augustine *insists* on it: "You 'turned her sadness into rejoicing,' into joy far fuller than her dearest wish, far sweeter and more chaste than any she had hoped to find in children begotten of my flesh," he assures his God (8.12).

"Time never stands still," writes Augustine (4.8). But once, before the end, they get it almost right, once time almost stands still. For a heartbeat— at the text's midpoint—Augustine and his mother rest together in the embrace of God's eternity: their Lives truly coincide.[71] Leaning from a window overlooking a garden, they converse, he recalls. (It is in the days just before Monica's death, but they do not yet know that.) The flame of their love draws them higher and higher. "And while we spoke of the eternal Wisdom, longing for it and straining for it with all the strength of our hearts, for one fleeting instant we reached and touched it." Afterward they imagine what it might be like to encounter God not through the veil of Scripture but directly voiced. "Suppose that we heard him himself, with none of these things between ourselves and him, just as in that brief moment my mother and I had reached out in thought and touched the eternal Wisdom which abides over all things" (9.10).

Augustine continues to long for the moment of naked truth, but the truth is that he has already touched his Bride. However briefly, he has glimpsed Lady Wisdom, there in the window with his mother. Augustine is not ready to die, but he is nonetheless happy to be standing on the threshold with Monica. Where Paula and Macrina on their own deathbeds hasten to their heavenly Bridegroom with joyous greeting, Monica uses her dying breath to renounce her desire to be buried next to her earthly husband (9.11). Is she saving herself for Christ or merely choosing Continence like her son? Choosing her continent son? Who is the bride, who the Groom, in this strange woman's Life? Augustine is grooming himself for Wisdom, but it is Monica who has accompanied him this far. It is Monica, the ever-revisable text, who enables him to recognize the woman with many faces. It is also Monica who teaches him how to submit to the chastening blows of divine desire (how to play the bride). It is Monica who teaches him not only about sin but also about *charity*. One day the Lady will reveal herself to him nakedly (she may even come as his Lord).[72] Now he gazes upon her veiled form, he unfurls her pages, and it is his own naked hunger that is revealed. He sucks, he gulps, he devours the inexhaustible maternal body of text. ("But the very simplicity of the language of Scripture sustains them in their weakness as a mother cradles an infant in her lap" [12.27].) He consumes Wisdom's material feast of words. ("I had learned that Wisdom and Folly are like different kinds of food" [5.6].) He makes something new of the ancient writing. He makes something new of himself. Writing, he reads. Sucking, he feeds. He feeds us. We eat him. We are eating him, reading him now. We are eating, reading *her* now.

Monica is already there at the beginning, and she is still present in the many-faced and many-named scriptural Wisdom in whom Augustine rests at the end—sign of constant love, figure of ongoing metamorphosis, creature of both excess and deficiency. Beyond that, it is hard to say: she is elusive, adaptive, mobile and multiple, a trickster skilled at evading domination, disguising desire, guiding by misdirection. She offers no easy solutions. *She demands a strong reading.*

Testimony to (Woman's) Survival

> *Allow me to call to mind an essential kind of generality: is the witness not always a survivor? This belongs to the structure of testimony.... This surviving speech must be as exemplarily irreplaceable as the instance of the instant from which it speaks, the instant of death as irreplaceable, as "my death," on the subject of which no one other than the dying person can testify. I am the only one who can testify to my death—on the condition that I survive it.*
>
> —Jacques Derrida, Demeure

> *In so far as any feminine existence is in fact a traumatized existence, feminine autobiography cannot be a confession. It can only be a testimony: to survival. And like other testimonies to survival, its struggle is to testify at once to life and to the death—the dying—the survival has entailed.*
>
> —Shoshana Felman, What Does a Woman Want?

Men, it seems, write their autobiographies from memory. The act of remembrance, however, is also a testimony to the death of a "self" that splits the subject—"for to end is to surrender to a memorial of what one has become," as Lynda Hart puts it.[73] "I" am dead; and "I" survive. "All that remains is the feeling of lightness that is death itself or, to put it more precisely, the instant of my death henceforth always in abeyance," writes Maurice Blanchot.[74] This passage occurs at the end of a work that exemplifies, for Jacques Derrida, the undecidability of the distinction between testimony and fiction and also "the impossibility of *remaining* in the undecidable."[75] "I can testify to the imminence of my death," muses Derrida, reflecting thereby upon "the singular concept of an unexperienced experience"[76]—a "concept" that seemingly inheres in "*passionate* trajectories of literature" in which martyrdom is always implicated. "Where the witness alone is capable of dying his own death, testimony always goes hand in hand with at least the *possibility* of fiction, perjury, lie. . . . If testimony is passion, that is because it will always *suffer* both having, undecidably, a connection to fiction, perjury, or lie and never being able or obligated—without ceasing to testify—to become a proof."[77]

Men, it seems, first write their autobiographies by giving testimony to the death of an Other, a woman. Jerome and Gregory, as well as Augustine, tell their own stories by reliving their grief for a friend, a sister, a mother. "She" is dead; "he" survives. But "she" also lives on (she gets a Life), even as "he" (the writer) surrenders to a memorial of what he has become. "And this is the colloquium," notes Derrida, "this is the dialogue between the two witnesses, who are, moreover, the same, alive and dead, living-dead, and both of whom in abidance claim or allege that one is alive, the other dead, as if life went only to an *I* and death to a *you*. Always according to the same compassion of passion."[78] But is "the compassion of passion" "the same" for feminine subjects? Is woman not always a *you* and never quite an *I*?

"Unlike men, who write autobiographies from memory, women's autobiography is what their memory cannot contain—or hold together as a whole—although their writing inadvertently inscribes it," asserts Felman.[79] She goes on: "I cannot confess to my autobiography as missing, but I can testify to it. I cannot write my story (I am not in possession of my own autobiography), but I can read it in the Other."[80] It is "the same compassion"—and it is also different (always already different). For in the "*passionate* trajectories of literature" in which we still stand (however unsteadily), it is the death of the woman that is witnessed; and *no one other than the dying person can testify to her death*. Female (auto)biography is, then, itself a privileged witness to the "necessary but impossible abidance of the abode" of writing, the deep complicity of literature and death.[81]

Reading, and thus ("inadvertently") writing, as a woman—*reading and writing for survival*— "I" cannot possibly find a stable place to stand in texts of men who erect their Lives like monuments upon the tombs of women. (But, then, "who" could?—a rhetorical question.) "I" (and "you" too) may, however, discover a transient joy in the instabilities of a fractured and scarred subjectivity ("a scared subjectivity," I almost wrote, for the truth is, I am afraid of pain)—"a joy that now cuts across limits to reverse the effect of the first cut, which established the discontinuous subject."[82] The killing knife that excises "me" from the text also cuts me back in; it opens me to, and in, the other. Tears and blood of uncontainable memory ink the page, letters like old wounds fade and eventually decompose with the skin on which they are inscribed, but now for a little while longer they can be traced with eyes, fingers—*they can be rewritten* (the pen cuts deeply, once again). I am *not* in possession of my own autobiography, but I may be possessed by the texts of others—Jerome, Gregory, Augustine. After all, they were always already possessed by those other others, "women."

Fragments of an Autobiography

Hair

Oddly enough, I was reading the following gossipy passage in one of Jerome's letters while sitting veiled under a hair drier at a beauty salon, eyes lowered demurely to the little red book in my lap. "In those days lady's maids used to arrange her hair, and her poor head, which had done no harm, was imprisoned in a head-dress crammed with curls. Now it is left alone and knows that it is sufficiently cared for when it is covered by a veil." (Earlier, Sandy, the stylist, had wrapped strands of my own reluctant hair in bits of shining foil, each containing a dye that would—she assured me—interject shades of golden brown and gleaming silver into the darker browns and duller grays already adorning my head.) I used to think being a real woman (and a good feminist) meant being "natural"—at all costs resisting being made a "sex object." At forty-two, I'm no longer so sure. Is it possible for me to be *sexual at all* without flirting dangerously with the terms of my own objectification—playing at the "feminine" so as to make myself "femme" so as to become *someone other* than either a "man" or his desired "object"? Blaesilla, the Roman lady who stopped seeing her stylist, was undergoing her own radical makeover—one that would end, sadly, in her death by starvation. Her mother, Jerome's friend Paula, gave up her makeup box and silk dresses in order to cultivate gauntness and grunge, wearing rough goat's hair and purposefully disfiguring her face. That is no more, or less, "natural" than cosmetics and curls—or highlights. It *is*, however, an acute articulation of the double bind of one caught in a "femininity" simultaneously suspected of sheer artifice and reduced to mere flesh. More than that, it is an effective act of resistance. In performing a denaturalized "body," risking a hyperembodiment of "culture," Blaesilla and Paula walk a dangerous edge, and it is one that I imagine I know.

Skin

Macrina's breast is marked by a scar. If she is Odysseus, her thigh also bears the sign. Charged zones: to show or not to show? (Just a glimpse of near-recognition—a flash of flesh—and fantasy takes flight.) Frequently, I am surprised to find my body still so blank. In compensation, I add more piercings to my ears; some of them refuse to heal. Do you have any scars? my daughter asks. She and I would both be satisfied, I think, if I could point to visible signs (on breast or thigh, for example) of the passing violence of her birth, the voracious tug of her feeding mouth. (Others would like to have left their marks too, it occurs to me.) My scars are still invisible, I say to her—except this one on my knee. Tell me about it, she demands. And I rehearse yet again the unremarkable tale of a twelve-year-old girl racing too quickly down sharp stone stairs. Did it bleed a lot? Yes. If you'd gotten stitches would there have been a scar? Perhaps not. Do you wish you'd gotten stitches? Not really. (It's the right answer: she runs her fingers over my knee with the tenderness and fascination of a lover.)

Like Macrina I was a runner. I still like to run (though it *is* hard on the knees). Muscles mold and remold my thighs—a layered history of internal scarring ("no pain, no gain"), just breaking the surface of visibility. It is important to be strong, I tell myself.

Eyes

Augustine bends God's ear but seeks his mother's eyes. Frequently they are overflowing with tears: he is the son of her tears, her ever-breaking maternal waters. He can't get enough, for his own have long since dried. (Then again, if she would dry up, maybe he could feel his own grief.) You too have the gift of tears, my friend tells me. (She is not similarly "graced.") My son teases me about weeping at movies. (And I wonder when it was that he stopped crying.) I cry in church—and in faculty meetings. I cry in public and in private. Is there no end to this grieving? I ask myself. Are all tears tears of grief? Where does joy begin?

But Monica's eyes are not only frequently tearful; they are also (like mine) both watchful and guarded. I watch Augustine watching her watch him. He wants her to watch him. He wishes she would stop. He does, and does not, want to see himself reflected in her eyes; he does, and does not, want to drown in the depths of her bottomless gaze. He is happiest to stand shoulder to shoulder, peering into the still more perfect mirror of an eternal sameness. He imagines he is looking through her eyes. I wonder what he thinks he sees.

It is not easy to look through the eyes of a woman. There is no identifiable "vantage point": views are particular, partial, multiple, perverse. Veiled, downcast, shifting, sidelong—or else brazen (*beyond* direct). The hardest thing of all, for *my* eyes? The mirror: to look at myself: to see myself looking back. The image doesn't hold together as a whole; I see nothing but fragments. I seem to myself like the dream of a martyr's relics.

Chapter 3
Hybrid Desire: Empire, Sadism, and the Soldier Saint

What I vividly recall are their grasp of the "sense of wonder," alienness, the feeling of being lost in a strange, new world of colour, gorgeousness and marvels not to be imagined.
—Stephen May, Stardust and Ashes: Science Fiction in Christian Perspective

Contemporary science fiction is full of cyborgs—creatures simultaneously animal and machine, who populate worlds ambiguously natural and crafted. . . .The cyborg is resolutely committed to partiality, irony, intimacy, and perversity. It is oppositional, utopian, and completely without innocence.
—Donna Haraway, "A Cyborg Manifesto"

Martin of Tours, a Pannonian ex-soldier credited with the militant conversion of Gaul to Christianity, is best known to us from the Life penned by the Aquitanian ascetic Sulpicius Severus. Much admired for its delicate engagement with classical traditions of historiography and biography, Sulpicius's *Life of Martin* also forcefully overwrites prior hagiographical texts. Like Jerome, Sulpicius takes up the task of refuting the singular claims of the *Life of Antony*, thereby also issuing a challenge to Jerome's own Lives of Paul and Hilarion—competitors in his competition with the Athanasian Life. The *Life of Martin* is thus written aggressively, but it is also written haltingly, in distinct stages, visibly crossing genres, in conversation and amidst disputation. It is a queer work, not only because its author's apparent desire to say it all—and also to have the last word—finally results in a series of intriguingly open-ended fragments. It is a queer work also because its hypermasculine polemic, condensed in the ferocious figure of the soldier saint, renders it perversely feminine: it is almost a woman's Life. Initially composed circa 396, before Martin's death the following year, this text, more than any other ancient male Life, is interjected with the intimacy of a distinctly autobiographical voice, marked by the author's palpable (and palpably erotic) investment in his improbable subject.[1] Reopened by Martin's death almost before it had come to a close, the wound in the initial Life—the lacking corpse—gives rise to supplemental letters of consolation, lamentation, praise, and pointed self-defense. Pierced by the swift darts of ongoing criticism, the martyred text spills its blood further into the myriad channels of the *Dialogues* (circa 404–406), in which the author's self-representation is a still more prominent aspect of the text, even as his voice is multiplied, displaced, and dispersed in the very effort to locate the (now absent) Martin—who was never quite believable anyway.

Sulpicius's Martin is above all a worker of miracles, a flamboyant performer of the impossible—and it was largely on that basis that his repeatedly repackaged Life was denounced by contemporaries as a pack of lies. Intriguingly (and not accidentally), Sulpicius's Martinian texts continue nonetheless to be mined for "evidence"—even if the evidence is sometimes deemed to be mostly negative. E.-Ch. Babut was the earliest and most severe of Sulpicius's modern critics, inclined to agree with his ancient detractors that the author had virtually invented his hero in order to support the cause of his own rigorist faction of Gallic ascetics.[2] While subsequent apologists defended Martin's historicity against Babut's attacks, Jacques Fontaine turned attention to the literary interest of Sulpicius's work.[3] Yet even Fontaine's literary-historical study hinges on the refutation of Babut and the defense of "la vérité historique" of the Sulpician portrait.[4] More recently, Clare Stancliffe has offered a careful and balanced historical assessment of Sulpicius's intentions in authoring his Martinian works and of the complex cultural context in which those works and their subject, Martin, became the matter of controversy. Nonetheless, for Stancliffe, even more than for Fontaine, understanding Martin himself remains the ultimate goal. She well comprehends the difficulty of what she names a "quest": "It follows the time-honored historical principle of starting from a definite body of material, in this case Sulpicius's Martinian writings, and of stretching out towards what is further from our grasp, in this case Martin and the impact which he made upon his contemporaries."[5] The historical Martin, elusive as he may be, is thus grasped at eagerly by modern commentators, seemingly confident of the positive powers of a healthy skepticism. (But that is the paradox of much historical criticism—its fundamental, unwavering positivism, its desire to *transcend doubt*.) Without denying the significant contribution of such social-historical studies, my own interest lies with a different, and (as it seems to me) relatively neglected, history—namely, the history of the modes of testimony mobilized within the hagiographical texts themselves.

Ancient readers were perhaps more able to recognize a work of fiction— and a disturbingly transgressive fiction at that—when they saw one. Like Jerome, but with even more vehemence, the sophisticated Sulpicius, initially playing at literary simplicity, implodes the ambivalence inherent in ancient traditions of prose narrative: the already compromised distinction between history and romance, truth and fiction, fantasy and lie is brought to a point of crisis. Sulpicius does not merely put the "real" into question; he places it in danger. The apparent referentiality of historical narrative is exposed as an illusion and in its place are offered "the possibilities of the imaginary that are located at the very limits of representation"—the "impossible real," as literary theorist Lynda Hart names it.[6] Indeed, it is the unsettling potency of the "impossible real" mobilized within the literary imaginary that Sulpicius outrageously *insists* on as he opens his biographical text onto the realm of the fantastic, where imagination does not merely reflect but continually reconstitutes reality, pressing readers past the limits not only of plausibility but even of possibility. Sulpicius's stark inscription of present wonders is tensely leveraged against the perspective of future hindsight:[7] he makes visible already the apocalypse that will have been.[8] If Jerome's Lives of men are fantasy romances, Sulpicius writes Martin's Life as science fiction.

Like much (though by no means all) science fiction, these texts are austerely masculine, covertly homoerotic, and finally strangely sexed—eminently queerable.[9] The realms of the erotic and the fantastic prove coextensive and inextricable, linked by their participation in the "unnatural"— which is also the "hypernatural." Bending his will against the laws of nature, Martin at the same time wildly defies the protocols of culture. In this violently catachrestic figuration of sainthood, the distinction between nature and culture (*between the native and the man of culture*) is thus forcibly broken down. Indeed, we seem to see in Sulpicius's portrait a precursor to Donna Haraway's cyborg figures—"densely packed condensations of worlds, shocked into being from the force of the implosion of the natural and the artificial, nature and culture, subject and object, . . . narrative and reality."[10] In the moments of violent breakdown, in the electrifying *shocks*, lies the power of the saint and his text. This is the "authority" that fascinates Sulpicius—like, but not identical to, the power that the woman's erotic death exerts on her biographer. Is it a "phallic" authority? (A question inevitably posed in relation to a sadistic saint who can scarcely be credited with a conversion from soldiering[11]—who is easily imagined with a sword, if not a machine gun.) Yes, but it is also perhaps a phallic authority bent on even its own destruction—bent also on *surviving* even its own destruction. Moreover: it is a phallicism that is beginning to recognize the profound unnaturalness of its own claims. ("It neither returns to the male body, originates from it, nor refers to it.")[12]

Domination and Submission in the Life of Martin

> *Promises are made to be broken.... The tense is the future anterior—the past that will have been. Still, I cannot quite get this right. I want so much to write in the subjunctive—the past that would have been—the mood/mode of subordination. That is why I am a top. But I am a writer only when I surrender.*
> —Lynda Hart, Between the Body and the Flesh: Performing Sadomasochism

Sulpicius would like to be viewed as a modest man. Following ancient literary convention, he protests to his "dearest brother Desiderius" that he did not really want to author this Life. He has done so only by request and out of love for his "brother"; he laments that the Life has not been written by someone whose eloquence was truly worthy of the subject. His humility begins to exceed convention, however, as he continues to whisper his fears into the reader's ear.[13] Desiderius has promised to "reveal it to no other," yet Sulpicius suspects nonetheless that he "will become the means of its publication to the world." (Perusing the published text, we accept this suspicion as a true prophecy and eagerly read on.) Why *is* he so afraid of the inevitable, after all? The style is "somewhat unpolished"; the language may grate on the ears, he worries out loud. The author may come off more like a Galilean fisherman than the Gallic orator that he in fact is.[14] (He has been neglecting his studies, he confesses.) Sulpicius has been found slumming—or perhaps going native. He has cleverly exposed himself in the act. Yet it is more "disgraceful that so great a man should remain concealed" than that Sulpicius should be disgraced. Caught on the horns of his carefully constructed dilemma, he concludes his dedicatory letter: "the book should be published, if you think right, with the author's name suppressed." Erase the title page, he instructs Desiderius; leave it blank; "let the book proclaim its subject-matter, while it tells nothing of the author" (*Life of Martin*, dedicatory preface).[15] But Sulpicius has already told us *so much*.

Launching his formal introduction, he shifts his strategy. Dismissing the aspirations of those who have sought glory by writing of the lives of great men (Hector or Socrates, for example), he does so not on the basis of a charge of false pride (as if implying that they too should have left their title pages blank) but rather on the grounds of their poor choice of subjects—authors, warriors, philosophers (ho-hum). Writing the *right* Life, "by which, indeed, the readers shall be roused to the pursuit of true knowledge, and heavenly warfare, and divine virtue," Sulpicius can hope to be remembered eternally—not only by mere mortals but by the very God (who, like the readers of the dedicatory epistle, can see the words inscribed on the blank title page). Thus it is that he will write the *Life of Martin*, topping the literary efforts of those who have come before. He does not know all that there is to be known about his subject (who was, he admits, not always a forthcoming informant); and much that he does know he will not set down (in the conventionally professed interest of avoiding tedium). But he implores the readers of the subsequent text to approach it with the promise that "I have written nothing of which I had not certain knowledge and evidence." He adds, "I should, in fact, have preferred to be silent rather than to narrate things that are false" (1). We are forewarned, then: later we may be inclined to question the accuracy of what *will*, by then, have been narrated (as he *would* have it?); but for now the author forcefully urges our complicity and, provisionally, we grant it, in the face of his threatened silence.

Martin was always already a servant of God, according to Sulpicius. Denied the satisfying drama of a conversion, he emerges as a peculiarly ambivalent figure, strangely indecisive, and thus initially marked by a hermeneutical undecidability. Son of pagans, already as a child of ten, "he betook himself, against the wish of his parents, to the Church, and begged that he might become a catechumen." He was not, however, baptized. By age twelve, "he desired to enter on the life of a hermit." Yet he was thwarted in this desire—due to his youth, Sulpicius reports, somewhat vaguely. At fifteen, he was drafted into the army, under the terms of an edict requiring all sons of veterans to serve in the military. "He, on the information furnished by his father (who looked with an evil eye on his blessed actions), having been seized and put in chains, . . . was compelled to take the military oath." Passive in the face of a diabolical paternal coercion, presenting itself in both familial and imperial guises, Martin reluctantly becomes not a Christian hermit but a Roman soldier. "During nearly three years before his baptism, he was engaged in the profession of arms" (2). In fact, Martin "continued, although but in name, to act the part of a soldier, for nearly two years after he had received baptism" (3). Nonetheless, even before his baptism, "he was regarded not so much as being a soldier as a monk," insists Sulpicius (2). Martin's baptism (to which we will return) thus did not mark a break with soldiering, any more than soldiering compromised his monastic identity; nor was his asceticism itself clearly signaled by either baptism or retirement from "the world."

As a soldier, Martin is thus already a saint—which is also to say, perhaps something of a sissy. He is "content with only one servant as his companion." Strikingly, he prefers to play bottom to his servant's top: "And even to him, changing places as it were, he often acted as though, while really master, he had been inferior." Sulpicius paints a vivid scene: "He drew off his [servant's] boots and cleaned them with his own hand; while they took their meals together, the real master, however, generally acting the part of the servant." (Is Sulpicius, we may wonder, repeating the act of voluntary, bootlicking submission to a lower-class man? Is this the disgrace with which he so self-consciously flirts in his dedicatory epistle? Later, this possibility will reemerge, and also reverse itself more than once.) Martin avoids the vices typical of soldiers; not only kind, he is wonderfully affectionate toward his fellows; "his patience and humility surpassed what seemed possible to human nature." (His capacity for humiliation is unnatural.) He gives away to the needy all his pay beyond what is required for his daily subsistence (2).

Martin's generosity is showcased in a well-known encounter with a beggar "destitute of clothing"—a condensed figure of abject poverty who evokes not only a layered biblical intertext but also the contemporary context of an economically devastated military frontier.[16] Martin is already practically naked himself, having given away so much. "Taking, therefore, his sword with which he was girt, he divided his cloak into two equal parts, and gave one part to the poor man, while he again clothed himself with the remainder." Many of the onlookers mock his ridiculous appearance ("he was now an unsightly object"), but that night Martin is visited in a dream by Christ himself, and in the vision Christ is wearing the partial garment with which Martin has clothed the beggar. Here Sulpicius has cleverly outdone prior hagiographical accounts of intimate exchanges of clothing between hermits: *his* "hermit" is wrapped in the same cloak as Jesus himself; indeed, they wear it at the same time—dreamer and dreamed, two equal parts sundered and rejoined in one holy union. Jesus speaks in gospeled tones: "Martin, who is still but a catechumen, clothed me with this robe" (cf. Matt. 25.40). Now it is that Martin, perhaps taking the hint, finally also seems to take action, rushing off to be baptized. "He did not, however, all at once, retire from military service." Why not? His tribune, "whom he admitted to be his familiar tent-companion," begged him to delay, promising to retire with him if Martin would wait out the expiration of his tentmate's term of office (3). As Fontaine points out, this is not the only known instance of "couples d'amis chrétiens" whose march toward conversion to an asceticized Christianity is imperfectly synchronized: Martin and his tribune anticipate not only Jerome and Bonosius and the two young *agentes in rebus* of Trier but also Alypius and Augustine (Augustine, *Confessions* 8.6).[17]

In the event, Martin leaves the military on rather different terms—with or without his tent-companion, we cannot say. (Sulpicius does not attempt to harmonize his narrative at this point and thus continues to proliferate ambiguities, blunting the sharpness of narrative turns.) The emperor, anticipating battle, is distributing a donative. Martin, so long passive, now seizes his chance to make his witness and thereby to take his leave from the military—or rather, to defect to another army. The event is closely modeled on tales of soldier martyrs.[18] "Hitherto I have served *you* as a soldier: allow me now to become a soldier to God," he proclaims, thereby neatly dividing the identities that Sulpicius has artfully seamed together in his initial portrait of the saintly soldier. "I am the soldier of Christ: it is not lawful for me to fight." Accused of cowardice, Martin vows he will fight without worldly weapons: "I will take my stand unarmed before the line of battle tomorrow, and in the name of the Lord Jesus, protected by the sign of the cross, and not by shield or helmet, I will safely penetrate the ranks of the enemy." Ever the soldier after all, Martin lays claim not only to divine protection but also to holy powers of penetration. He is a real man now, in word if not in deed. (For he is saved by less dramatic means, when the barbarians surrender on the following day: God is not as battle-hungry as his servant, it seems [4].) Martin has not converted, and he does not need to convert: he was always a soldier and always a man of God. But he has learned to play the top. Now *God*'s soldier, his identity is sewn up more tightly than ever. He has made his decision.

At this point in the text, linear narrative begins to give way to the punctual recitation of anecdotes: signs and wonders proliferate as the soldier goes off to do battle with the powers of evil at work in the world. Still, Sulpicius carries the tale a bit farther before eschewing linear narrativity altogether, recounting Martin's visit to bishop Hilary of Poitiers (who perceptively appoints him exorcist) (5), his return to his native land of Pannonia (where he converts his mother but not his father); misfired attempts to establish a hermitage at Milan and to pursue an ascetic life "with a certain presbyter as his companion" on the island Gallinaria (6); his return (following upon the return of the exiled Hilary) to Gaul and the founding of a hermitage at Ligugé outside Poitiers (7); and finally his surprising and controversial election to the episcopate of Tours. (In a vivid passage that recalls earlier jeers at his half-cloak, we are told that some suggested "that Martin's person was contemptible, that he was unworthy of the episcopate, that he was a man despicable in countenance, that his clothing was mean, and his hair disgusting" [9].) As Stancliffe points out, even Martin's election to the episcopacy is not marked as a sharp turning point, although it does bring the main narrative portion of the Life to an end: as a bishop, Martin—who finally succeeds in establishing a successful monastery at Marmoutier just outside Tours (10)—is still a monk as well as a soldier, and the focus remains on the continuity of his identity, now fully revealed.[19]

What finally demands our attention is less Sulpicius's chronological presentation of the course of Martin's life than the cumulative energy of the hero's recounted acts, which rapidly overwhelm the initial narrative. The first such "act," which takes place as Martin is traveling to visit his parents, concretizes the ambivalent clash of powers that will characterize the saint's deeds throughout. Martin is in the Alps, an extended, jagged borderland notorious for offering "hideouts for bandits"—a charged zone of transition in which, historically, the distinction between an emperor or general and a local strongman or "bandit" frequently broke down.[20] Martin is himself beset by bandits as he enters this terrain of contested wildness. After he narrowly avoids the blow of an ax aimed at his head, his hands are bound behind his back and he is handed over to one of the gang "to be guarded and stripped." (This is not the first or the last time that Martin—saint of decloaking—finds himself in danger of bodily exposure.) Yet again playing at martyrdom, Martin answers a question about his identity by proclaiming his Christianity. Aren't you afraid? the bandit asks pointedly. Martin responds that he has never before felt so safe and that it is rather the bandit who should fear. Thereupon Martin preaches the gospel and the bandit, predictably, converts. (Indeed, it is from the converted bandit that Sulpicius has received the tale [5].) Martin has tricked the trickster. The reader is scarcely surprised when, in the very next breath, Sulpicius recounts Martin's meeting with the devil himself, who vanishes into thin air in the face of the soldier's uncanny courage (6). Martin has, then, also outdeviled the devil. Time grows short, and cosmic conflict is played out in the worldly sphere. In Martin, heaven and earth, the holy and the unholy, coincide in a pure burst of power. The triumph, however, is never conclusive: omnipotence would kill the Life. Martin dances with the devil and his minions (who will, necessarily, return again and again, surviving their own destruction). They always recognize each other. They are not unlike.

Martin does battle even with death. Silently evoking the rugged figure of a more ancient man of God—the prophet Elisha—Sulpicius recounts Martin's raising of a monastic companion, seemingly his first "disciple" at Ligugé,[21] who has died of a fever during the master's brief absence. "He orders the others to quit the cell in which the body was lying; and bolting the doors, he stretches himself at full length on the dead limbs of the departed brother." The young man is tremblingly resuscitated after several hours of prayerful effort. This intimately earthy, covertly erotic, closeted encounter—which Sulpicius has dressed, down to its last detail, in the threads of the biblical account (cf. 2 Kings 4.32–37)[22]—is the immediate source of Martin's fame: "From this time forward, the name of the sainted man became illustrious, so that, as being reckoned holy by all, he was also deemed powerful and truly apostolical." The resurrected man is also Sulpicius's first informant, we are told—the "impossible real" indeed, a man who can testify to his own death because he can also testify to his resurrection (who *cannot*, however, be a credible witness to the closeted scene described above, it might be noted). Playing a double role in the public production of the saintly performance, the resurrected man partly collapses the interval separating the "original" from its "representation." The two-timing witness both reveals and reveils the authorial sleight of hand—the *craft* of Sulpicius's own claim to fame—even as the precise biblicism of the self-consciously literary account draws the time of "this time forward" into the tight weave of a competing textual temporality (7). As if to diffuse the dizzying effect, Sulpicius repeats the trick, relating in quick succession how Martin raised a slave who had hanged himself: "Martin entered the cell in which the body was lying, and, excluding the multitude, he stretched himself upon the body, and spent some little time in prayer" (8). The echo, displaced from the Elisha text, is now safely contained in the (historical) life—or is it the (literary) Life after all that harbors *all* of Martin's fame? Has Sulpicius constructed his hero wholly out of biblical cloth?

This fast-paced action precedes Martin's episcopacy and the founding of the monastery of Marmoutier, where the manly brothers follow the saint in cultivating wildness, living in holes carved out of the native rocks and wearing nothing softer than the imported roughness of camel's hair (10). Yet neither episcopal nor monastic duties cause the single-minded soldier to break his militant stride. In this distinctly unpastoral text, the violence has only just begun. Three particularly queer miracles are erected like portentous signposts of Martin's weird ways. In the first, Martin visits the site of a supposed martyrium and there dramatically invokes an unexpected apparition, namely, the shade of a bandit—or perhaps of a hero of the Bagaudae?[23]—"of mean and cruel appearance" who had been "beheaded on account of his crimes." Although no one else can see the ghost, the good Christians gathered hear his voice and thus stand convicted of their own crimes of misplaced piety. Martin, meanwhile, marks his odd triumph by ordering the removal of the altar (11).

If this "miracle" seems nearly pointless—as the rough-and-ready saint now converts a martyr into a robber, whereas previously he had made a witness of a bandit—the following performance of power positively exults in arbitrary reversals. Martin sees from a distance of nearly half a mile a crowd engaged in some kind of rite. Sulpicius emphasizes Martin's ignorance: "it was difficult to discover what the spectacle he beheld really was." The man of action does not hesitate, however. (Ready—fire—aim!) He sees that it is a rustic gathering, perceives linen cloths blowing about in the wind, darkly imagines veiled images of "demons" being paraded through the fertile fields. Raising the sign of the cross, he commands the people to stop and lower their burden. (Zap!) The little crowd of pagans is literally paralyzed. "The miserable creatures might have been seen at first to become stiff as rocks." Comically, they try to move forward but cannot; still they clutch their burden. Then "they began to whirl themselves about in the most ridiculous fashion, until, not able any longer to sustain the weight, they set down the dead body." The whirlers are understandably "thunderstruck." But so are we: for "they are simply a band of peasants celebrating funeral rites, and not sacrifices to the gods." The imperturbable Martin regally raises his hand and allows them to move forward and retrieve the corpse. "Thus," comments Sulpicius with apparent satisfaction, "he both compelled them to stand when he pleased, and permitted them to depart when he thought good" (12).

In the third episode, Martin finally takes careful aim as he once again demonstrates that nature itself is on his side in the battle against demonic powers (whether "real" or perceived): manifesting a veritable "psychosis of crusade *avant la lettre*,"[24] he intensifies the rigor of his campaign to eradicate native cults. Here Martin is the hypernatural man of uncouth wildness. His opponents are archetypal tree-huggers. Having already witnessed the destruction of their temple, these villagers cling fiercely to their sacred pine, a tree associated with the Gallo-Roman cult of Cybele.[25] Finally, as if making a pact with the devil, the villagers strike a dangerous deal with the scary soldier saint: they will cut the tree down themselves, if he will stand under it as it falls. Martin is securely bound "in that spot where, no one doubted, the tree was about to fall." The spectators, both monks and villagers, catch their breath as the pine totters and crashes. Martin plays the scene for all it is worth, withholding his response until the last possible moment: "while it was just rushing upon him, simply holding up his hand against it, he put in its way the sign of salvation." Now it is the tree that whirls as impotently as the crowd of mourners, "after the manner of a spinning top," veering to the opposite side, where it nearly crushes a huddle of country folk. Martin's "magical" powers, put to the test, are thereby also confirmed. "The heathen were amazed by the miracle, while the monks wept for joy," reports Sulpicius (13). Continuing to sharpen the definition of a monastic movement placed strategically in the service of the "spiritual colonization of the countryside,"[26] Martin unleashes his chaotic rage on a series of subsequent village temples, "converting" the rural populace in the process—small wonder (14–15).

Accounts of healings and exorcisms (15–19) do not soften Martin's image. His methods are sometimes brutal, the results occasionally grotesque. In "curing" an unfortunate man possessed by a demon, Martin thrusts his fingers into the man's gnashing teeth, forcing the demon to flee in the opposite direction: "he was cast out by means of a defluxion of the belly, leaving disgusting traces behind him" (17). True, the saint, perhaps betraying his own class-consciousness, takes a milder approach to the healing of the cataracts of the aristocratic Paulinus, who is credited with no demonic infestation; but the honor of Paulinus's visit is itself perhaps sufficient evidence of Martin's power, at least in Sulpicius's eyes (19). The carefully scripted scene of Martin's dinner with the usurping emperor Maximus, "a man of fierce character," demonstrates nonetheless what the opening scene with the converted bandit already hinted: unlike the servile clergy who shamelessly flatter the ruler, Martin, man of power, gives way to no competitor, on the tense, indeed virtually apocalyptic battlefield of late ancient Gallic society, where outlaws, emperors, bishops, and demons all jostle for position (and enemies cannot always be easily distinguished from allies—certainly not from a half mile's distance). Receiving a golden cup from the emperor's servant, Martin is well aware that the emperor expects to be honored by receiving the cup in turn from Martin's right hand; "but Martin, when he had drunk, handed the cup to his own presbyter." Even the emperor must admire this act of audacity. Martin, however, is not finished with his performance until he—a man who has the power of resurrection—has predicted the emperor's own death (20).

Whispering with angels, jousting with devils, Martin sees clearly the complex webs of force and resistance that remain invisible to other eyes. Thus it is that he moves so gracefully within the cosmically charged field. His Life, which has no need for improvement, no interest in progress—which can only keep repeating its testimony to a power that traverses all realms and transgresses all boundaries, holy and unholy—must nonetheless come to an end, after a few more signs and wonders. But the saint is not yet in his grave when Sulpicius writes. The author cannot therefore invoke a funereal context for his oration of praise. In place of a corpse over which he might extend his own revivifying body of text, he offers the long-delayed account of his intimate intercourse with the *living* saint. (Perhaps it is Sulpicius who shares Martin's cloak, as Paulinus quips.)[27] Proof of his worthiness as a witness: this is what we have been anticipating since the beginning, whether we have realized it or not. When it finally comes, surprisingly little remains to be said. The narrative is oddly condensed. Its initial framing creates a tight enclosure, as the encounter that results in the Life is already hemmed in by Sulpicius's authorial aspirations: setting out on "what was to me a pleasant journey," he recalls, "already my mind was inflamed with the desire of writing his life." Closeted with his carefully chosen subject, the desiring author is deeply gratified by Martin's humility and kindness. "He went so far as in person to present me with water to wash my hands, and at eventide he himself washed my feet; nor had I sufficient courage to resist or oppose his doing so." Here Sulpicius is not only casting himself as a disciple to Martin's Jesus (cf. John 13)[28] but also, crucially, playing servant to the soldier in Martin's battlefield tent. The thrill lies not in simple inversion but in the simultaneous conjunction of multiple, incompatible axes of power: the unkept monk washes the gentleman's feet (and Sulpicius has, after all, come to subject Martin to his writerly author-ity); yet it is Sulpicius who finds himself overwhelmed by passion's passivity, unable to resist the saint's authority in this electrifying scene of foot washing. "In fact, I felt so overcome by the authority he unconsciously exerted, that I deemed it unlawful to do anything but acquiesce in his arrangements." Martin lays down the law for Sulpicius, who would surely have happily agreed to wash the master's feet, if only commanded to do so. Martin's "arrangements," however, take the shape of an exhortation that Sulpicius follow the esteemed Paulinus and give up all that he has—that he give extravagantly as only the wealthy can give (as only a "woman" can give?).[29] Sulpicius by now can do no more than ejaculate: "What power and dignity there were in Martin's words and conversation! How active he was, how practical, and how prompt and ready in solving questions connected with Scripture! . . . I never heard from any other lips than those of Martin such exhibitions of knowledge and genius, or such specimens of good and pure speech." The excitement derives from the improbability of the speaking subject: such eloquence and wisdom are "remarkable . . . in a man who had no claim to be called learned" (25).

Sulpicius is a worthy witness because he has *surrendered to his subject*. Momentarily restoring a sense of decorum (as if rebuttoning his rhetorical clothes), he concludes with a carefully conventional speech of praise, showcasing a provocatively improbable Antonine portrait of Martin as a sage figure of serenity. One last, telling outburst of Martinian rage is, however, reserved for Martin's detractors. "I shall, however, by no means feel ashamed if any people of that sort include myself in their hatred along with such a man as Martin," he finishes with a flourish. Shameless by now, the cultured Sulpicius has thrown in his lot with the savage soldier. His book, he promises, "will give pleasure to all truly good men." As for the others, let the devil take them: "if anyone read this narrative in an unbelieving spirit, he himself will fall into sin" (cf. Rev. 22.18–19) (27). The reading of the Life, then, gives rise to a contest of wills, issues a challenge—a test for the readers. Here, at the end, we must look back, take the measure of the depths of our own resistance, explore the abyss of our submission. In the diabolical world of the saintly Martin's Life, it would be a sin to deny the pleasure inhering in the very play of power.

Sulpicius's Passion

> "Passion" implies an engagement that is assumed in pain and suffering, experience without mastery and thus without active subjectivity. Because this passion, which is not active, is not simply passive either, the entire history without history of the middle voice—and perhaps of the neuter of the narrative voice—is opened in passion.
> —*Jacques Derrida*, Demeure

Almost before the ink has dried, Sulpicius finds it necessary to supplement his *Life of Martin* with three letters that more strongly than ever inscribe Martin as a martyr while also representing his Life as a passionate text, its author as a true witness. As with the Lives of women, the epistles focus the gaze on the shining spectacle of the corpse—seen through the sharp lenses lent by a dream's vision, slipping sensuously from mortal existence into the glory of resurrection. Riveted by the death, the letters are also pierced by the bittersweet cries of irrepressible lamentation. Even more powerfully than in the Lives of women, in this homosocial world of text the erotic bond between the suffering saint and the grieving author (multiplied in the figures of other male disciples) threatens to displace the anticipated heavenly union of saint and Christ in the potent moment of death's witness. That bond—that bondage—is suffered joyfully insofar as it is also resisted. Grief is figured as erotic resistance; grief itself is resisted (but not utterly overcome). The reader is invited to resist the text and also to succumb to its power; the text itself suffers.

104   Chapter 3

The first letter is written before Martin's death. The postmortem testimony here centers on the literary Life, dead in the closure marked by its publication, now resurrected in the epistle, which deliberately reopens the text by performing its subjection to the agonies of contested readings. In the midst of a visit from a group of monks, "mention was made of the little work which I published concerning the life of that saintly man Martin," reports Sulpicius, modestly. "I was most happy to hear that it was being eagerly and carefully read by multitudes," he continues, less modestly (Ep. 1.1). The text, however, is not only being celebrated; it is also being attacked. The conflated suffering of the Life and its subject, Martin (and, by implication, its author, Sulpicius, as well), stands at the center of the markedly martyrial epistle. The immediate context is provided by the charge that the Life's claims for Martin's miraculous powers are refuted by the recent event of his near-death by fire (Ep. 1.2).

What such attackers—such *poor readers*—fail to understand, notes Sulpicius contemptuously, is "that almost all the saints have been marked, in respect to their virtues, rather more by their dangers" (Ep. 1.6). Sanctity is properly perceived in the sign of its endangerment, its suffering, its passionate passivity. Virtue, or *power* (the power of virility), is the result of something more complex and actively resistant than mere endurance of threat. It involves *passing through* the very depths of peril, *surviving destruction*. Sulpicius develops this theme through an intricately intertextual (and distinctly *elemental*) reading of scriptural passages that converge in the image of near-death not by fire but by water, locating the saint at the nexus of powers both natural and supernatural—or perhaps, again, rather more *hyper*natural, defying the bifurcation of "nature" and "culture" (or "cult"). He begins with the account of Peter's imperfect imitation of Jesus' feat of walking on water: "I see indeed, Peter strong in faith, walking over the waves of the sea, in opposition to the nature of things, and that he pressed the unstable waters with his footprints." Here the delicate ambiguity of the image of the imprint of Peter's feet breaking the aqueous surface overwrites the heavier scriptural account of Peter's sinking failure and subsequent rescue (cf. Matt. 14.28–33).[30] Quickly, Sulpicius shifts figures while sticking closely to the topic, denying the "lesser" status (or stature) of "the preacher of the Gentiles" (cf. Gal. 1–2; Rom. 11.13), "whom the waves swallowed up; and, after three days and three nights, the water restored him emerging from the deep." The image of sinking and resurfacing, suppressed in relation to Peter, is thus superimposed on the overlarge figure of the apostle Paul—but it is a peculiarly *Jonahlike* Paul (cf. Jon. 1.17, 2.10). Now Sulpicius gives voice to a daring suggestion: "Nay, I am almost inclined to think that it was a greater thing to have lived in the deep, than to have traversed the surface of the sea's depths" (Ep. 1.6).[31] The unnamed figure of Jonah is also attached to Peter, in a passing, humorous reference to "the dangers connected with shipwrecks and serpents." But again, it is the apostle to the Gentiles who bears the burden of interpreting Peter's ambiguous performance. Mining the textual resources of the Pauline vaunting of strength in resistant subjection (cf. 2 Cor. 11.23–33, where the author has also found watery excuse for his initial Jonah interpolation), Sulpicius recalls how the apostle "gloried in his nakedness, and hunger, and perils from robbers."[32] Now he can close in on his punch line, having succeeded in making Martin the successor to Paul (who himself forcefully supersedes Peter). *All* the saints endure—and conquer—such dangers, suffer such trials; the height of their power can be precisely measured by the depth of their suffering (Ep. 1.7). "Hence this event which is ascribed to the infirmity of Martin is, in reality, full of dignity and glory, since indeed, tried by a most dangerous calamity, he came forth a conqueror." Nor will Sulpicius be outflanked by his detractor's criticism that he omitted this "event" in his Life: "in that very work I openly acknowledged that I had not embraced all his acts" (Ep. 1.8).

Only after having taught us how to interpret it correctly is Sulpicius ready to render his own account of Martin's ambiguous trial by fire, thereby prolonging the Life. We continue to be trained in the art of double vision, led to perceive both the illusion of realism and the impossible reality sustained in the "true" witnessing of the event. In one view, a series of natural accidents: a faulty stove lit to warm a visiting monk's cell; a careless toss of a straw mattress to make way for an ascetic night on the bare floor; a rusty bolt hindering the sleepy saint's exit from the fire-filled room; a subsequent break-in by a monastic rescue party, who drag their visitor out of the flames in the nick of time. In another view, a scene of purposeful testing and triumph: a fiery furnace where "the snares and the urgency of the devil" mislead Martin to aim for mere survival by grappling with the bolted door; his subsequent recovery of his senses and resort—in the nick of time—to the power of prayer, which renders the flames incapable of further harm. Like Peter and still more like Paul, Martin is initially swallowed by his own elemental fear. Like Peter and still more like Paul, he emerges from the depths stronger than ever. "Martin was indeed tried by that danger, but passed through it with true acceptance," concludes Sulpicius (Ep. 1.10–15).

The second letter, crossing the abyss of Martin's death, shifts the focus to Sulpicius's own trial by grief. Addressed to a friend, Aurelius, it first relates a striking vision, perceived in the ambiguous borderland between sleep and waking, in which Sulpicius experiences—through the mediating immediacy of dream—the departure of his saint from the world of the living. "I seemed suddenly to see St. Martin appear to me in the character of a bishop, clothed in a white robe, with a countenance as of fire, with eyes like stars, and with purple hair." Sulpicius struggles to describe the quality of the strikingly apocalyptic figure crystallizing at the limits of imagination.[33] Martin both does and does not appear in his familiar aspect—he both is and is not continuous with his known fleshly form. "He could not be steadfastly beheld, though he could be clearly recognized." Smiling gently, he seems to answer the author's deepest desires: "he held out in his right hand the small treatise which I had written concerning his life" (Ep. 2.3). Sulpicius clutches the saint's "sacred knees" and begs for the customary blessing. "Upon this, I felt his hand placed on my head with the sweetest touch." Martin mingles his blessing with countless repetitions of "the name of the cross so familiar to his lips": his pleasurable words are ever traversed by violence. Sulpicius cannot get enough of gazing at him, but even as he becomes aware of the insatiability of his longing Martin is whisked away. Sulpicius's eyes strain to follow his passage "through the vast expanse of air" until the ascending saint finally eludes his gaze (Ep. 2.4). "Impudently desiring to follow," Sulpicius wakes up abruptly instead (Ep. 2.5). Thereupon he learns that two monks have just brought word of Martin's death (Ep. 2.6).

The rest of the letter flows with the copious tears of Sulpicius's lamentation. He begs his friend to make common cause with his mourning, even as he has shared his love of Martin. He acknowledges, shamefacedly, that there is nothing lamentable about Martin's triumphal ascent to heavenly glories. "Nevertheless, I cannot so command myself as to keep from grieving" (Ep. 2.7). Singing the praises of Martin's bloodless martyrdom, he comforts himself with the thought that "he loved me in a special manner, though I was far from meriting such affection" (Ep. 2.14). This memory causes another burst of tears, an issue of groans from the bottom of his heart. "In what man shall I for the future find such repose for my spirit as I did in him? and in whose love shall I enjoy like consolation? Wretched being that I am, sunk in affliction, can I ever, if life be spared me, cease to lament that I have survived Martin? Shall there in future be to me any pleasure in life, or any day or hour free from tears?" (Ep. 2.15) Sulpicius's words recall Jerome's Antony exuberantly lamenting Paul's departure; they also anticipate Jerome's own, rather more ambivalent mourning of Paula as she slips away into the embrace of Christ. The result is a rare intensity in the expression of a desire rendered in the autobiographical voice as the biographer confronts and protests the death of his holy—and wholly masculine—subject.

Sulpicius finds queer satisfaction in the writing of this letter of lamentation, in "conversing" with his dear friend, in whom he imagines he stirs up "tears and lamentation," which Sulpicius desires to comfort in turn. "He will not be absent from us," Sulpicius reassures his addressee. "Believe me, he will never, never forsake us, but will be present with us as we discourse regarding him, and will be near to us as we pray" (Ep. 2.16). Shared grief and love draws these "brothers" close. Confiding his fears, Sulpicius confesses, "I shall never be able to climb that difficult ascent, and penetrate into those blessed regions" (Ep. 2.17). Pressed down with the weight of his own mournfulness, he nevertheless pins his hopes on Martin's prayerful patronage. He closes with a glance at his overfull page. Writing the letter is an attempt to prolong a communion of sorrowful love, he acknowledges; yet paradoxically, it also defers desire's satisfaction: "Why, brother, should I longer occupy your time with a letter which has turned out so garrulous, and thus delay you from coming to me?" (Ep. 2.18). (Is this, after all, the man in whom he shall now find repose for his spirit, as he formerly did in Martin? Only if they share the embrace of the saint.)

Soon, however, Sulpicius is writing again. His last Martinian letter seems to draw the now thrice-supplemented life to a symmetrical close by repeating the ploy of the dedicatory epistle, in an elaborate reperformance of authorial reluctance. This time—for the first time—Sulpicius addresses a woman, however. (Perhaps her alien, and thus alienating, eyes will finally put the seal on his repeated acts of literary self-exposure.) Playing the lawyer, Sulpicius pretends to take his mother-in-law Bassula to court "on a charge of robbery and plunder." He protests that she has "left him no little bit of writing at home, no book, not even a letter." She has stolen his most familiar, private scribblings so as to "publish them to the world" (Ep. 3.1). Devious trickster, planting secretarial spies in his most intimate domain, this woman (who is also, evidently, his patron) has outed his closeted secrets. It becomes clear that it is the lamentable letter "which I recently wrote to Aurelius the Deacon" that he has in mind (Ep. 3.3). He wonders how she can possibly have gotten her hands on it. Despite Sulpicius's sly (and hopeful?) insinuation that the whole world is perusing his private correspondence, Bassula's act of betrayal is betrayed solely by her own familiar letter's charge that the epistle to Aurelius is incomplete, omitting to convey "the manner in which that saintly man [Martin] left the world." (The dream vision is, evidently, not fully satisfying—she wants the real thing.) Sulpicius continues to grumble that he never meant anyone but Aurelius to read it; he protests that he will not write another word about Martin to Bassula, either, "lest you publish me everywhere" (Ep. 3.4). On the other hand, if she promises not to tell, Sulpicius will deign to satisfy the curiosity of a woman.

His subsequent account does indeed provide the kind of closure that the reader of a woman's Life (or a womanly reader of a Life?) might desire. In fact, it has the distinct air of being destined for publication from the start. But, first, en route to demonstrating Martin's foreknowledge of his own death, Sulpicius seizes the opportunity once again to present his hero in the act of bending the vicious course of nature—here, by diverting the flight of birds. Beholding a number of waterfowl feeding on fish in a river, Martin sees an illustration of the insatiability of the demons who devour human souls. Entering into the script of his own metaphorical confabulation, Martin "commands the birds to leave the pool in which they were swimming, and to betake themselves to dry and desert regions." Sulpicius attempts to negotiate the strangeness of this conflation of cosmic and earthly realms (of the realms of the symbolic and the literal), noting that Martin here uses "the very same authority with which he had been accustomed to put demons to flight." What the clearsighted onlookers perceive, however, is one who "could even rule the birds" (Ep. 3.8). This is not, then, exactly a metaphor, and Sulpicius himself is not, seemingly, fully in control of a text in which Martin's weirding ways continue forcefully to reconfigure the real and the natural. Commenting on the biblical density of the parabolic text, Fontaine notes, "The universe contemplated through the eyes of the sacred authors becomes for Martin in turn a 'mirror of asceticism,' where the discerning monk can perceive constantly how better to fight against his Adversary."[34]

Having dismissed the birds, Martin quickly informs the flock of gathered brethren that his body is "on the point of dissolution" (Ep. 3.9). Now Sulpicius's previously closeted lamentation begins to find an appropriate public forum. (Perhaps this was what the wily Bassula intended all along.) "Then indeed, sorrow and grief took possession of them all," the author reports. The monks cry out (much like Macrina's virgins): "Why, dear father, will you leave us? Or to whom can you commit us in our desolation? . . . We know, indeed, that you desire to be with Christ; but thy reward above is safe, and will not be diminished by being delayed; rather have pity upon us" (Ep. 3.10). Martin (unlike the manly Macrina) is deeply moved; he "is said to have burst into tears" (Ep. 3.11). Sulpicius's own competing desires now emerge as he imagines Martin's torn heart—and imagines himself one of the monks who tempt Martin to dally longer with the living. "Thus, hovering as he did between anticipation and grief, he almost doubted which he preferred; for he neither wished to leave us, nor to be longer separated from Christ" (Ep. 3.12). Giving his decision over to God (cf. Matt. 26.39), Martin spends several more nights in fevered prayer; he displays his feeble limbs to his admirers, laid out on a "noble" couch of sackcloth and ashes. Characteristically, he uses his last breaths to repudiate the devil, whom he sees standing nearby: "Why do you stand here, thou bloody beast?" He continues, as his spirit flees: "Abraham's bosom is about to receive me" (Ep. 3.16).

Martin's corpse glows like a bride's, caught up in the embrace of the Bridegroom's bosom. His face seems the face of an angel; "his limbs too appeared white as snow"; in his flesh is manifested "the glory of the future resurrection" (Ep. 3.17). (He is as difficult to gaze upon as a figure in a dream, yet still recognizable.) His funeral (like those of Paula and Macrina) draws a "multitude" from the city of Tours and the surrounding area. Particularly audible, in Sulpicius's empathetic rendition, are the lamentations of the nearly two thousand monks in attendance. "Then, too, there was the choir of virgins, abstaining out of modesty from weeping"—but where tears were suppressed, "affection forced out groans" (Ep. 3.19). Joy battles with grief, manly tears mingle with womanly groans, but finally all join in "singing hymns of heaven" (Ep. 3.20) as Martin is brought to his place of burial in what resembles, more than anything, Sulpicius professes, the triumphal procession of a conquering general. Richly and publicly celebrated, Martin, the author is sure, "looks upon me, as my guardian, while I am writing these things, and upon you while you read them" (Ep. 3.21). Writer and readers are thus drawn together in the intimate gaze of the protector saint. Time condenses, collapses in on itself. Surfacing desire out of the depths of grief—suffering its own desire—the text, already supplemental, is opened in passion in its very moment of closure.

The Hagiographer, the Ethnographer, and the Native

> *Summing up the characteristics of a novelistic hybrid, we can say: as distinct from the opaque mixing of languages in living utterances that are spoken in a historically evolving language . . . , the novelistic hybrid is an artistically organized system for bringing different languages in contact with one another, a system having as its goal the illumination of one language by means of another, the carving-out of a living image of another language.*
>
> —Mikhail Bakhtin, The Dialogic Imagination

Sulpicius cannot seem to get enough of writing Martin: some seven years later, he once again puts pen to page in celebration and defense of the soldier saint. His *Dialogues* carry the charged and contested intimacy of ascetic friendship already performed in his letters into a broader, more flexible, and still more self-consciously theatrical arena. Overt competition and polemic, as well as relations of "love," are dramatically enacted within a polyglossal literary format that allows (and to an extent *requires*) that not only the present witnesses but also their absent interlocutors be identified by name.[35] At the same time, the paradox of an artfully constructed testimony to the stark "facts" of Martin's portentous history is well accommodated by the venerable tradition of the philosophical dialogue—a loosely novelistic and distinctly hybrid genre always (since its Platonic beginnings) hovering in the borderland between history and fiction,[36] where a merely plausible staging of events might claim to convey a more transcendent truth about reality. Finally, the structured temporality of the dialogue, miming the "natural" flow of conversation modestly molded by daily rhythms, allows Sulpicius to resist the temptation of narrative closure—even if he must, eventually, cease to write. That his Martin should ultimately exhaust and exceed every textual frame is Sulpicius's own ambitious authorial desire: "As to Martin, you ought not to expect that there is any limit to one talking about him: he extends too far to be comprised fully in any conversation" (*Dialogues* 3.27).

In the *Dialogues* the "extent" of Martin is registered topographically, though the terrain mapped from the perspective of the Aquitanian author's complex (as we shall see, veritably "postcolonial") positionality is both layered and shifty. The text itself divides rather easily into three parts. Although the first two dialogues were probably written at the same time and claim to encompass the conversations of a single day, they split neatly between the ethnographic report of Sulpicius's friend Postumianus concerning his travels to the monastic communities of the east and the subsequent Martinian discourse of Sulpicius's own, quasi-local native informant—"the Gaul." The third and final dialogue, interrupted by a night's sleep and the arrival of a larger crowd of visitors, continues the Gaul's account. Perhaps published somewhat later, this text is more stridently defensive in tone and more local in its concerns.[37] But first, let us consider the complex dynamics of the competing performances of *Dialogues* 1 and 2—the speeches of the ethnographer and the native.

Sulpicius is closeted with Gallus when the first dialogue opens. The Gaul is "very dear" to Sulpicius, both because of his close link to Martin and "on account of his own merits" (1.1). Much like one of Jesus' disciples, Gallus is compelling as a witness due to his prior historical proximity to the now-departed saint. Having been formed by the master, "his own merits" mirror Martin's; yet the mimesis is necessarily inexact, and Gallus is also compelling in the interval of his distinctness and difference. Martin, hailing from Pannonia, has conquered Gaul. Now Gaul can, in turn, claim him as its own, and the authority of Sulpicius's *Dialogues* is grounded in the stolidly native identity of the one called simply "the Gaul," singularly denied a "proper" name. This "nativity" becomes visible—is made a spectacle—when Gallus is taken out of context and brought into contact with the adaptive and culturally fluent elite of romanized Aquitania, sophisticated men who model sackcloth as the latest Mediterranean fashion.

Indeed, the dyad of Sulpicius and Gallus is *immediately* interrupted: "my friend Postumianus joined us." The Gaul has not yet spoken or moved. Postumianus, in contrast, crashes into the scene at full tilt and with the ease of one at home—as Gallus, by contrast, is not. "Having embraced this most affectionate friend, and kissed both his knees and his feet, we were for a moment or two, as it were, astounded," Sulpicius enthuses. "And, shedding mutual tears of joy we walked about a good deal." Eventually the mobile gentlemen settle: "by and by we sat down on our garments of sackcloth laid upon the ground." It is a prettily pastoral scene. Postumianus speaks first, relating his dream of Sulpicius, which has summoned him back to his friend. "Do thou only, for whose sake I have sailed over so many seas, and have traversed such an extent of land, yield yourself over to me to be embraced and enjoyed apart from all others." Sulpicius takes up his part in this amorous exchange with apparent gusto: "I, truly, . . . while you were still staying in Egypt, was ever holding fellowship with you in my mind and thoughts, and affection for you had full possession of me as I meditated upon you day and night." The armchair traveler continues to urge his love for the footloose Postumianus, following conventions of rhetorical hyperbole: "Surely then, you cannot imagine that I will now fail for a single moment to gaze with delight upon you, as I hang upon your lips." He agrees that no other will be admitted to their place of leisured "retirement" in the country hideaway that Sulpicius refers to, with modest presumption, as his "remote cell." No other will be admitted, that is, but the Gaul who is already there: Sulpicius is sure that Postumianus will not "take amiss the presence of this friend of ours." "That Gaul will certainly be retained in our company," agrees Postumianus magnanimously, meanwhile grasping Sulpicius "with both his hands" (1.1). Later, however, as he launches his narrative,

Postumianus inches the sackcloth robe on which he is sitting "a little nearer" to Sulpicius, as if to signify a prior claim on the author's affections (1.2).

Perhaps the irrepressibly charming Postumianus can see no serious rival in the laconic Gallus. He unwinds his novelistic travel narrative for the connoisseur's appreciation: Sulpicius is the targeted audience for a tale that culminates in an exotic meal served by a ragged hermit on the coast of Cyrene to four marooned travelers—a half of a barley cake and "a bundle of herbs, of which I forget the name, but they were like mint, were rich in leaves, and yielded a taste like honey," recalls Postumianus. "Our hunger was fully satisfied," he marvels (not without a hint of irony). Sulpicius smiles and, for the first time, draws his *other* friend into the conversation: "What, Gaul, do you think of this? Are you pleased with a bundle of herbs and half a barley cake as a breakfast for five men?" Gallus blushes. The humor, he readily recognizes, is at the expense of his own countrymen, notorious for their hearty appetites—a subject on which, he protests gently to his "friend," "you never miss any opportunity which is offered you of joking." The butt of the already overplayed joke, "the Gaul" has no choice but to continue to play along. His sharp wit proves more than adequate to the challenge issued. Under the cover of friendly banter, he names the coercion implied by the smiling question: "It is unkind of you to try to force us Gauls to live after the fashion of angels." He also enacts his resistance, venturing the hypothesis that "even the angels are in the habit of eating"—that angels, in other words, are rather more *Gallic* than well-traveled Aquitanian gentlemen can imagine. Perhaps the men of Cyrene are not naturally endowed with hearty appetites, and the storm-tossed travelers were probably too seasick to desire food, he observes with deceptive lightness. "We, on the other hand, are at a distance from the sea; and, as I have often testified to you, we are, in one word, Gauls." Having made his witness—planted his feet solidly in his own native soil—the implacable Gallus next suggests that they may be wasting their time with these jokes: Postumianus should continue with his tale (1.4). Postumianus cannot resist one more round of repartee: the Gauls seemingly are a bit sensitive when it comes to the subject of abstinence, he remarks, with a rhetorical twinkle; thus, he adds mockingly, he will omit his planned recitation of subsequent Cyrenian "feasts," "lest Gallus should think that he was jeered at" (1.5). Later in the day, the Gaul will find occasion to reassert the argument that Postumianus has refused. He offers the opinion that "the love of eating is gluttony in the case of the Greeks, whereas among the Gauls it is owing to the nature they possess" (1.8). If gluttony is a sin cultivated by the cultured in defiance of natural need, and fasting best suited to weaker natures, where does this leave the peripatetic Postumianus? "Greek" or "Gaul"? More to the point: how large is *Sulpicius*'s natural appetite?

The dramatic tension subtly building between the figures of Gallus and Postumianus, triangulated by the coyly aloof Sulpicius, is complicated by the invocation of Jerome, who proves to be a crucial figure in this first dialogue. Divining the precise significance of the ambivalent figure is, however, not easy. Postumianus mentions him first in the context of describing his own encounter with the Origenist controversy of the east, noting that Jerome, "a man truly Catholic and most skillful in the holy law, was thought at first to have been a follower of Origen, yet now, above most others, went the length of condemning the whole of his writings." Postumianus does not wish to be seen judging rashly. (He is a generous and affectionate man.) He himself is inclined to view Origen's deviations as "error" rather than "heresy." Furthermore, he finds the repression of the Origenist party not merely impractical but, worse, counterproductive: "it never could have spread itself so far and wide, had it not gathered strength from their contentions." Those directly indicted are the persecuting bishops; yet Postumianus has already mentioned Jerome as "above most others" in the strength of his condemnations (1.7). Having insinuated a critical difference, he goes on, nonetheless, to describe the high regard and love in which he holds Jerome, noting that his works must be familiar to Postumianus's own audience (1.8).

This is the context for Gallus's reiteration of the defense of the Gallic appetite. It happens that Jerome's published critique of monastic gluttony had, some five years earlier, stirred up much controversy in the monastic communities of the west. Unlike an unnamed "Belgian friend, who is accustomed to be very angry" (and also unlike Postumianus, who is habitually light-hearted), Gallus interprets Jerome forgivingly by reading him strongly: "I am of the opinion that he had made the remark rather about Eastern than Western monks." Upon Sulpicius's asking whether Jerome's writing targets gluttony alone, the Gaul responds quickly to the contrary: "In particular he inveighed against avarice, and no less against arrogance" (1.8). (One wonders whether either of the other two flinches at that). Gallus now launches into a hearty endorsement of Jerome's denunciation of "familiarities which take place between virgins and monks, or even clerics." At this point, Sulpicius *does* visibly flinch (but how artful is the gesture?), rebuking the Gaul quite sharply and urging Postumianus to resume his tale. "You are going too far, my Gallic friend: take heed lest someone who perhaps owns to these things, hear what you are saying and begin to hold you, along with

Jerome, in no great affection." Postumianus, for his part, continues to sing Jerome's praises, in terms seemingly less controversial (1.9).

Postumianus's initial recounting of monastic life in the Egyptian desert provokes one more interruptive outburst from Gallus, in response to the mention of a monk who was never angry. Bitterly decrying the anger of a man known all too well by both himself and Sulpicius, he also coyly praises the forbearance of another man (also unnamed), who "rather pitied than inveighed against" an "ungrateful freedman" who abandoned him. Sulpicius (for it is evidently he who was abandoned and forbore inveighing) modestly agrees that he would have been angry, had not the law forbidden it. Again, he appears to suppress the Gaul's voice, encouraging Postumianus to continue his narrative (1.12). But by now we may be wondering whether Gallus has not been burdened with the task of conveying Sulpicius's unutterable thoughts.

Postumianus promises "to stint nothing" in satisfying their desires with his subsequent discourse. And, to be sure, his words paint a delightful canvas of text, depicting a desert that might please a man like Jerome—though not, perhaps, a hungry Gaul, ill-positioned to appreciate the merits of sun-boiled vegetables, he cannot resist hinting (1.13). Indeed, it is difficult to imagine the gallicized Martin appearing on the scene of Postumianus's confabulation, if only because his appetite for violence would not have been met. The setting is pastoral, and the exotic beasts are all implausibly *gentle*, even *genteel*: a lion is hand-fed freshly plucked dates by one monk (1.13); a she-wolf accustomed to break bread with another hermit experiences repentance and receives forgiveness when she swipes a loaf (1.14); a lioness seeks and receives a miracle of healing for her blind whelps from yet another holy man, whom she rewards with a gift of her own (1.15); an ibex helps a starving anchorite distinguish between edible and poisonous plants (1.16). The Hieronymian resonances of these wondrously benign bestial figures are confirmed when Postumianus refers to his visits not only to Antony's monasteries but also "to that place in which the most blessed Paul, the first of the eremites, had his abode" (1.17). If the *Life of Martin* hints at a more direct competition with Jerome's miracle-studded *Life of Hilarion*, Postumianus's fabulous desert discourse invokes—and indeed, in its immediate context, seems to pay tribute to—his *Life of Paul*. Although dismayed by the polemicist, Postumianus admires the biblicist and hagiographer in Jerome.

Postumianus himself seems to sense the dangerous drift of his discourse; he begins, perhaps, to discern the gravity of the threat that the savage Gallus represents. He does not lose his humorous and subtly amorous touch altogether. (At one point, reporting on a saint who subsisted "on only six dried figs" daily, he remarks, "I will whisper this, Sulpicius, into your ear lest our friend the Gaul hear it" [1.20].) Yet he now hardens the lines of his monastic portraits, placing greater emphasis on the working of miracles, the battling of demons, and the severity of temptation. Having finally managed to achieve the sharp tone of a Hieronymian polemic against pride, he attempts to conclude: "But let us leave all these things to be described more pungently by that blessed man Jerome" (1.21). Gallus, however, is now bursting with strategic praise: he doubts that Postumianus has left anything for Jerome to say; perhaps western monks "will not require in future to be kept in order by the books of Jerome." Having chosen the right "Jerome" to imitate, Postumianus can displace the (after all, suspiciously orientalizing) ascetic authority of the west. It is, however, not Postumianus but the real (the purely native) Gaul who is now calling the shots. And it is the inscrutable Sulpicius who is writing the script.

The good-natured Postumianus finally gives up the floor and graciously submits to the inevitable, requesting of Sulpicius "the recompense you owe, by letting us hear you, after your usual fashion, discoursing about your friend Martin" (1.22). The author—who is also an actor in his own drama—feigns surprise: "'What,' replied I, 'is there not enough about my friend Martin in that book of mine which you know that I published respecting his life and virtues?'" Postumianus produces a well-traveled copy from the folds of his robe and testifies loyally that the book is known and admired throughout the world. For some of Sulpicius's admirers, however, there is still not enough in the book, he confesses. Indeed, he now reveals, Postumianus has been commissioned to persuade Sulpicius "to supply those particulars which you stated in your book you had passed over concerning the virtues of the saint" (1.24). If the Life is not enough, there will be no end of supplements, as the reader of the letters already knows. Here Sulpicius will let himself be lured into giving his readers still more, after all: he is inspired by the comparisons with the eastern saints, he explains, whose virtues Martin exceeds at every point. (Martin, for example, does not merely tame wild beasts but faces them down in their savage fury [1.25].)[38] This time, however, Sulpicius will write the Life in a different voice—in the voice of the Gaul.

As the second dialogue opens, Gallus has already announced that he will carefully avoid repetition of any incidents already related by Sulpicius, furthermore reporting only what he himself has witnessed. This self-imposed discipline not only underlines the inexhaustible plenitude of the Martinian

Life; it not only emphasizes the distinctness and authority of the "Gallic" testimony ("speak either in Celtic, or in Gaullic, if you prefer it, provided only you speak of Martin," exclaims Postumianus); it also results in the production of anecdotes that subtly mimic and embellish the prior, explicitly suppressed narratives of the Sulpician Life and Letters. (Yet we dare not forget, and indeed are not very much tempted to forget, that the artfully dodgy Sulpicius is still our author [1.27].)

The first mininarrative is a case in point, adding a tricksterish spin to the tale of the sundered cloak that so dramatically unveiled Martin's sanctity in the initial Life. Once again, a poor man begs clothing; Martin, already a bishop, directs his chief deacon to provide for him "without delay"; the bishop himself subsequently retires to his churchside cell to prepare himself for services. (And there the tale might have ended; but if it had, it would not have been worth telling.) Martin is "in his own seclusion," "in his retirement," when the poor man rushes "into this private apartment of the blessed man." The deacon has, after all, delayed, despite his master's command, but Martin does not: "secretly" removing his inner tunic, the "holy man" clothes the beggar and dismisses him. In the meantime, the church has filled with waiting worshipers, and the deacon comes to fetch Martin—who is now naked but for his cloak. Martin, proving his mastery of doubletalk, "said to him in reply that it was necessary that the poor man ... should be clothed, and that he could not possibly proceed to the church, unless the poor man received a garment." Understandably irritated by *this* delay, the deacon hurries out and buys the cheapest possible garment, "short and shaggy"; he lays it, "in wrath, at Martin's feet." In privacy, Martin dons the rude shift, "striving with all his might to keep secret what he had done." The Gaul concludes: "But when do such things remain concealed in the case of the saints desiring that they should be so? Whether they will or not, all are brought to light" (2.1). This forceful recounting not only gives a new twist to the already familiar theme of Martin's threadbare generosity but also nakedly unveils the aggression of the "outing" itself. To write the Life is to uncover what the saint desired to keep secret; Sulpicius, through his Gallic mouthpiece, strips Martin of his cloak to reveal his unclothed body. Yet that revealed body is itself a veil, a "short and shaggy" garment, more seductive than ever.

A subsequent narrative likewise surfaces an ambivalent desire to violate the saint while once again working variations on prior Martinian themes. A procession of soldiers (comporting themselves, as we shall see, like bandits) passes Martin on the road. Their beasts of burden perceptively shy away from the man in the "shaggy garment, with a long black cloak over it." (They see the wildness beneath the dour disguise.) The soldiers, enraged by the disruption, "began to belabor Martin with whips and staves." His "incredible patience" merely incites further violence, and the soldiers do not stop until he falls "almost lifeless to the earth, . . . covered with blood, and wounded in every part of his body." Returning to their conveyance, they discover, however, that the stubborn mules "all remained fixed to the spot, as stiff as if they had been brazen statues." Repeating their violation of Martin, "they waste all the Gallic whips" at their disposal; they strip the neighboring forest of wood with which further to cudgel the beasts cruelly; yet "the animals continued to stand in one and the same place liked fixed effigies." Finally these military men accept defeat, acknowledging both Martin's superior power and their own consequent shame. "He kindly granted them forgiveness; and restoring their animals permitted them to pursue their journey." If this narrative replays the story of the "frozen" funeral procession (its beasts arguably as innocent as the mournful villagers), its vicious edge is more purposefully directed, in a distinctly sadomasochistic enactment in which the hyperbolic violence of the worldly soldiers is finally topped by the all-suffering soldier saint.

A more covertly violent, "antisexual" misogyny loosely links a later series of anecdotes, reviving Gallus's support for Jerome's harsh criticism of the easy social intercourse enjoyed by some ascetic men and women. The first such narrative only seems to disrupt expectations established earlier, thus setting Postumianus up to revoice Gallus's former concerns, in nearly exact counterpoint to Sulpicius's previous cautionary chastisement of the Gaul: "I really fear lest those persons who freely mingle among women should to some extent defend themselves by that example" (2.7; cf. 1.9). The example in question is one set by the usurper Maximus's wife: yet again, Martin reluctantly dines with the emperor. "The queen hung upon the lips of Martin, and not inferior to her mentioned in the Gospel, washed the feet of the holy man with tears and wiped them with the hairs of her head." She begs her imperial husband to dismiss all other servants so that she alone may honor Martin with "her servile attentions." Gallus does not forbear to elaborate in minute detail those meticulous acts of bodily service, charged with the excitement of such an extreme social reversal (2.6). Small wonder, then, that Postumianus takes the bait. The Gaul eagerly reels in his catch, responding with a mimicry of cultured pedantry: "Why do you not notice, as grammarians are wont to teach us, the place, the time, and the person?" Only once, for good political reasons, and as a man of advanced years, did

Martin allow himself to be "served" by a woman. Crucially, she was not an ascetic—"a free sort of widow" or a "wanton virgin"—but a matron, a woman securely under the rule of a man and thus also easily subjected to Martin's dominance. "Let a matron serve and not rule you; and let her serve but not recline along with you," the Gaul pronounces (2.7).

Perhaps the moral of the tale of the servile queen remains a bit too ambiguous—the tale itself, once explicated, more than ever erotically charged, less by its gendered dynamics than by the enactment of extreme and reversible power differentials that those dynamics only partly convey. Postumianus's response is colored by more than a hint of irony. "If we were to follow the ways of Martin, we should never need to defend ourselves in the case of kissing," he protests, admiringly. (Who is kissing whom? we may wonder. "I kissed both his knees and his feet," Sulpicius has already reported of his reunion with Postumianus [1.1].) Postumianus continues: "But as you are wont to say, when you are accused of being too fond of eating, 'We are Gauls,' so we, for our part, who dwell in this district, will never be reformed either by the example of Martin, or by your dissertations." Once again, the Gallic appetite is on the table. Whether that appetite is for food or servility—better yet, table service—it is not the same as the Aquitanian taste, which runs rather toward munching kisses. Turning the tables, Postumianus is ready to admit that his own natural appetites will not be "reformed" and thus may have to be curbed. But where (we wonder again) is Sulpicius located in this colonial topography of desire? Postumianus himself draws attention to his friend's "obstinate silence." Sulpicius the actor (and also the author) dodges again—but his gesture takes a "Gallic" turn, as he explains his silence to be the result of enmity incurred "on the part of all the women and all the monks" when he once attempted to intervene in a case of apparently "indecent" relations between a virgin and "a certain young man who was dear to me." (Ah, those dear young men! "Aquitanian" after all?) Reverting to his usual ploy, Sulpicius begs Gallus to resume his narrative (2.8). Yet, refusing to take Postumianus's point, perhaps he has after all taken a stand—though his two feet may not be on the same side of the shifty border. Slyly sidestepping the question posed by "Aquitanian" desires ("kissing"), he reveals the "secret" of his long-established distaste for heteroerotic minglings. Where desire is implicated in (social) intercourse with a "woman," Sulpicius can denounce it as lustily as a Gaul. And if his appetite thus begins to take on Gallic proportions, it is no surprise that he (unlike Postumianus?) may find satisfaction in the portrait of an utterly submissive empress.

Gallus, for his part, obliges Sulpicius with a few diversionary miracle tales, populated with appropriately vicious (reassuringly non-Hieronymian) beasts—including a demonic *cow*—who freeze satisfyingly in their tracks at Martin's masterful command (2.9). Soon, however, the Gaul has worked his way from the animal kingdom to human marriage—better than fornication, worse than virginity (2.10)—and thus back to the question of proper relations between men and women. He tells the cautionary tale of "a certain soldier" who has left the army to take up the life of a hermit. Although Martin has ordered his wife to a nunnery, the former soldier desires to resume cohabitation with a partner to whom he now feels bound not by marriage but by shared military oath: he protests "that he was a soldier of Christ and that she also had taken the oath of allegiance in the same service; and that the bishop therefore should allow to serve as soldiers together people who were saints, and who, in virtue of their faith, totally ignored the question of sex." Martin recognizes the devil when he hears him. Nor are his own eyes sex-blind. The veteran saint appeals to the soldier's own battle experience. "Did you ever in a line which was prepared with arms for battle, or, having already advanced near, was fighting against a hostile army with drawn sword—did you ever see any woman standing there, or fighting?" The soldier takes the point of the "true and rational analogy." He thereby rejects his own false analogy of ascetic wife to saintly comrade-in-arms. Martin then reiterates the point, for the benefit of the crowd that has gathered: "Let not a woman enter the camp of men, but let the line of soldiers remain separate, and let the females, dwelling in their own tent, be remote from that of men." A "tent" is perhaps not enough to prevent the men being made "ridiculous" by the admixture of a "female crowd": "Let the woman keep herself within the protection of the walls." No camp prostitute, but a wife, her goal is the protection of her chastity, "and the first excellence, as well as completed victory, of that is that she should not be seen" (2.11). The proper role of a woman is, thus, simply to disappear, clearing the field for the purely (queerly?) masculine comradery of saints.

Gallus follows up quickly with the account of a virgin who has perfected the disappearing act. She "had so completely withdrawn herself from the eyes of all men, that she did not admit to her presence Martin himself, when he wished to visit her in the discharge of duty." The interest of the event lies in the awkward positioning of Martin himself: the virgin's wondrous and wholly admirable refusal of her visitor—her refusal to *be seen*—may seem to expose the inappropriateness of the saint's own scopic desire. Indeed, Gallus emphasizes the difficult point: "Let the whole world listen attentively to this: a virgin did not permit herself to be looked upon by Martin." At the same time, the sharply inscribed distinction of sex is also troublingly blurred, for if the virgin may now seem to have outdone Martin in ascetic rigor, Martin may be called upon to match her act. Gallus resists this implication—but surprisingly he does not do so on the basis of sexual difference: "no deduction is to be made from the excellence of those others, who often came from remote regions for the purpose of seeing Martin, since indeed, with the same object in view, even angels ofttimes visited the blessed man" (2.12).[39]

Martin wishes to visit the virgin. Angels visit Martin—and not only angels. Gallus calls Sulpicius himself as fellow-witness to the startling fact that Martin is known to have conversed familiarly in his cell not only with Peter and Paul ("who were pretty frequently seen with him") but also with virgins— "Agnes, Thecla, and Mary." Angels, apostles, and virgins are, then, Martin's tent-companions—"demons" too. ("He found Mercury a cause of special annoyance, while he said that Jupiter was stupid and doltish" [2.13].) These are portentous visitations indeed, passing strange minglings in the soldier's camp, scarcely believable. Perhaps Martin is not quite Gallic after all (if he is also no longer simply Pannonian)—though it may take a Gaul's martial eyes to rend the veil of impending apocalypse, exposing the cosmic battle that is already being prepared when angels and demons converse with saints: "you may conjecture, then, how nearly about to happen are those things which are feared in the future." Gallus, speaking "emphatically," is still building to his climax—he "had not finished what he intended to relate"—when the author strategically interrupts the fiery discourse by introducing a servant who coolly announces the arrival of one Refrigerius. Aquitanian hospitality counters the claims of Gallic emphaticism. "We began to doubt whether it would better to hear the Gaul further, or to go and welcome that man whom we so greatly loved." Undaunted, Gallus again seizes the initiative: the unfinished discourse will be put to bed for the night; "tomorrow we shall proceed to what remains" (2.14). Apocalypse, announced, is deferred; night will give way to dawn; visitors are welcomed; conversation among dear friends will continue.

The third dialogue, however, opens onto a changed scene. Word has spread, and the country retreat is now mobbed by crowds of clerics, ascetics, and laity eager to hear Gallus give witness to Martin's virtues. After a bit of squabbling among Sulpicius's friends about who should be admitted—not, it is decided, the common lot—the Gaul resumes his narrative (3.1). He will not repeat himself, but he does reiterate the competitive framing established on the previous day: "Postumianus expects something new, intending to make known what he hears to the East, that it may not, when Martin is brought into comparison, esteem itself above the West" (3.2). Yet rather more local disputes seem to loom larger in this final, overtly apologetic and frequently agitated discourse. "I am enraged in heart, believe me, and through vexation, I seem to lose my senses," exclaims Gallus. "Do Christian men not believe in the miraculous powers of Martin, which the demons acknowledged?" (3.6). (Here, huddled under the triumphal banner of Martin, Gaul and the asceticized landscape of its ambiguously romanized Aquitanian margin draw close.) Once again Martin the miracle worker is at the center of controversy, and the witnesses—"persons who are still alive and well" (3.5)—are called to take their stand. Gallus piles up his own testimony to Martin's powers and to his triumph over all adversaries, human and demonic. Yet Christ has his Judas, and Martin too suffers a familiar betrayal, he acknowledges (3.15). The Aquitanian ascetics themselves are also hard-pressed nearer to home, Postumianus interjects (3.16). Sulpicius, having released the clamor, brings it to an artificial end by calling attention to nature's compelling rhythms: "The day is gone, Postumianus," he announces abruptly. The animated discussants freeze in their tracks, if only temporarily. Here it is that Sulpicius exposes the artificiality of all limits to talk about Martin: "he extends too far to be comprised fully in any conversation." In the meantime, Postumianus is made heir to the apostolic mission: he will carry the Gaul's witness to Martin's exceeding sanctity to the ends of the earth— or at least of Mediterranean civilization. Sulpicius even supplies him with a verbal map (3.17).

The *Dialogues* end on a queer note of reproachful grief, as Sulpicius imagines Postumianus on far-distant shores, visiting the grave of a beloved— yet betraying—friend. Doomed not to repeat himself, Sulpicius cannot lament *Martin*'s death again. Is the substitution of his oddly self-centered (and nearly vindictive) mourning for a hitherto unmentioned companion merely another performance of the artificiality—and inconclusiveness—of all narrative endings? Or does the displacement betray a still deeper authorial doubt? "We at length departed, certainly with a profound admiration for Martin, but with no less sorrow from our own lamentations" (3.18). An odd balance of admiration and sorrow is thereby struck: perhaps it is the elusive Martin who has abandoned Sulpicius, here at the unsettling end. The provincial hagiographer, for his part, has also seemingly abandoned (effectively superseded?) the "native" claims of the Gaul, even as he has thereby been rendered doubly alien in his own (already long since colonized) land while sending Postumianus forth to foreign places ("Greek," or simply "east"), imbued with the self-proclaimed cultural authority of a romanized west now effectively recolonized by asceticism. When at length we readers must ourselves depart (for the text does eventually come to an end), we leave Sulpicius fractured by the inherent ambivalence of his position, torn between violence and tenderness, split between the locations of writer and written text. He is not, finally, *unmasked*, any more than Martin is, not exposed even in his transgressive identification with Martin (not self-identical with his ever-elusive object of desire). Sulpicius remains suspended in the telling of Martin, the violated and violating writing of Martin—a rent cloak, a torn text, a manhood torturously, felicitously undone by the true love of an impossible saint. That such "love" blazes at the savagely transgressed borders of class, gender, and ethnicity, in texts that register the effects of late Roman imperialism (in texts that are traversed by the complex currents and countercurrents of cultural colonization and resistance), is a matter that calls for further consideration here at the end.

Witnessing Ambivalence

> *Culture, as a colonial space of intervention and agonism, as the trace of the displacement of symbol to sign, can be transformed by the unpredictable and partial desire of hybridity.*
> —Homi Bhabha, The Location of Culture

> *Taking the question of historical agency seriously ("How . . . is authority displaced?") entails interrogating more than the ambivalences of form; it also entails interrogating the messy imprecisions of history, the embattled negotiations and strategies of the disempowered, the militarization of masculinity, the elision of women from political and economic power, the decisive foreclosures of ethnic violence and so on. Ambivalence may well be a critical aspect of subversion, but it is not a sufficient agent of colonial failure.*
> —Anne McClintock, Imperial Leather

Erotically charged stagings of domination and submission, boot cleaning and foot washing, fascination with the unkempt body and its "natural" appetites, the abjection of the female, and the performance of the transgressive reversibility of class and sexually gendered positionalities are the stuff of Sulpicius's Martinian writings, as we have seen. The parallelisms of ancient and modern imperialisms and their symptomatic (or, indeed, constitutive) eroticisms are by no means exact. The multiple resonances are, however, suggestive. Anne McClintock's subtle analysis of the Victorian love affair between the barrister and "man of letters" Arthur Munby and the domestic servant Hannah Cullwick, for example, similarly allows a glimpse of how imperial colonialism and its discourses of race and nativity invade and inflect a transgressively cross-class and queerly gendered erotic relationship characterized by "a variety of fetish rituals: slave/master (S/M), bondage/discipline (B/D), hand, foot and boot fetishisms, washing rituals, infantilism (or babyism), cross-dressing, and a deep and mutual fascination with dirt."[40] The categories of the "fetish" as well as the "sadomasochistic," although distinctly modern, are nonetheless usefully invoked here again for interpreting (by way of analogy, if not also of *genealogy*) a late ancient theater of desire that likewise involves "the displacement of a host of social contradictions onto impassioned objects" while simultaneously revealing "that social order is unnatural, scripted and invented."[41] If such (interpretive) enactments do not themselves bring about "colonial failure" (then or now), they do nonetheless (re)perform "the unpredictable and partial desire of hybridity," which always troubles the totalizing desire of empire and sometimes also effects local transformations.

Rereading Sulpicius as a "*post*colonial" figure, I do not intend to inscribe a neatly linear (and dangerously optimistic) narrative of historical supersession of colonialism—though the term may indeed point toward a "late" and distinctly chaotic moment in the unfolding drama of succeeding ancient Mediterranean empires. The primary usefulness of the label lies in demarcating a complex and ambiguous sociocultural terrain, the structuring of which defies the tidy binary of "colonizer" and "colonized," "Roman authority" and those subjugated by it.[42] In such a context, to mark the "hybridity" of *all* subjects of desire is not to blunt the edge of theoretical precision or political critique but rather to attempt to accommodate the complex and unstable differentiation of positionalities produced and negotiated "in a colonial space of intervention and agonism."

Postcolonial theorist Homi Bhabha marks "three conditions" underlying "the *process of identification* in the analytic of desire." First, colonial desire relates to "the place of the Other": "the phantasmatic space of possession that no one subject can singly or fixedly occupy, and therefore permits the dream of the inversion of roles." Second, that place of identification is a "space of splitting" constituted by "the disturbing distance in-between"—the colonizer's artifice inscribed on the native's body. Third, the subjectivity produced by the demand of identification "entails the representation of the subject in the differentiating order of otherness," returning "an image of identity that bears the mark of splitting in the Other place from which it comes."[43] These abstract formulations take on flesh in Sulpicius's texts. If, for Sulpicius, "the place of the Other" is northern Gaul, it is a place traversed and fractured by the savagely alien figure of the soldier-bandit Martin, spiritual conqueror of a territory already colonized by demonic forces. Martin is a split screen ("a space of splitting"), not only (or indeed primarily) because a gallicized Pannonian, but also (and more importantly) because doubled in and by the unsettling mimicry of the demonic. When, in the *Dialogues*, a figure of repressed "native" identification—"the Gaul"—returns with near-vengeance, he is already haunted (and thus compromised in his "nativity") by his relation not only to Martin but also to Sulpicius—no simple tree-hugger, he. Sulpicius himself, repeatedly self-performed as an Aquitanian, that is, Gallo-Roman, man of letters, likewise emerges to view ambiguously in "the disturbing distance in-between" the coproduced, complexly overlapped "places" of imperial conquest and barbarian subjugation, whence returns "an image of identity that bears the mark of splitting." Doubled in the figure of Postumianus (who is himself doubled and further distanced by the admired and finally disavowed Jerome), Sulpicius mimics the ambitions of empire, aspiring to conquer the world through the ethnographer's "imperial eyes"[44] while at the same time (and under the same Martinian banner) simulating the resistant stance of the lusty "native." What is effected through this iterative hybridization of the subject is both more and less than the commonly perceived rivalry of local claims to a triumphal transcendence. Sulpicius's complex and open-ended literary "process of identification" intensifies the disturbance already mobilized in the ambivalent claims of an overtly fictive, subversively hybridized "Greekness."[45] It thereby issues a further challenge, simultaneously subtle and strident, *both* to the longstanding cultural hegemony of "Greece" (now revived, from Sulpicius's perspective, in ascetic performances staged in the desert theaters of Egypt and Palestine)[46] *and* to the holistic and originary subjectivity insinuated by the pan-Mediterranean dominion of "Rome."[47]

The implicit political challenge is conveyed by the covert eroticism of Sulpicius's texts, as it has seemed to me. At this point, McClintock's attention to "the messy imprecisions of history" and the complicating factoring of class and gender into the ethnicized equation of colonial desire helps to bring "the unpredictable and partial desire of hybridity" of Bhabha's universalizing Lacanian formulation into sharper historical focus. If Sulpicius's "process of identification" is concretely conveyed via the literary enactment of his desire for Martin, that desire is itself ever traversed by the charged and dangerously reversible dynamics of power. The virtually fetishized, unkempt, rudely dressed (repeatedly undressed) body of the soldier saint—a body uncannily transformed, yet still recognizable, in death—continues to fascinate, bringing together "a host of social contradictions" that embrace complex, conflicting impulses both to dominate and to submit, even as the miracle-working Martin himself takes both domination and submission over the edge, to the point that they are no longer clearly distinguishable. In the Life, Sulpicius sets out to subject Martin to his authorial pen; yet when Martin submits extravagantly in a ritual of foot washing, it is Sulpicius who finds himself surrendering to the power of the holy man—"abandonment at the very moment of dependence," as McClintock describes the experience courted in the rituals of sadomasochistic sex.[48] Other scenes staging more straightforward class reversals layer themselves under and over this one—Martin cleaning his servant's boots, the empress washing Martin's feet. The queerness of a reversal that is no reversal in terms of worldly class is thereby intensified: class itself has been queered when the irreducibly savage Martin conquers by serving the aristocratic Sulpicius. But what of gender? The containment of gendered positionalities within the homoerotic play of class reversals is both disrupted and provisionally reconfirmed by the insertion of the "native," who relates the story of the empress and other tales of feminine subjection. The Gaul exposes the violent suppression of women that underlies Sulpicius's sublimely sadomasochistic desire; at the same time, the "native's" savage patriarchalism—simultaneously embraced and disavowed—differentiates itself from the carefully modulated, effete manhood of the Aquitanian ascetics, through a circulation of ambivalent mimicry. The desired native man and the abjected imperial woman remain the least assimilable elements in Sulpicius's topography of desire, yet perhaps they thereby all the more powerfully mark the "splitting" in the hybrid subject of desire—the desire of hybridity—produced in the Martinian writings.

Invoking Bhabha's postcolonial theory (as well as Luce Irigaray's feminist theory), Lynda Hart has argued that contemporary sadomasochism constitutes "not mimesis but mimicry," disturbing the illusory reality of the subject by performing the "impossible real": "sexuality is always, I think, about our desire for the impossible-real, not the real of the illusion that passes for reality, but the Real that eludes symbolization."[49] By replaying frequently oppressive scripts (and thereby recognizing them *as* "scripts"), the ritualized eroticism of s/m acknowledges that "the struggle is not to avoid repetition but to repeat with differences that are transformative."[50] In Sulpicius's Martinian writings, ancient stagings of quasi-ritual scenes of domination and submission condense the subversively transformative aspirations of the impossible reality enacted in Sulpicius's repetitious, even relentless, insistence on Martin's miraculous powers, which both mime and undermine the violent hierarchies of empire and ethnicity, class and gender.

Pointedly rejecting the fantasy literature of Jerome's hagiography (marked implicitly as "Greek"), Sulpicius's ambivalently "Gallic," stridently antipastoral narrative loosely resembles, I have hinted, recent ("postmodern") waves of science fiction that likewise explore the sites of excess and breakdown in the hegemonic exercise of power. Martin's "science" is the hypernatural technology of exorcism and wonder-working; his open-ended narrative thereby brings the once-future apocalypse into the present moment, breaking down the distinction between the real and the imaginary (between worldly and spiritual realities, earthly and extraterrestrial domains). It remains, of course, for the reader to decide whether the textual performance of Martin (like much science fiction) finally merely reinstates the implicitly masculine (phallic, as well as imperial) transcendence of the subject in even more extreme terms;[51] whether, alternatively, it performs (and prefigures) a paradoxical death of transcendence that is also the end of history, the collapse of critical difference, and the annihilation of desire itself;[52] or whether (as I have desired to read it) Sulpicius's oeuvre, "trading in signs and wonders," achieves through its figuration of Martin a version of Donna Haraway's "modest witness" that acknowledges "alliances with a lively array of others, who are alike and unlike, human and not, inside and outside what have been the defended boundaries of hegemonic selves and places of power."[53] Haraway's robustly—indeed, robotically—eclectic (if by no means idealized) "postmodern" science fictional figure of the cyborg[54] is not "the same" as Bhabha's poststructuralist theory of hybridity as the strategic failure of mimesis, yet each may contribute to a rereading of Martin the soldier saint as a sign of (im)possibilities ever rematerializing in a complex and violently agonistic field of culture "transformed by the unpredictable and partial desire of hybridity." If it is arguably the "savage" heterogeneity of my own eclectic, transdisciplinary interpolations (better yet: interpellations) that has hailed such a monstrous figure into new existence, is this witness to Martin not also "true"? "Witnessing is a collective, limited practice that depends on the constructed and never finished credibility of those who do it, all of whom are mortal, fallible, and fraught with the consequences of unconscious and disowned desires and fears," notes Haraway.[55] Some of those desires and fears, traversed by unearthly hope, might even break the surface of "consciousness" for one who begins to own up—and thereby also to surrender—to the fearsome excitement, the fractured and fracturing violence, of Martin's sacred passion.

Chapter 4
Secrets of Seduction:
The Lives of Holy Harlots

The strength of the feminine is that of seduction.
—Jean Baudrillard, Seduction

Women are seduced by more than the promise of sexual pleasure or escape from poverty, or even eternal devotion. They are seduced as well by the stories men have told about those seductions and by the vision of women which may be derived from such stories. . . . Women can no more escape being adulterated than they can escape being adulteresses.
—Jane Miller, Seductions

The peculiarly promiscuous Lives of loose women are not easy to tie down to a particular time, place, or even textual version, in large part because their immense popularity led quickly to multiple translations and uncertain attributions of authorship. Thus, although the Syriac tale of Mary, part of a longer *Life of Abraham* also transmitted in Greek and Latin versions, was traditionally assigned to the fourth-century poet-theologian Ephrem, it is almost certainly a fifth-century text, and its author must remain anonymous.[1] The *Life of Pelagia* claims to be authored by one Jacob, the deacon of the bishop Nonnos, yet neither the place nor the date of Nonnos's episcopacy can be identified with any confidence, and the earliest witness to the (possibly fifth-century?) Greek original, transmitted in several linguistic versions, including Latin, is a Syriac translation.[2] The Greek *Life of Mary of Egypt*, seemingly reflecting fourth- and fifth-century desert traditions and texts, is attributed (somewhat uncertainly) to Sophronius, patriarch of Jerusalem from 634 to 638.[3] Like the other two hagiographies, it was translated into several languages, and a Latin rendition seems to have been available in the west as early as the seventh century.[4] Eluding both authorial and linguistic propriety, these seductive Lives circulated both swiftly and widely.

To the extent that the Lives of Pelagia and the two Marys represent a distinct subgenre of ancient hagiography—namely, the "Lives of Harlots"—this is less the product of their initial composition than of their subsequent reception, for the three texts betray no awareness of each other and indeed, as we shall see, are narratively and stylistically quite distinct. Furthermore, none of them is particularly well described *literally* as the biography of a *harlot*: the Syrian Mary is a seduced nun who takes up prostitution as penance, Pelagia an actress who becomes a monk, and the Egyptian Mary a woman who enjoys sex too much to reduce it to an economic transaction.[5] Nonetheless, their stories have continued to be read collectively, together with other briefer, protohagiographical narratives of desert fathers and repentant prostitutes.[6] As a collectivity, the Lives of sexually transgressive women have colluded to produce the harlot as a paradigmatic *figure of conversion* who offers hope not only for the few but for "Everyman." In two essays introducing her English translations of ancient harlot Lives, Benedicta Ward, for example, locates these texts squarely within the "literature of conversion" most famously represented by Augustine's *Confessions*, on the one hand, and the accruing legends attaching to the figure of Mary Magdalene as a repentant prostitute, on the other.[7] Lynda Coon repeats the emphasis on conversion and repentance: "Only the conversion of sexually depraved women, such as Mary of Egypt and Pelagia of Antioch, could teach Christian audiences that redemption is possible even for the most loathsome sinners."[8]

Coon's particular reading of the Harlot Lives as narratives of conversion and repentance rests its case heavily on the hagiographical penchant for biblical typology, first, by rendering self-evident "the double-edged biblical *topos* of impenitent woman as sinful humanity and repentant woman as harbinger of universal salvation" and, second, by imbuing the topos with extraordinary explanatory power.[9] Yet, how is one to "explain" (if not by a suspiciously circular logic) the fact that the biblical figures are themselves thereby forced to repent of their "depravity," whether through the interpretive efforts of the ancient hagiographers or through more recent readings of the hagiographical texts? The famously seductive Queen of Sheba, who "came to Jerusalem to test [Solomon] with hard questions, having a very great retinue and camels bearing spices and very much gold and precious stones" (2 Chron. 9.1), metamorphoses, in Coon's own text, into a "contrite woman." The Shulamite, whose irrepressible desire for her male lover rings out lustily in the Song of Songs, is made over not only as a "bride" but still further as a sublimely disembodied "soul" reveling in "the intimate experience of divine love" (and also, presumably, repenting of her prior carnality). The sensuously "sinful woman" who anoints Jesus' feet with costly oil and tears is converted into "the biblical harlot who represents human apostasy from God"; moreover, when Jesus affirms her for having "loved much," for which reason "her sins, which are many, are forgiven" (Luke 7.37–50), we are led to see "Christ's conversion of a polluted woman."[10] (Is "sin," in the case of a woman, so easily identified with "harlotry"? And, at the same time, with implicitly Jewish notions of "pollution," a feminized code of carnality itself requiring conversion in Christ?) In each interpretive moment, the drama of salvation history is replayed, as the "Madonna-like chastity" of a repentant whore "reverses Eve's fall from grace."[11] Indeed, on Coon's ambiguously celebratory reading, this soteriology of penitential conversion may almost be seen to supersede the more robust (and implicitly more elitist?) optimism of male Vitae in which "the lives of the lofty God-men approach celestial status on earth" through a progressive restoration of "Adam"'s *pre-lapsarian* grace.[12]

Sebastian Brock and Susan Harvey are more attuned to the historical particularities of "oriental" cultural presuppositions that strongly shape narratives like that of Mary, the niece of Abraham, or Pelagia of Antioch. "Here women are portrayed as weak-natured, wantonly sensual, darkly sexual beings. Saved from the error of their ways by the grace of God (and by men wiser and stronger than themselves), they live out their holy careers with a penance of violent proportions." If biblical traditions play an undeniably strong role in hagiographic compositions, they do not in themselves wholly account for the fact that, as Brock and Harvey put it, "in hagiography women often represent the extremes of sinfulness and sanctity."[13] Such attentiveness to the specificity of the late ancient historical context may lead in turn to more nuanced literary readings of these ancient Lives. Opening our eyes to the exegetical inventiveness of the texts (rather than presuming their biblical determination), we may also begin to see that "conversion" itself is less the answer proffered than the question posed by the hagiographical works.

On almost any reading, the Lives of overtly seductive women defy the temptation to inscribe gender neutrality onto a de-eroticized female hagiographical subject.[14] Their interpreters nonetheless seem to surrender to another temptation, namely, the privileged abjection of the hypereroticized woman, who becomes emblematic of the carnal desire that must be converted to "divine love" in *all* human souls. This temptation too should be resisted, I am suggesting, first, at the point where the interpretation frames "sinfulness and sanctity" as mutually exclusive, oppositional binary terms, one of which ("sanctity") negates and succeeds the other ("sinfulness") and, second, at the point where the sex of the woman is, after all, retroactively neutralized, as the "harlot" is universalized as a symbol of sin and repentance. It is, rather, the *coincidence* of the "extremes of sinfulness and sanctity" in a *seductively feminized* figure that marks the similarities between these texts. Failing to register the profound ambivalence of such a figure, scholars have scarcely begun to plumb the depths of attraction that the Lives of women *in extremis* exert.[15] We have, perhaps, been unwilling to surrender to the power of the unabashed (possibly even unrepentant) pleasure that inheres in the texts. For what is conversion itself, if not a form of seduction—a conquest matched by an acquiescence to conquest, whether by a man or a God? Are the asymmetrical relations of power effected by seduction not, furthermore, peculiarly reversible? (Is the saint not marked equally by her seductiveness and her seducibility?) The zeal to isolate and contain a single, repressive moment of "repentance" marking a decisive rupture with "harlotry" has occluded the distinctive, even constitutive power of the hagiographical figure of the sexually "sinful" woman—namely, the *continuity* of her seductive seducibility, the *enviability* of her convertibility, the *lure* of her capacity to desire. Put simply, my argument is that the "holy harlot" of ancient hagiography is just that: already holy, and still, unrepentantly, a "harlot."

Jane Miller remarks on the similarity between the concept of "seduction" and Gramsci's influential notion of "hegemony," each of which evokes the complex collusion of (vulnerable) force and (resistant) compliance. She also comments on their difference: "Behind seduction lie the private, the hidden and personal, the secret and sensual, the erotic, and pleasure. Gramsci's version of hegemony bestrides a map of metaphor involving force and military conquest, massed and public and—inevitably—male belligerence."[16] If Sulpicius's miracle-working Martin emerges to view on the ambiguous battlefield of "hegemony," as we have seen, the "Lives of Harlots" are enacted on the similarly, and also differently, power-charged field of "seduction," I am suggesting. Whereas the hypermasculine soldier saint finally exceeds the terms of mere masculinity, the hyperfeminine "harlot" will also transgress the bounds of a fixed femininity—not least by parodying prior traditions of women's Lives while at the same time mimicking the queerly romantic Lives of desert *fathers*. Some of the these "harlots" are even transvestites: they masquerades as monks. "Perhaps the transvestite's ability to seduce comes straight from parody—a parody of sex by its oversignification," muses Jean Baudrillard (thinking, however, of a *male* transvestite). "The prostitution of transvestites would then have a different meaning from the more common prostitution of women. It would be closer to the sacred prostitution practiced by the Ancients."[17] Perhaps the prostitution of women—the harlotry of the feminine—is *always* an "uncommon" and potentially "sacred" act, an instance of discursive subjectification that gives rise to a singularly disturbing possibility, namely, the irruption of a *feminine desire* as a surplus of "seduction" that exceeds closed economies of sex and sexuality, whether ancient or modern. This disturbance is registered differently in the elaborated hagiographies of three ancient "sex radicals," each written on the very cusp of an already "late" antiquity and at the explosively multilingual borders of empire—the Lives of Mary, niece of Abraham, Pelagia of Antioch, and Mary of Egypt.

The Lamb, the Wolf, and the Fool: Mary, Niece of Abraham

> *It is neither simply true, nor indeed false, to claim that the little girl fantasizes being seduced by her father, since it is equally valid to assume that the father seduces his daughter but that, because (in most cases, though not in all) he refuses to recognize and live out his desire,* he lays down a law that prohibits him from doing so. . . . Henceforth, how could the daughter recognize herself in her desire, particularly her desire for her father?
>
> —*Luce Irigaray,* "The Father's Seduction: Law But Not Sex"

> *It may be historically necessary to be momentarily blind to father-love; it may be politically effective to defend—tightly, unlucidly—against its inducements, in order for a "relation between the sexes," in order to rediscover some feminine desire, some desire for a masculine body that does not respect that Father's law.*
>
> —*Jane Gallop,* The Daughter's Seduction

The narrative of Mary, intimately enfolded in the embrace of her uncle Abraham's Life, is a stunning literary miniature, at once simple in its style and intricate in its craft. The tale begins with the report that the girl Mary, orphaned at age seven, is sent to live with the ascetic Abraham. The guardian's domestic arrangements are somewhat unusual: "Abraham told her to live in the outer part of his home, while he lived as a recluse in the inner part." Inverting the conventional architectural topography of gender, the uncle claims the woman's place in the interior of the dwelling, while little Mary is housed in the more ambiguous, liminal zone marking the space of interface between private and public domains. Nonetheless, she turns her face resolutely toward the interior, where "a small window" opens a slender band of guarded communication between uncle and niece. The opening allows Mary to care for Abraham and also to be made his disciple in ascetic practice. "Willingly she trained herself in all the excellent ways of her blessed uncle, and he in turn delighted to see her fine intention, her tears and her humility, her quiet and gentle nature, and her love of God." For twenty years they live happily as an ascetic couple, and Mary remains "like a chaste lamb, like a spotless dove" (17).[18]

Unfortunately, there is a snake in this paradise. (But where—and who—is it?) A man who is "nominally a monk" pays regular visits to Abraham. "One day he happened to see the blessed girl through the window." The angle of vision here described is intriguing: the monk, closeted with Abraham, is peeping not *in* but *out*, for Mary, by her uncle's design, is already in the "outer part" of the house. The angle of vision is thus Abraham's, the window of tempting opportunity his own. However, when the monk, who "fell in love with her at the mere sight and wanted to get hold of her and sleep with her," finally gains access to Mary after a year of passionate suffering, it is not through the interior window. "The girl eventually opened the door of the house where she lived as a recluse and came out to see him." Guarding his own desires, Abraham has left Mary exposed to the world. Eventually, she opens. The consequences are immediate and drastic: the false monk "assaulted her with his blandishments, bespattering her with the mud of his lust." Is this a scene of rape or of seduction?

If "seduction is something other than a rape, it may also be thought of as a deflected or renamed rape, a rape annulled by an ambiguous assertion of conquest," notes Jane Miller. "The language of seduction spells out the ambiguities within an apparently shared responsibility. The seducer tempts. The one who is seduced yields to temptation."[19] The sheer outrage of Mary's rape, we realize, is already deflected and annulled by the ambiguities of seduction: she opens; she hears the monk's flattering words; thus the mud of lust with which she is bespattered is at least partly her own. Her response confirms, even as it also interrogates, the insinuation of her complicity. "Alas, how did I fall? How did my mind and senses become so darkened without my realizing it? How my downfall occurred, I was unaware; how I became corrupted, I do not know. A dark cloud overlaid my heart, preventing me from seeing what I was doing." This is no theology of "original sin"; it is rather a poignant expression of the psychic violence of seduction. Mary does not understand how it happened or where it all began, but she knows that she has been made complicit in her seducer's desire and has thereby been "corrupted." As a result, she has "died to God and men." No more the lamb of snow-white innocence, Mary exclaims: "I can no longer go near that window, for how can I, a sinner, full of horrid stains, speak with that saintly man? If I made bold to approach the window between us, then fire will issue forth and consume me" (18). But why should she fear *Abraham*? What is the fire that threatens to consume her through the window, now that she is "full of horrid stains"? Who is the seducer in this tale? Who fears seduction? (Who will pay the price?)

Enacting her own social death and performing her shame for the world to see, Mary quickly leaves town and sets herself up as a prostitute.[20] Her chosen penance is thus also a seduction, and the ambivalence of desire is more than ever her own. The woman's choice to reenact the trauma of the primal scene—to repeat it, with a difference—not only sharply critiques but also subtly transforms her apparent victimization. Meanwhile, Uncle Abraham has "a fearful vivid dream." In the dream, a "disgusting serpent" swallows a dove and returns to his lair. The old man wonders at this apocalyptic vision but cannot fathom its depths. (He remains in his lair, puzzling over the mystery.) Two days later, he receives another vision. This time, the serpent leaves its dream-lair and enters Abraham's own house, placing its head under his feet in a gesture of surrender. The serpent's belly, "ripped open," gives birth to the dove. "The blessed man stretched out his hand and took the dove, which was still alive and unharmed." The serpent who swallows has now been displaced by the man who protects; the dove is still intact. (Perhaps, having "lost" her virginity, she is more intact than ever.) Abraham is not, however, quite ready to take the point. Instead, upon waking, the careless guardian calls out to his charge: "My daughter, why are you so negligent: for two days you have not opened your mouth to praise God." Only when she fails to answer does he begin to register the import of his dreams. "Alas for my lamb, the wolf has snatched her away." Calling upon Christ to "return the lamb Mary to the fold of your flock," Abraham embarks on his own two-year trial of anxious supplication while his niece pursues her destiny "in the world" (19).

The story takes an astonishing turn when Abraham learns where his niece is living and practicing her new profession. Donning military costume, the reclusive ascetic flamboyantly takes on the role not only of a soldier but also of a seducer, as he turns his horse toward the brothel. Here he seems to enter into the script of the virgin martyr of Antioch, who, in Ambrose's recounting, is consigned to a "house of shame," whence she is rescued with virginity intact by a soldier who (proving himself a sheep in wolf's clothing) exchanges clothes with the girl and thus enables her to escape the brothel in order to claim a proper martyr's death (Ambrose, *On Virgins* 2.4).[21] Abraham, however, saucily rewrites the script, taking the trickster's role to daring extremes never imagined by Ambrose. "He spoke to the tavern keeper with a smile on his lips, 'My friend, I've heard you have a pretty lass here; I'd like to see her.'" When the tavern keeper points him to Mary, Abraham's face positively glows, as he commands: "Summon her, so that we can enjoy ourselves together with her today. From what I've heard of her I am much attracted by her." Mary, duly summoned, approaches to take up her part in the play. "When Abraham caught sight of her dolled up and dressed like a prostitute, his whole body nearly began to run with tears." (Or is it with the "mud of his lust"? is a question the reader may find difficult to suppress, under the spell of the virtuoso performance of "this amazing old man.") They drink; they chat; Mary embraces Abraham and kisses his neck. It is Abraham's "ascetic" smell that almost gives him away. Choking, Mary gasps, "Woe is me, me alone!" Still attempting to evade discovery (but to what end?), the old man demands angrily, "Why do you have to recall your sins now that I've come?" His question is as explosive with multiple significations as a figure in a dream (21).

Next the ascetic orders and consumes a hearty meal, at which even "the angel hosts stood in astonishment." Through the narrator's eyes, we are led to see the sublime wisdom in the acts of a holy fool (22). The fool becomes still more foolish after supper, entering Mary's bedroom and not waiting for an invitation to sit down beside her on her large and luxurious bed (23). As she begins to remove his shoes, he directs her to shut the door, and she complies. "My lady Mary, draw close to me," urges Abraham. Then, grasping "her firmly so as to prevent her escaping and, as though he wanted to kiss her," he finally removes his soldier's mask, in a thrilling denouement. "My daughter Mary, don't you recognize me? Am I not your father Abraham? My beloved daughter, child of my dearest relations, don't you know who I am? . . . I brought you up as my daughter: why didn't you tell me when you committed the sin? I would have done penance for you. . . . Who is without sin, apart from God alone?" Mary, not surprisingly, "became like a motionless stone in his hands, petrified with terror and fear." (Abraham may seem finally to have translated his dreams into her worst nightmare.) The old man continues to press his entreaties until midnight, promising that he "will be the one to do penance for this sin." When Mary finally finds the courage to speak, she proclaims her own shame. Abraham, however, assures her of the power of repentance. She weeps until dawn (24).[22]

Brock and Harvey point out two striking aspects of this extraordinary scene: first, "the close links, brought out by Abraham's bizarre action, between sanctity and folly" and, second, the concept of "the saint standing surety for someone else."[23] The themes of holy folly and substitutionary penance may themselves be closely linked—and also more double-edged than they appear at first glance. Surveying the ancient "fool's" tradition, Derek Krueger argues that early Christian representations of holy folly center on the concept of concealed sanctity; with Leontius's seventh-century *Life of Symeon*, the figure of the foolish saint for the first time also lays explicit claim to the more subtle subversiveness of the Cynic's performance of shamelessness.[24] The *Life of Abraham* conforms to the notion of folly as hidden holiness, in its insistence that the saint's foolishness is always strategic and thus, implicitly, a mere cover for wisdom. Yet the text also anticipates Leontius's cynicizing representation of the saint, insofar as it exults in the genuine ambivalence of Abraham's trickster role (or rather, his role as a "trick"): "Full of wisdom, or of folly? A man of discernment or someone who has lost all sense of proportion? ... We hesitate to utter a single uplifting word to those present" (23).[25] This rhetoric of ambivalence is matched by a narrative logic that suggests that Abraham has truly played the fool in relation to Mary: is it, then, only by entering into his own folly *parodically* that he may finally *become* wise? If so, the penance that he takes on is as much his own as it is Mary's. Moreover, his penance *begins* with his performative shamelessness (his virtuoso Cynicism), and the brothel is configured as the womb of his own salvation, as well as of the salvation that he brings.

Indeed, the narrative of repentance is cleverly doubled and intricately interwoven in the enfolded Lives of Mary and Abraham. Whereas Mary's decision to play the prostitute both reenacts and transforms her seduction, Abraham's decision to play the lover both reenacts and transforms his ambiguous complicity in that seduction. (Thus it is that he has to take it *almost* "all the way.") Both Mary and Abraham are "holy fools," and for both penance proves continuous with seduction, while the only "conversions" that take place remain *within* the field seduction. Abraham's action when he arrives back home with his niece is telling: "he enclosed her in the inner part of the house where he had previously lived, while he took up residence in the outer part, which had formerly been her place." Reversing the folly of his initial domestic arrangements, Abraham now holds the dove gently in his hand, taking up the fool's place in the outer part of the house, where *he* may now face the serpent's temptation (which was, perhaps, always also his own). In the inner part, Mary perfects the act of repentance: "compared with hers, our repentance is a mere shadow; compared with hers, our supplications are just dreamlike." Might it be that her penance is as much Abraham's as her own? (Compared to hers, his repentance remains confined to dream and the shadowy realm of theater.) Perhaps the woman seems imprisoned more securely than ever—chaste, chastened, subjugated to a (foster-)father's "law." Yet has this distinctly unvirginal Mary not also wedged open a space for a feminine subjectivity in the very heart of her "father's" house? Enclosed within the "inner part"—occupying the place of the hysteric's trembling womb—perhaps the "daughter" does more than expose the ambiguous truth of the father's seduction.[26] Perhaps, by making herself "momentarily blind to [a] father-love" that demands her complicity in the repression of desire, she also gives birth to an other "love," to a seduction outside the law, to a pleasure that is peculiarly her own.[27] Seducer and seduced, seduced and seducer, neither Mary nor Abraham can boast an unadulterated purity: they are not gods but fools. Abraham has effectively performed his penance for the blindness of his own love. It is, however, the lamb Mary, converted in seduction, who possesses the full power of repentance, whose prayers of supplication can persuade the divinity itself. "God, the compassionate and the lover of mankind who receives the prayers of the penitent, accepted her back" (25). Even God cannot resist the alluring saint. In—not despite—her "sin," she is perfected.

Seduction of the Eye: Pelagia of Antioch

> *The transvestite . . . is both terrifying and seductive precisely because s/he incarnates and emblematizes the disruptive element that intervenes, signaling not just another category crisis, but—much more disquietingly—a crisis of "category" itself.*
> —Marjorie Garber, Vested Interests: Cross-Dressing and Cultural Anxiety

The *Life of Pelagia*, a drama unfolding in three acts, raises the curtain on a dazzling theater of scopic desire, in which the action turns on scenes of charged (mis)recognition. The leading lady performs the roles of Marganito, Pelagia, and Pelagios—jewel-bedecked starlet, white-robed bride of Christ, and cross-dressed eunuch-monk. Nonnos is the bishop with the keen eyes to perceive the depths that dance on the shifting surface of a woman's seductive performance. Jacob the deacon is the seemingly hapless narrator, emplotting a tidy narrative of "the conversion of the prostitute" that almost (but only almost) overlooks, and thus partly (but only partly) suppresses, the profound ambiguity of saintly identity and the disquieting crisis of categorization enacted within his own text.

The first act opens onto a gathering of bishops in Antioch, among whom the ascetic Nonnos, Jacob's own bishop, is acknowledged for his outstanding spiritual gifts. Sitting outside a shrine on the edge of town, the bishops are reveling in Nonnos's wise discourse, when "all of the sudden, a rich prostitute, the leader of a troupe of actors, happened to pass by us," reports Jacob. Exhibiting a professional's expertise in enticing self-display, the actress is inevitably deemed guilty of prostitution, if only by association. "This prostitute then appeared before our eyes," repeats Jacob, "sitting prominently on a riding donkey adorned with little bells and caparisoned." The woman's dramatic appearance, borrowing heavily from novelistic traditions,[28] also, as Patricia Cox Miller points out, evokes two wildly incompatible and differently gendered biblical figures, simultaneously recalling the bejeweled "whore of Babylon" on view in Revelation 17.4 and the entry of Jesus into Jerusalem as depicted in Matthew 21.1–9.[29] (The public procession of the actress is furthermore, as we shall see, a parodic anticipation of the woman's subsequent secretive approach to that same holy city, dressed in an ascetic garment borrowed from a bishop.) Jacob continues: "In front of her was a great throng of her servants and she herself was decked out with gold ornaments, pearls, and all sorts of precious stones, resplendent in luxurious and expensive clothes." He misses no sartorial detail in his minute description of the well-accessorized woman's costume (a costume indeed seeming to consist solely of "accessories"):[30] "On her hands and feet she wore armbands, silks, and anklets decorated with all sorts of pearls, while around her neck were necklaces and strings of pendants and pearls" (*Life of Pelagia* 4).[31] He concludes: "Thus it was that her beauty and finery lured everyone who saw her to stare at her and at her appearance" (5).

Dizzy with the scent of the woman's perfume and cosmetics, "the bishops as they sat there were amazed at her and her clothes." Oddly enough, what amazes them most is the virility protruding nakedly from this spectacle of feminine adornment: "she went by with her head uncovered, with a scarf thrown round her shoulders in a shameless fashion, as though she were a man; indeed in her haughty impudence her garb was not very different from a man's." Thus, the prostitute already masquerades as a man, by virtue of her public exposure. Elaborately dressed for success, she also exposes femininity itself as an artifact of culture, an effect of the theater.

We are now told that the bishops, embarrassingly caught in an act of extended gazing, "averted their eyes from her, as though she was some sinful object" (6). The ambiguous qualification—"*as though* she was some sinful object"—gently prepares the way for the more violent shock of the holy Nonnos's rather different response to the woman—*as though* she was an appropriate object of desire. Only when the actress has passed beyond view does Nonnos, having gazed in open wonder, turn *his* face away. Filling his lap with tears of grief, the bishop, Jacob concludes, is "lamenting greatly for her." Yet Nonnos's own words hint otherwise: "To be honest, fathers, did not the beauty of this prostitute who passed in front of us astonish you?" (Ward plays up the romanticism of the text: it is "a matter of 'love at first sight.'")[32] The bishops, perhaps wisely, "kept silent and did not answer a word" (7). Nonnos continues to weep copiously, until even his hair shirt is soaked through. (Our fashion-conscious narrator notes: "He always wore a hair shirt next to his skin, hiding it with a soft woolen garment on top.") Again (and almost comically) Nonnos questions his fellow bishops: "I beg you, my brothers, tell me, did you lust in your minds after the beauty of that prostitute who passed in front of us?" Admitting that her ornaments are "a stumbling block leading to perdition," Nonnos expresses his hope that God will turn her toward chastity (8). This hope, it appears, is inspired less by her deep depravity than by her sublime seductiveness. "I imagine she must have spent many hours in her boudoir putting on her eye-black, making herself up and dressing in her finery; she will have looked at her face in the mirror with the greatest attention, making sure there is not the slightest speck of dirt on it, or anything that might not please those who behold her," muses Nonnos (9). "In this prostitute we should reprove ourselves," he exclaims. His meaning gradually becomes clear: the prostitute is a reproving exemplum because she knows how to please a lover, whereas the ascetic bishops, affianced to a Bridegroom who is no less than divine, have sorely neglected the arts of seduction. "It is he we should please, but we fail to do so; it is for him that we should adorn our bodies and souls but we totally fail to do so. . . . We have paid no attention to our souls in the attempt to adorn them with good habits so that Christ may desire to dwell in us." The prostitute has seen what the holy men have overlooked: "We should have been trying to please our Lord in all things with even greater effort than she has expended on her embellishment and adornment." Nonnos concludes with an audacious suggestion: "Maybe we should even go and become the pupils of this lascivious woman" (10).

Back in the lodging that he shares with Jacob, Nonnos begins to lament in earnest.[33] His lamentation is first and foremost for himself. "What the prostitute has accomplished in a single day in beautifying herself surpasses everything I have ever achieved during all the years of my life." Yet the prostitute's zeal is "in trying to please Satan" (12). If Nonnos prays that he may yet please his divine lover, he prays also that the woman may be changed (13). Converted, then? Yes, but from what, and to what? Nonnos prays not for the woman's conversion from seduction but rather for her conversion as a seductress. If Nonnos has willingly made himself the prostitute's disciple in the arts of love, Nonnos hopes that she will in turn be guided to a Lord whose absolute worthiness matches her infinite capacity to please. He begs God to seduce, and thus save, them both.

Like Mary's uncle Abraham, Nonnos, disturbed by a woman, dreams of a dove. His dove, however, is already bespattered with mud. "It was as though I was standing beside the horns of the altar, and all of a sudden a black dove, befouled with mud, flew above me. I was unable to endure the disgusting stench of the mud on this dove." Flying away when the deacon commands the catechumens to depart before the eucharist, the dove returns after the service is concluded, whereupon Nonnos grasps it and hurls it into a basin of water. "Once I had thrown the bird in, I saw in my dream that it left behind all the mud, washed off in the water, and the foul stench disappeared." Thereupon the bird ascends to invisible heights (14–15). The dream, as related by Nonnos to Jacob, fairly obviously foretells the prostitute's conversion from abject carnality to the spiritual purity effected by the grace of baptism. It thus seems forcefully to rewrite Nonnos's own prior assessment of the woman's exemplary virtue, as his disquieting admiration for the prostitute is now translated into a more seemly disgust. Yet if the dream represents a disgust absent earlier in the text, that disgust is invoked so as to be semiotically revised. Nonnos has, in essence, already "baptized" the woman with his eyes, recognizing the sanctity inhering in her powers of seduction. The dream thus does not merely foretell but also recapitulates. At the same time, it refamiliarizes the shock of Nonnos's eager response to the prostitute, redressing it in the conventional garb of ecclesiastical ritual and inscribing it in a triumphalist narrative of conversion.

As an interpretive text of foretelling, as well as revisionary recapitulation, the dream sets the script for the second act. Self-disgust, once provoked in "the city's famous playgirl" (18), will inspire a change in costume and lead to a new walk of life. Only God's providential care can account for the fact that the woman, unprecedentedly, shows up in church when Nonnos (whom she does not yet know) happens to be preaching. His inspired words strike her heart. "Their immediate appreciation of one another is shown in these two moments of encounter—Nonnos sees her riding by; Pelagia hears his words in church," notes Ward. "The delicate theme of the love between them pervades the account as seen through the amazed eyes of [Jacob] the

Deacon."[34] Groaning with contrition for her "sins" (as she now perceives them), the woman leaves with the catechumens before the eucharist, as foretold by the dream. Subsequently, having sent her servants to spy out the location of the bishop's lodgings, she inscribes on a wax tablet "a passionate and moving message with a plea concerning her salvation." For the first time we learn her name: "To the holy bishop Nonnos, from the sinful woman Pelagia who is a disciple of Satan, many greetings." Pelagia's flattery and self-abjection match (indeed, outdo) the bishop's: in Nonnos she perceives a man who loves God with all his heart, even as Nonnos has seen in her a wholehearted love that he, lamentably, lacks (20). Nonnos has never seen his God "with the physical eye"; yet that same God, Pelagia has heard, "spoke with the Samaritan woman at the water well, with the Canaanite woman who cried out after him, with the woman who was smitten with illness, whom he healed, with Mary and Martha whose brother he raised." (Presumably, he looked at these women, and they saw him too, even if Nonnos has not.) Pelagia now entreats the bishop: "I ask to appear before you and to see you in person, in case there is a possibility that I might be saved at your hands" (21). (She wants to see, and be seen by, Nonnos). Nonnos, before whom she has already appeared, with momentous effect, does not disown his own seducibility but does mark its dangers. He writes back: "Do not try to tempt me who am both insignificant and weak; for I am a sinful person and one who has never been righteous." He proposes that they meet under the chastening eyes of "the seven holy bishops." At this point (if not before), commentators have been tempted to speculate knowingly about Nonnos's vulnerability: "Much of his prayer and lamentation and feelings of inadequacy probably arose because in reality he was drawn to her carnal beauty as much to her spiritual potential."[35] Indeed, Pelagia's boldness in pursuing Nonnos does seem to assimilate her to the role of the "temptress" also familiar from pagan romance.[36] Yet Nonnos's conscience appears rather more robust than such a reading allows: in his eyes, the woman's "carnal beauty" the admirable effect of her careful self-adornment—is the manifestation of her actual spiritual power. In the end, his concern is less for his own virtue than for his public: he cannot see Pelagia alone, "lest the simple, who lack understanding, stumble and be offended" (22).

Now the initial scene is repeated: again, the bishops gather at the shrine. This time, however, Nonnos is directing the action, as he gives Pelagia her cue to approach (23). The pleasurable shock of Pelagia's first proud epiphany is overwritten by the painful predictability of a prescribed performance of self-abjection. Whereas Nonnos previously drenched his clothes with his tears of repentance, now Pelagia soaks his feet with her own tears of grief, inadvertently wiping "onto herself the dirt from his feet." The formerly gleaming dove is thus muddied, as dictated by the dream, but the mud is from the bishop's feet. "I am a prostitute," she confesses, "a disgusting stone upon which many people have tripped up." She continues, building rhetorical momentum: "I am a ravenous vulture. . . . I am a sly she-wolf. . . . I am a deep ditch of mire. . . . I am a destructive moth, and I have gnawed into many bodies. . . . I am an abyss of evils." The overplayed scene hovers at the edge of parody; it exceeds even the stern requirements of the dream. Perhaps the actress is still after all calling some of the shots, even if she has been handed a lousy script. Demanding baptism, Pelagia commands Nonnos: "Stand up, my lord, and strip off from me the dirty clothing of prostitution; clothe me with pure garments, the beautiful dress for the novel banquet to which I have come" (23). Pelagia has set her sights high indeed, if she intends to make improvements on the lavish wardrobe already so admiringly catalogued by Jacob—if, moreover, she intends Nonnos himself to undress and dress her. Small wonder that the bishops hesitate, questioning whether the baptismal gown will possibly satisfy this woman. But she will not be denied. "No, you must baptize me at once, and so make me a stranger to my evil deeds." She resorts to threats: "You will become a stranger to your holy altar and deny your God if you don't make me a bride of Christ this very day." The bishops are muttering about sponsors. God himself will be not only her Bridegroom but also her sponsor, declares a woman confident of her power to please any lover (26). The bishops and all the other onlookers are by now persuaded—indeed, they are seduced. They "gave praise to God when they saw how the mind of this sinful prostitute was set on fire and was burning with the love of God." (She is still "sinful"; she is still "burning"; they give praise!) Nonnos orders Jacob to make arrangements for an immediate baptism (27).[37]

Pelagia's tearful prebaptismal confession reiterates the hyperbolic declaration of her sinfulness while also reemphasizing her solidarity with the marginalized women of the Gospels, whom God received gladly (29). At this point, Nonnos asks for her name, "so that I can offer it up to God." Repeating the self-designation already inscribed on the wax tablet addressed to Nonnos, she asserts, "My actual parents called me Pelagia." She also, however, reveals her stage name: "the entire city of Antioch, where I was born, called me Marganito [Syriac for pearl], because of the quantities of jewelry I wore and prided myself on." If Nonnos seems to be having trouble learning her name, perhaps it is because he has to make a choice. "From birth your name was Pelagia?" he asks. "Yes, my lord," she replies. Pelagia it will be, then, who marries the Lord, and Marganito is renounced with Satan (30). Satan, however, is not happy to be abandoned by so desirable a woman, and he makes a dramatic cameo appearance, "furious, in the form of a scowling man with tangled long sleeves and his hands on his head" (32). After reviling Nonnos, he addresses Pelagia/Marganito directly: "How can you do this to me: you've made me a laughingstock to this old white-head and to everyone who hears that you have jilted me. . . . Why have you turned against me and tricked me like this? Why have you done this to me and jilted me, just because of a few misleading words from this ill-starred old man?" Nonnos has seduced Satan's woman (34). She, in turn, steadfastly repudiates Satan, sticking by her decision to play the role of Pelagia, bride of Christ (35).

The role, as it happens, lasts only as long as the honeymoon, a week of "bridal days" that follow her baptism (41), during which time she dismantles her household and gives her riches to support the widows and orphans of Antioch (36–40). On the Monday afterward, Pelagia visits Nonnos under the cover of predawn darkness. Blessing her, he gives her permission "to take off her holy baptismal garments." Seemingly still unconcerned about her modesty, the actress is nonetheless worried about her wardrobe. "The holy Pelagia earnestly besought the priest of Christ that she might receive her clothing from some of his, rather than put on something else." Nonnos agrees, giving her "a hair shirt and a woolen mantle," Jacob notes carefully (although he was not, by his own admission, present at this intimate encounter). Pelagia, shameless as ever, fears neither the exposure of her femininity nor the presumption of her virility: "Straightaway she took off her baptismal robes and put on his clothes." Pelagia has now become Pelagios. "That night she left dressed as a man and secretly went off without our being aware of it." Only Nonnos knows her secret. He does not even tell Jacob (41).

The third act in the drama of Pelagia takes place three years later. For the first time, Jacob himself plays a leading role. He feels an urge to make a pilgrimage to Jerusalem. Nonnos grants permission, adding casually: "Be sure to make inquiries there about a certain monk Pelagios, a eunuch; when you have ascertained he is there, go and see him, for there is much that you can benefit from him. For he is a true and faithful servant of God, a monk who is perfect in his service" (43). Once in Jerusalem, Jacob dutifully tracks down the monk, who is residing in a cell on the Mount of Olives. There is no door on the cell, but only a small window. Jacob knocks. Pelagia, who appears through the window "dressed in the habit of a venerable man" (44), recognizes Jacob and greets him joyfully; he, however, does not recognize her, "because she had lost those good looks I used to know." He elaborates: "Her astounding beauty had all faded away, her laughing and bright face that I had known had become ugly, her pretty eyes had become hollow and cavernous as the result of much fasting and the keeping of vigils. The joints of her holy bones, all fleshless, were visible beneath her skin through emaciation brought on by ascetic practices. Indeed, the whole complexion of her body was coarse and dark like sack cloth, as the result of her strenuous practice." Jacob's ever-sharp eyes see much through the small window; yet still he does not "notice anything about her that resembled the manner of a woman," and when he receives his blessing, cued by Nonnos, it is "as if from a male eunuch" (45). As Patricia Miller notes, Pelagia's femaleness is "castrated" in her depiction as a eunuch, even as her virility is perversely enhanced;[38] the layered depiction of Pelagia as both female transvestite and eunuch doubles the ambiguity of her gender.[39] Pelagia asks her visitor if he is not Jacob, deacon of Nonnos, and when he responds in the affirmative, she requests that he send her greetings to Nonnos "and all his companions." Still, Jacob does not guess the truth. "Since she was dressed as a man, I did not recognize her" (46).

In this scene, the initial, dazzling appearance of Pelagia is again replayed and revised. (For a third time, Jacob observes her closely and yet fails to recognize her; where formerly he has seen only a "prostitute," then a "convert," now he perceives merely a "man of God.") Here her abjection materializes before our eyes. Her voluptuous flesh melts away to nothing, her brightness is extinguished, and all that remains is the image of a skeleton loosely covered in skin as coarse as sackcloth. Corruption, running its inevitable course, gives way to the purity of clean-picked bones. But Pelagia has accomplished this natural metamorphosis through a most unnatural effort: she has made herself over as a living corpse (outdoing even Jerome's Paula). Jacob's horror at the spectral image is retrospective, even improbably nostalgic, layered atop vivid memories of the Antiochene beauty. Meanwhile, he has let us in on Nonnos's secret, and we already see with the double vision he later acquires, beholding a grotesque body that seems to transgress all boundaries and confuse all efforts of categorization. If it is only when recognized as female that it is perceived as grotesque, it is also only by being simultaneously misrecognized as male that it provokes such nauseating unclarity.[40]

The public exposure of Pelagios's true sex occurs at "his" death—as is not infrequently the case in the lives of transvestites who "pass." That death conveniently takes place while our reporter, Jacob, is still on the scene in Jerusalem. "The bishop and entire clergy of Jerusalem, together with the honorable abbots, approached and opened up the holy Pelagia's cell; they took out her body, laid it on a bier, whereupon the bishop and all the local holy men came close to anoint it decently with fragrant unguent." The moment is as erotically charged as that of Abraham's unmasking in the brothel. What do they see? Enough to tell that she is a woman, evidently. Their surprised response seems somewhat incoherent: "Praise to you, Lord; how many hidden saints you have on earth—and not just men but women as well!" The sanctity of Pelagios/Pelagia has not been hidden, however: "he" is widely acclaimed "as a righteous man" (49). What has been concealed is solely "his" sex. Perhaps this leaves the clerics and other local holy men feeling a bit foolish; indeed, they desire to continue to "hide this astonishing fact from the people." But the truth will out: "this wonder immediately became known to the entire people" (50). "Why this attempted cover-up?" queries Miller. What kind of "wonder" is contained in this unsuccessfully suppressed exposure of Pelagia's carefully guarded secret? we might further ask. Is it simply the (not inconsiderable) miracle of the masquerade itself— the very fact that a *sinful woman* could pass as a *holy man*?[41] If so, what are the implications of this "fact"? Is gender finally transcended, in the Life of a "harlot" saint? Perhaps not.

Many contemporary scholars prefer to locate the miraculous in the relatively mundane, noting (with varying nuance of emphasis) the practical benefits of Pelagia's transvestitism, which frees her from the social constraints historically imposed on women and allows her to pursue a life as a solitary without threat of violence.[42] Without denying either the validity of such an interpretation or the significance of the historical phenomenon thereby described, we might still resist its tendency toward what cultural critic Marjorie Garber describes as a "normalization of the story of the transvestite" in which cross-dressing is effectively "explained away." Garber herself finds the normalizing reading "both unconvincing and highly problematic." Her reasons are specified: "Unconvincing, because they ignore the complex and often unconscious eroticism of such self-transformations and masquerades (whether or not they are to be called versions of 'fetishism') and because in doing so they rewrite the story of the transvestic subject as a cultural symptom. Problematic, because the consequent reinscription of 'male' and 'female,' even if tempered (or impelled) by feminist consciousness, reaffirms the patriarchal binary and ignores what is staring us in the face: the existence of the transvestite, the figure that disrupts."[43] Indeed, in the case of the *Life of Pelagia* we would do well to let ourselves be challenged by Garber's critique. As Miller remarks (in answer to her own question about the attempted cover-up), the Life is not successful in suppressing the femaleness of its subject, but it is also not entirely successful in promoting a sheerly female model of holiness: the figure of Pelagia, perched "at the limits of intelligibility," draws "the representational function of hagiography" into crisis.[44] Indeed, the transgression of desire and the troubling of gender that bring about such a "crisis" are crucial to the power of a tale of a disturbingly "abnormal," nearly unrepresentable, saint who is manifested (sequentially, but also simultaneously) in the bejeweled finery of an actress-courtesan already strangely virilized, the white gown of a baptismal bride, and the borrowed threads of a eunuch-monk.

The Latin version of the Life gives a hint as to what the holy men see when they break down the door of the cell and remove the saint's corpse, in the potent instant before they know that "he" is really a "she": "They carried out his sacred little body as if it had been gold and silver that they were carrying." Here (viewed through "Jacob's" perhaps after all knowing eyes) Pelagia appears as *both* the virtually virile, voluptuously adorned Marganito—her very flesh alchemically converted to the sheer adornment of "gold and silver"—*and* the delicately effeminate, excruciatingly emaciated eunuch Pelagios—a "sacred little body." The wonder is not so much that "he" is really a "she" but rather that the oversexed figure remains irreducibly unstable and indeterminate—and thus disturbingly seductive—to the very end.[45] Even when condensed through ascetic discipline into little more than precious (fetishized?) relics of gleaming bone, the saint refuses reduction to a single essence. Disrobed, nearly fleshless, cut back to her corporeal core, does she not still dazzle us with a surface of ornamentation—her wasted body itself more than ever like gold and silver, armbands and anklets rich enough to catch the eye of the very God? We look, we cannot stop looking: Pelagia/Marganito/Pelagios continues to entice the gaze. We drop our eyes in confusion, overwhelmed by a monstrous spectacle of conflicting images that refuse to resolve into a visual "whole": Pelagia/Marganito/Pelagios is hard to look at. She does not transcend gender; she flamboyantly transgresses it—a woman, and then some. She does not renounce the "sin" of feminine seduction; she takes it to extremes—a "harlot," and more. What we behold when we view this disquieting figure ("this perch at the limits" of visibility) is, as Miller suggests, a grotesquerie: a *holy woman*.[46] If we are to see her at all, we must, like Jacob, borrow Nonnos's fearless gaze.[47] We must abandon ourselves to the seduction of the eye.

Sacrifice in the Desert: Mary of Egypt

> *There is a certain amount of ritual sacrifice in seduction. . . . Something has to die but I don't see it as having to remove someone—perhaps desire or love must die. Sacrificing a woman in the desert is a logical operation because in the desert one loses one's identity. It's a sublime act and part of the drama of the desert. Making a woman the object of the sacrifice is perhaps the greatest compliment I could pay her.*
> —Jean Baudrillard

> *What is the point of such a gratuitously provocative statement?*
> —Suzanne Moore and Stephen Johnstone, in Baudrillard Live: Selected Interviews

At the center of the *Life of Mary of Egypt* is an astonishing autobiographical narrative, a parodic tale of a lusty pilgrim's progress. In the depths of the Transjordanian desert, where her journey both ends and begins again, the woman's path is intercepted by that of a monk named Zosimas, who has been mysteriously impelled to undertake a pilgrimage of his own. The account of Zosimas's journey frames Mary's reported speech; it does not—cannot possibly—contain it, however. The Egyptian Mary, unlike Abraham's niece or Nonnos's actress (unlike even Antony's Paul), will not suffer enclosure. She is as vast—and as uncompromisingly elemental in her passions—as the desert itself.

The author appends to the Life a matter-of-fact explanation of his scribal role: "The monks continued to pass on these events by word of mouth from one generation to the other. . . . I have put down in this written narrative what I had heard by word of mouth" (*Life of Mary of Egypt* 41).[48] His preface, however, is both less modest and more overtly defensive: "No one should disbelieve me when I write about what I have heard, either thinking that I am talking altogether about marvels, or being amazed by the extraordinary occurrence. For God forbid that I should give false account of or tamper with a story that mentions God" (1). Anticipating disbelief, the writer nonetheless fearlessly follows the divine imperative to expose all holy works. Indeed, no secret will remain hidden, as we shall see.

As the tale opens, the fifty-three-year-old Zosimas, having lived in a Palestinian monastery since his earliest childhood, finds himself facing the terrible possibility that he has achieved a perfection so complete that it cannot be improved upon. "Is there a monk on earth who can teach me anything new, or who has the power to help me in any form of ascetic discipline that I do not know or have never practiced?" Zosimas asks himself. "Is there any man among those leading a contemplative life in the desert who surpasses me in ascetic practice or spiritual contemplation?" As he is thinking such desperate thoughts, a stranger appears before him and offers him both assurance—"there is no man on earth who has achieved perfection"—and direction—"go to that monastery which is situated near the river Jordan" (3). Zosimas obeys and is accepted by the abbot (4). In this remote, virtually unknown monastery he finds "fellow travelers who were admirably re-creating the divine paradise" (5). The secret of their success lies in the observance of an unusual rule, and it is "on account of [this] rule, I think, that God led Zosimas to that particular monastery," opines the narrator. During Lent, the otherwise strictly cloistered monks all exit the gates of the monastery (6). Crossing the Jordan, they disperse into the desert, each observing strict solitude and turning aside if one chances to encounter another in the vast space (7). On Palm Sunday they return to the monastery. Observance of the rule consists as much in the monks' silence in the monastery as in their solitude in the desert: "No monk asked another anything whatsoever about how or in what way he had exerted himself in his struggle. This was the rule of the monastery" (8).

The situation presents the perfect challenge for an author bent on exposing what has been concealed. It would also seem to complicate Zosimas's search for an observable model of monastic perfection—a search, we might note, that appears doomed in advance by the very possibility of its success, since the threat of achieving perfection is what has driven Zosimas to the remote monastery in the first place. Eagerly setting out for the "inmost part of the desert," Zosimas, however, still hopes "to find a holy father dwelling there who could help him to find what he longed for." The knowing reader appreciates the irony: what Zosimas will in fact find is a "mother" who will not so much fulfill as intensify his longing and thereby finally—blissfully—shatter his self-satisfaction.

On the twentieth day of his wandering, he stops to chant psalms at the appointed hour (9). While chanting, he glimpses out of the corner of his eye "the shadowy illusion of a human body." He shivers, wondering whether it is a demonic apparition.[49] Having protected himself with the sign of the cross, he realizes, however, "that in fact someone was walking in a southward direction." The person comes into view: "What he saw was a naked figure whose body was black, as if tanned by the scorching sun. It had on its head hair white as wool and even this was sparse, as it did not reach below the neck of its body" (10). The scorched skin recalls Jerome's description of himself as transformed by the burning sun of the desert into the black beauty celebrated in Song of Songs 1.6 (Jerome, Ep. 22.7). But look again: is this not also the "one like a son of man" whose "head and . . . hair were white as white wool, white as snow" (Rev. 1.13–14)?[50] As Miller remarks, this queerly hybrid figure, like Pelagia, "will continually pass in and out of focus."[51]

Despite the fact that his monastic rule dictates solitude, Zosimas races joyfully after the creature. Seeing itself pursued, the creature flees, turning "toward the innermost part of the desert." Seeming to perform a fast-paced parody of Antony's pursuit of Paul in the tracks of the she-wolf (cf. *Life of Paul* 9), "Zosimas, as if unmindful of his old age and with no thought for his fatigue from his journey, hastened and exerted himself to overtake the creature that was running away from him." Gradually he narrows the distance between himself and his prey. Having finally gotten close enough to make himself heard, he cries out tearfully, "Why are you running away from this old and sinful man? O servant of the true God, wait up for me, whoever you are. . . . Wait for me, weak and unworthy as I am" (11). Eventually the two halt on opposite sides of a dry streambed. The exhausted Zosimas can go no farther. His weeping and sighs of grief echo loudly in the stillness of the desert (12).

The figure finally speaks, though it does not yet face him. "Father Zosimas, forgive me in the name of the Lord; for I cannot turn toward you and be seen by you face to face, for as you see I am a woman and I am naked, and I am ashamed to have my body uncovered." "It" is a "she," then, we are (perhaps) surprised to discover. The uncanny creature asks him to throw her his cloak. "Shivering fear and astonishment overwhelmed Zosimas"—not, as it happens, because he finds himself facing a naked woman in the desert, but because she seems to know his name (12). (It will be some time before he learns hers.) Deciding to interpret this otherwise inexplicable knowledge as a sign of divine grace rather than demonic cunning, "he quickly did her bidding and, removing the old and torn cloak which he was wearing, threw it to her while he stood with eyes averted." Donning the cloak, with which she covers "only certain parts of her body," the woman half-dressed in a man's garment may now resemble Marganito as much as Pelagios, virilely feminine in her semiclothed state. She turns finally to face Zosimas with a challenging question: "Why, Father Zosimas, did you decide to look at a sinful woman?" In lieu of an answer, he kneels down and asks for a blessing. Matching his move, she kneels too. "Both remained on the ground, each one asking the blessing of the other" (13). (We are reminded of Antony and Paul, arguing for an entire day over who will first break bread [*Life of Paul* 11].) The competition remains deadlocked for some time, but the woman finally yields "to the monk's persistence" and offers a brief blessing. (By acceding, she takes on the superior role.) Now she repeats her question: "Why did you come to see a sinful woman?" This time Zosimas avoids answering by asking her to pray for his sins and for the sins of the whole world. Out of respect for his priesthood, she complies (14). He cannot hear her words but, peeking up furtively from his own prayers, is dismayed to observe that she is "elevated about one cubit from the earth, hanging in the air and praying in that way." Once again he wonders whether she might not be an evil spirit. Seeming to read his mind, she assures him, "I am not a spirit but altogether earth and ashes, and flesh" (15). (She is, as we shall soon see, indeed no figment of his imagination but rather the very enfleshment of the kind of fantasy that once plagued Jerome in the desert.) Zosimas is now overwhelmed by the desire to know *all about her*. "Do not conceal anything from your servant, who you are and where you came from and when and in what way you came to dwell in this desert. Do not conceal from me any detail of your life, but tell me everything. . . . Tell me everything in the name of the Lord" (16).

Despite her professed shame, the woman agrees. "Since you have seen my bare body, I shall lay bare to you also my deeds. . . . And I know that when I start telling you the story of my life, you will avoid me, as one avoids a snake" (17). (Her words, as we shall see, will prove false: Zosimas will learn to love the serpent of temptation.). Her deeds are not few and the story of her life cannot be told briefly. It begins in Egypt when, at age twelve, she leaves her parents, lured by the excitement of life in the big city. It is in Alexandria that she has not merely lost but actively "destroyed" her own virginity. "I threw myself entirely and insatiably into the lust of sexual intercourse." Trying to make a long story short, she summarizes: "for more than seventeen years . . . I was a public temptation to licentiousness." She is not a prostitute but something still worse: "I did not accept anything although men often wished to pay me." She thereby converts her lust into "a free gift," as she puts it. Nor does she refuse money because she does not need it: "You should not think that I did not accept payment because I was rich, for I lived by begging and often by spinning coarse flax fibers. The truth is that I had an insatiable passion," she insists.[52] Her lust is pure, then, no mere means to an end but an end in itself: what she desires is to desire, without limits, transgressing all bounds. "This was and was considered to be my life, to insult nature" (18). Does such abandonment within seduction, exceeding (or simply refusing) economies of exchange and production, whether "natural" or monetary, not already begin to draw "closer to the sacred prostitution practiced by the Ancients"?

The woman now lingers over a particular incident. "One summer I saw a huge crowd of Egyptian and Libyan men running toward the sea." She learns that they are going to Jerusalem to celebrate a holy festival. She has no money for fare or food but confesses herself confident that "I shall go and get on one of the boats they have hired, and they shall feed me whether they wish it or not, for they will accept my body in lieu of the passage money." The motivation for her pilgrimage, as she describes it, is simple: to obtain still more lovers for her "lust" (19). (At this point, the woman begs to be allowed to end her shameful narrative, lest Zosimas himself be corrupted. Fortunately for him, it is too late. "Speak, my mother, in the name of the Lord," he cries out desperately. "Speak and do not interrupt the flow of such a beneficial narration.") She continues, then, describing how she runs down to the harbor. There, gazing about with practiced eye, "I saw some young men standing at the seashore, about ten or more, vigorous in their bodies as well as in their movements, who seemed to me fit for what I sought," she recalls. Pushing into the midst of these fit young men, she entices them with her shocking proposals. The ploy succeeds: "Seeing my penchant for shamelessness, they took me and brought me to the boat" (20). The subsequent Mediterranean cruise leaves no room for disappointment. "What tongue can declare, or what ears can bear to hear what happened on the boat and during the journey and the acts into which I forced those wretched men against their will? There is no kind of licentiousness, speakable or unspeakable, that I did not teach those miserable men." (What reader does not at this point strain to imagine the unspeakable?) Once she reached Jerusalem, the traveler engages "in the same practices or even worse." Far from satisfied with the beautiful young men on the ship, she "corrupted many other men, both citizens and foreigners" (21). What a woman! But where can she go from here?

As usual, she follows the crowd. They are heading to the cathedral for the festival of the Exaltation of the Precious Cross. Elbowing her way expertly through the mob, she finds herself repelled by a mysterious force that prevents her from crossing the threshold (22). After three or four tries, she gives up, puzzled to meet such unanticipated resistance. Unable to get something she wants, for the first time the seductress gives thought to her own "filth." Then it is that she sees the goddess in the temple—or rather, "the icon of the all-holy Mother of God." She entreats the Virgin, now offering different enticements: "Command, my Lady, that the door may be opened also to me that I may venerate the divine cross. . . . I shall no longer insult this flesh by any shameful intercourse whatsoever" (23). The Virgin is persuaded, the doors are opened, the woman's pledge is sealed (24). A voice speaks to the now-holy harlot: "If you cross the river Jordan, you shall find a fine place of repose" (25). Leaving the church, she is given three pennies, with which she buys three loaves. Thus provisioned, she sets out on the next stage of her journey. Led by her virginal Guide, she crosses into the desert. "So I came to this desert, and since then to this day 'I have fled afar off and lodged in this wilderness, waiting for my God'" (cf. Ps. . 54.7–8), she concludes (26).

But Zosimas is still bursting with questions. How long has she been in the desert? Forty-seven years, she thinks. What has she eaten? The same (long since stale) bread she carried in. Has the violence of the change not caused her great distress? She hesitates to answer this last. "Do not hold back, my lady, anything that you might tell me," presses Zosimas. "Indeed I have asked you before to tell me everything without any omission" (27). At the monk's urging, the woman thus prolongs her tale. Or does she begin again? "For seventeen years I wandered in this desert struggling with those irrational desires, as if with wild beasts." Is this the same seventeen years as before or a subsequent span? The latter, it seems, as her desires replay themselves in the desert with even less chance of satisfaction than in the city. She longs for meat, fish, wine, but does not even have water. She longs for song and for sex. The Lady helps her bear her bittersweet suffering (28). "In this way seventeen years passed by, during which I encountered countless dangers" (29). The chronology wobbles suggestively. The initial figure of forty-seven years marking her desert sojourn has, seemingly, been attracted to the figure of seventeen years marking her time of lust. The time in the Lady's desert thus doubles, repeats, and reinterprets the time in the city of men. (In the meantime, thirty succeeding years are swallowed by a seemingly unspeakable serenity.)[53] Like a doubting Thomas,[54] Zosimas continues his cross-examination: "Did you not need any food or clothes?"

She answers, "After I consumed those loaves of bread, as I said before, during those seventeen years, I then fed myself with wild plants and whatever else can be found in the desert." (Yet she has told him no such thing: only now do we realize that her time—"seventeen years" and then some— is nearing its end, eked out on desert herbs.) Even as her bread has given out, so too her clothing has long since worn away. She adds: "I have endured cold and again the flames of summer, scorching in the burning heat and freezing and shivering in the frost" (30). A burst of scriptural allusions that concludes this second narrative causes Zosimas to marvel at her learning. The woman smiles gently at that, assuring him that she is illiterate; nor has she ever heard anyone read from the Scripture (31). If she speaks like the Bible—if she looks like a grotesquely hybrid creature of intertextual interpretation—this is the "natural" product of the long years of her desert training.

Having once again begged the monk to pray for her sins, the holy woman sends him back to his monastery, much as Paul dismisses Antony in Jerome's Life (*Life of Paul* 12). Like Paul, she also arranges for a subsequent rendezvous. (Outdoing Paul, she will draw it out into two stages.) Zosimas is to meet her on the bank of the Jordan the following year "on the holy night of the Last Supper," bringing with him the eucharistic elements so that the woman can "receive the life-giving gifts." Since crossing into the desert, "I have been unable to receive this blessing up to this day," she explains. "But now I long for this with unrestrained fervor" (32). After a suspenseful year's wait, Zosimas (who longs with unrestrained fervor for the woman herself) arrives punctually at the appointed place. The woman is teasingly late for their date (34). When she finally appears on the opposite bank of the river, Zosimas is nearly frantic with worry that she will not be able to cross. His worry is wasted: "Then he saw her making the sign of the holy cross over the Jordan—for, as he told us, there was a full moon that night—and at the same time she set foot on the water and walked on it, approaching him." She comes to him like Jesus approaching the disciples, yet it is from him that she begs a priestly blessing.[55] Having received the sacrament, she cries out to God that she be allowed to depart in peace (35). Before she goes, however, she requests that Zosimas come again the next year to the dry streambed where they met the first time. Zosimas responds, "I only wish it would be possible for me to follow you from now on, and look always upon your holy face." When she leaves—walking on water once again—he realizes that he has forgotten to ask for her name (36).

Once again, a year passes, and Zosimas hurries off to his secret appointment as to a lover's tryst. Finally reaching the designated place, he discovers the woman dead, "her hands folded in the proper manner and her body lying in such a way that she was facing toward the east." Unlike Antony, who immediately embraces and kisses the corpse of Paul (*Life of Paul* 15), Zosimas dares touch no more than the woman's feet, which he bathes with his tears (37). (Now *he* is cast as the "sinful woman.")[56] After singing some psalms and saying a prayer, he wonders whether it is proper to bury her. "While he was saying these words, he saw some writing impressed on the ground beside her head. . . . 'Father Zosimas, bury the body of the humble Mary in this place. Return dust to dust and pray always to the Lord for me. I died . . . on that very night of the Passion of our Savior, after I received the holy Last Supper.'" Queer words indeed, for so many months preserved in the shifting sand, written by a woman not only illiterate but also (seemingly) already dead. Zosimas, overjoyed to have finally learned the woman's name, discerns yet another marvel in the gritty text: "He realized that as soon as she had received the divine sacrament at the Jordan, she came immediately to this place where she died. In fact, the distance Zosimas had covered in twenty days of laborious walking Mary had traversed in one hour, and had then departed straightaway to God" (38).

At this point, the allusions to Jerome's *Life of Paul* are unmistakable. Just as "Antony grieved because he had no shovel to dig a grave" (*Life of Paul* 16), so Zosimas asks himself, "How will you dig a burial pit, you poor man, since you have no tool at hand?" Finding a small piece of wood, he begins to scratch at the arid earth, but "it did not yield at all to the old man who was trying hard to dig." Already drenched with the tears of his grief, now he is drenched with the sweat of his labor (so much improbable wetness in the dry desert!), but both tears and sweat are expended in vain. Heaving a great sigh, Zosimas looks up and is startled to see "a huge lion standing beside the dead body of the blessed woman, licking the soles of her feet." Like Antony when confronted with a similar apparition, he "shakes with fear." Even as he is calming himself with the thought that Mary will keep him safe, the lion begins "to fawn upon the monk." Then Zosimas, as if suddenly recalling the Hieronymian script ("next, the lions began to paw the ground nearby, competing with one another to excavate the sand" [*Life of Paul* 16]), asks the beast to put its claws to work. "As soon as he said these words, the lion dug with its front paws a pit deep enough for the burial of her body" (39). Zosimas then scatters earth on Mary's body, "which was naked as before"—although "certain parts" are still covered with the remnants of Zosimas's tattered cloak, we are assured. He and the lion depart, "the lion withdrawing like a sheep into the innermost part of the desert, while Zosimas returned to the monastery." Back in the monastery (where he remains until his death nearly half a century later), Zosimas is, seemingly, no longer constrained by the rule of silence. "He told the monks everything, without holding back anything of what he had heard and seen" (40).

Here at the narrative's end, Mary's corpse sports Zosimas's rags, yet she is still described as unclothed. Zosimas, unlike Jerome's Antony, has received no garment in exchange. Is he now "naked" too? Jerome's queer romance has been subtly revised by an uncompromising tale of seduction that finally evades even a parodic "marriage." It is surely no accident that there is only *one* lion in *this* tale, and that solitary lion, uncoupled, disappears like Mary into "the innermost part of the desert."[57] In the "drama of the desert" in which the "sacrifice" of a woman is ritualized, perhaps the monk who once clung ambivalently to his own "perfection" finally succeeds in losing his "identity" as well. But what of the woman herself? Lynda Coon remarks that "Mary's *vita*, like Pelagia's, mocks the charity, chastity, and pilgrimages of most holy women." In Coon's view, the seductress must finally repent of her mockery; thus it is that she can teach by example that "redemption is possible even for the most loathsome sinners."[58] But if one takes seriously the element of sacrifice inhering in seduction, rather than reading seduction as that which must itself be sacrificed, it may be possible to understand Mary's very "mockery" as redemptive. Indeed, Mary takes charity, chastity, and pilgrimage to ever more perverse extremes. Her "lust" is always already converted into a "free gift" to all; her refusal to be bound to a husband translates fluently into single-hearted devotion to a Virginal God(dess); and her promiscuous mobility meets its consummate end in the dissolution of a nakedly yearning body, mingled with the innumerable grains of sands in a desert as vast and open as her desire. Uncoupled, and coupling with all, this wild woman runs free as a lion. Queerly unstable in her gender, she is all the more seductive in her "femininity." Jerome's Paul is "an unattainable model," notes Coon, "whereas Mary's is accessible to the sinner."[59] Perhaps Coon has missed (as Zosimas seemingly did not) the surpassing boldness of the "sin" demanded of one who would attain the holiness of the harlot.

The Joy of Harlotry

> *When it finally did occur to me that I was a hooker, and I got over the initial shock, I enjoyed the idea.*
> —Annie Sprinkle, Post Porn Modernist

Reading the Lives of Harlots with unrepentant pleasure is risky business. It is not my desire to romanticize prostitution, rape, or incest. At the same time, I cannot deny the seductive allure of that sexiest of saints, the holy whore—a figure who cannot easily be dislodged from scenes or scenarios configurable as prostitution, rape, or incest, as it happens. In successive, mutually supplemental interpretations of the Lives of the Syrian Mary,

Pelagia, and Mary of Egypt, I have sought to "rescue" the feminine figure of desire from her victimization at the hands of a repressive interpretive tradition—in other words, to resist her inscription as a "victim"—without, I devoutly hope, simply staging yet another series of repressive "conversions."[60] If the Syrian Mary uncovers in prostitution a theater in which to "act out" and thereby re-script the layered histories of a daughter's seduction, the actress Pelagia delivers virtuoso performances of the reversibility of sex and power concealed within the play of seduction, while the Egyptian Mary nakedly exposes the secret of seduction as a "free gift" that radically disrupts the claims of the masculinist economy of sexuality as production and consumption. Reading these "harlots" without shame, even shamelessly *reading as a harlot*—once I got over the initial shock, I enjoyed the idea. In a sense, this "idea" and its "joy" (*jouissance*) pervades not only this final chapter but the entire book.

Jean Baudrillard suggests that "seduction"—which he asserts to be "of the order of the feminine, understood outside the opposition masculine/feminine"—is "an alternative to sex and to power."[61] These cryptic words requiring unpacking. This is all the more the case because their rhetorical context is explicitly antifeminist. Targeting the work of Luce Irigaray in particular, Baudrillard argues that "feminism," in its very search for a distinctly "feminine" speech or subjectivity, remains mired within an essentializing Freudianism that inscribes "anatomy as destiny." He cites with palpable distaste Irigaray's counterphallic (and disquietingly graphic) morphology of female pleasure as multilocal, dispersed, and nonunitary.[62] Baudrillard's "feminine" is, he assures us, not the same as feminism's "feminine." It is not found within the irreducibly masculinist discourse of "sexuality" but "is, and has always been, somewhere else."[63] Women—"feminists"—are forfeiting the secret of their strength "by erecting a contrary, feminine depth," he charges. *His* "feminine"—his "*seduction*"—does not merely refuse depth but, more than that, is characterized by "indistinctness of surface and depth."[64] It is a "principle of uncertainty"; like transvestitism, it plays "with the indistinctness of the sexes." It is "not soluble in power"; "it is not even subversive, it is reversible"; it is not "productive" but "seductive." It is not "hidden" or "repressed" but "secret."[65] "There is no active or passive mode in seduction, no subject or object, no interior or exterior: seduction plays on both sides, and there is no frontier separating them. One cannot seduce others, if one has not oneself been seduced."[66]

Allowing myself to be momentarily seduced by Baudrillard (indeed almost mesmerized by his incantations), I also remain enthralled by Irigaray,

I confess. And why not? Perhaps Baudrillard can seduce "others" ("women") because he has himself already been seduced by Irigaray. As Sadie Plant observes, Baudrillard's monograph *Seduction* "is written with close reference to [Irigaray's] work, and it is not merely the disparaged discourse of female sexuality that he takes from her writing."[67] For her part, Irigaray never denies the strength of her own seductive seducibility. Like Baudrillard, she flirts with "essentializing" language—that is to say, flirts with the power of language itself. Unlike him, she openly, even flamboyantly admits to the flirtation: "the option left to me was to *have a fling with the philosophers.*"[68] Avoiding direct contradiction (for that would be simply to "erect" another "depth"), Irigaray subtly mimics and mocks the fathers of sexual discourse, above all Sigmund Freud.[69] Baudrillard, however, actively suppresses Irigaray's seductive mimicry by reading it mockingly as faithful mimesis: "There is nothing here radically opposed to Freud's maxim."[70] He thereby seems inadvertently reduced to miming Irigaray's moves while claiming them as his own—seduced, after all, even if he persists in denial. The "subject" of sexuality is always "masculine," Irigaray has insisted[71]—a sentiment that Baudrillard echoes faithfully. In relation to discourse, the feminine "remains somewhere else," she notes repeatedly.[72] Emerging (almost) into view in the shifting play of the borrowed masks of her objectification, in the multifaceted dazzle and burning radiance secreted within linguistic concavity, Irigaray's "feminine"—like Baudrillard's—disrupts the distinction of surface and depth, appearance and reality: if "women" are not to be reduced to the "cheap chivalric finery," the "decorative sepulcher" in which they have been stiflingly enclosed,[73] it is also the case that "they do not have the interiority that you have, the one you perhaps suppose they have."[74] With this last remark, Irigaray seems almost to be anticipating Baudrillard's "supposition" about "feminism," and perhaps this is no accident, for the passage occurs shortly after the one that Baudrillard cites as evidence of feminism's false resort to a "contrary depth"—his own contrary projection of an "interiority" that Irigaray has, in fact, already disowned. Neither surface nor depth, neither revealed nor hidden, the feminine constitutes a folded and enfolding terrain—a thick surface—of heterogeneous eroticism that Irigaray has earlier described as "far more diversified, more multiple in its differences, more complex, more subtle, than is commonly imagined." It is also more secret, stubbornly evading linguistic transparency: "It is useless, then, to trap women in the exact definition of what they mean, to make them repeat (themselves) so that it will be clear; they are already elsewhere in that discursive machinery where you expected to surprise them."[75]

Irigaray is perhaps the harlot in Baudrillard's text. He knows she is always "elsewhere"; indeed, he has placed her there. He expects to surprise her with his knowledge of her whereabouts, to appropriate her with his seductive knowing, to convert her from the error of her ways. (If he brings her inside his own interiority, he must also push her back out again.) Although he professes that "one cannot seduce others, if one has not oneself been seduced," he does not really want to submit to seduction. "Baudrillard flatters seduction, attributes to it the greatest powers, bestows upon it the greatest honours, but does so only in an effort to contain its power and so protect himself against its wiles."[76] Like the elusive authors of ancient Harlots' Lives, Baudrillard seems to be surprised by "the strength of the feminine" in his own text.

For the reader who is willing to surrender to their charms, the Lives of Harlots do not perform the repressive confession of a debased desire but enact the unending triumph of the sublime seduction celebrated (however ambivalently) by Baudrillard. The plunge of the executioner's sword—which is also the authorial pen—that makes a woman (or a man) the bride of Christ by marking the singular moment and place of "her" (de)flowering is robbed of its irreversible decisiveness—its incontrovertible witness—when the virgin becomes indistinguishable from the whore. Paradoxically, perhaps, these overtly erotic Lives are the least violent of ancient hagiographies: saintly sex is no longer affixed by the penetrating truth of martyrdom but rather displayed in the enticing spectacle of harlotry. Or rather, the violence of the Lives of Harlots—the violence of seduction—is different, "an escalation of violence and grace"[77] that eclipses the drive to dominate: for domination—even, or especially, *divine* domination—would spell the death of desire, the annihilation of difference, and the extinction of hope. "Love is a challenge and a prize: a challenge to the other to return the love. And to be seduced is to challenge the other to be seduced in turn," muses Baudrillard. "The law of seduction takes the form of an uninterrupted ritual exchange where seducer and seduced constantly raise the stakes in a game that never ends. And cannot end since the dividing line that defines the victory of the one and the defeat of the other, is illegible. And because there is no limit to the challenge to love more than one is loved, or to be always more seduced—if not death."[78] *If not death*: if not even death sets a limit on love, the sacrament of seduction is infinitely suspended; it is, in every sense, nonteleological. This is the secret of sanctity: to play the harlot; to defy the law of sexuality and submit to the rule of seduction; constantly to raise the stakes in a game that never ends. The romancing of the harlot is thus also the romancing of God. (Is it even possible that "God is a whore," as Bataille suggests?)[79] "One *seduces* God with faith, and He cannot but respond, for seduction, like the challenge, is a reversible form. And He responds a hundredfold by His grace to the challenge of faith."[80] Seduction is God's challenge to the saint and also the saint's challenge to God—the very wager of all theology, as well as all asceticism.

Postscript (Catching My Breath)

Countereroticism will not tolerate conclusion. There can be no end to love in the lives of saints, no end to the reading and rewriting of holy Lives. Nonetheless, readers, writers, and lovers alike honor the power of the interval, the necessity—even the intense desirability—of the pause. Let us pause, then, in the midst, in between. Let us catch our breath.

Inspire: write and be read! Expire: let go of the self! In the midst, in between such daunting imperatives, our lives transpire. Heavy breathing, shallow breaths, suspenseful breathlessness: so we might measure the soulful, sensual embodiment of what Christians have traditionally named the "Spirit of God." More modestly, we might also note the persistent vitality of mortal creatures who continue—at times, seemingly against all odds, and thus not after all so modestly—to hope, to desire, to strive . . . to keep on breathing, for a little while longer. Such improbable aspirations!

Can breath be "caught"? It is neither prey nor disease. Yet we speak of "catching the wind": which is to say, being caught up by the wind, borne on breath—transported. "Catching the spirit": being caught up by the spirit. What else? A divine seduction.

When my first child was born, after an exhausting twelve hours of mutual labor, he paused delicately—such a beautiful in-between blue, I thought dreamily. The doctor shocked him into his newborn senses: he breathed; indeed, he screamed. My second child, secretly tutored, arrived in half the time and already ruddy, with full mastery of her lungs—or perhaps already mastered by their power. Sometimes I too catch my breath. Sometimes I find, to my surprise, that I am already screaming. Either way, breath comes as a shock—it *comes* in shocking repetitions—as pleasure and pain, spirit and flesh, collude and commingle in a mysterious rhythmic attunement. Life draws close to death and death to life: we inhale; we exhale. (We make love, however we can.) We keep on doing it for a little while longer: the mortal measure of eternity, the impossible stretch of desire, the ambitious span of a life.

We inhale the exhalations of other mortal creatures: this is the logic not only of ecosystems but also of history. Our children breathe our own breath in turn. Some of the fumes of the past—and these are not absent from ancient hagiography—have proved toxic, issuing in so many crimes of passion, homophobic, sexist, racist, ethnocentric, nationalistic, religious. Other holier breezes, equally ancient and equally fired by passion, may also blow our way—may, in grace, even blow us away, catch us up in the spirit. Yet the countereroticism that breathes through the ascetic Lives, simultaneously sensual and sacred, creates risk. Dare we inhale such dizzying drafts of desire?

Inspired by the saints, perhaps we will take the dare.

Our love will not, of course, be "the same" as theirs. The ascetics of late antiquity cultivated purposeful disciplines of embodiment and textuality, pedagogy and prayer, which freed desire from the constraining and often violently oppressive structures of familial, civic, and imperial domination. For the most part, this was accomplished through ambivalent mimicry of those very structures—through enactments of resistance within power rather than simple opposition to power, through subversion rather than inversion. Ancient Lives of men—specifically, those penned by Jerome and Sulpicius Severus—typically focus on the erotic relationship of disciple and master, replicated in the relationship of the writer to his hagiographical subject, as well as in the relationship of the saint to Christ (a divine figure who remains, however, intriguingly distant in the context of the homosocially contained eroticism of these male Lives). The fundamentally asymmetrical structure of classical pedagogical pederasty is thereby invoked and transformed, in the proliferation of reversals, repetitions, and displacements that both intensify and defuse dynamics of desire and power, while radically destabilizing the social hierarchies reflected in "active" or "passive" roles (and thereby also destabilizing the implicit "gendering" of these roles). Lives of women—Jerome's Paula, Gregory's Macrina, Augustine's Monica—balance the erotic union of a woman with Christ against the intimate relationship between the male narrator and his female subject, where the author becomes a character in his own history or, in the case of harlot Lives, where the holy woman is viewed from the perspective of a male ascetic who figures prominently in her Life and whose own ascetic journey is closely linked with her own. Here too traditionally asymmetrical relations of power—in this case, explicitly marked by gender—are invoked only to be repeatedly reversed and displaced, so that gender itself is rendered complex, unstable, and fluid. Hagiography thus continually generates new worlds of text in which love of

God—a sacred eroticism—disrupts subjects and traverses the sex(ed) lives of men and women, disclosing the joy at the heart of existence.

Christianity did indeed change the state of things in the history of western sexuality, with its sternly ecstatic revising of lives translated into holiness at the shifting borderlines of sexual difference, in the movement of eros across the constructed limits of subjectivity. (This, finally, is my answer to Foucault's evocatively ambiguous rhetorical question.) Yet Christianity—to the extent that it continues to inspire new life, to inscribe new Lives—is itself ever in a state of transforming love. The eroticism performed and celebrated in ancient Lives was bought at a cost. Certain prices—such as the refusal of more earthily sensual pleasures—some of us will be unwilling to pay, least of all at a time when the planet sickens from the effects of humanity's haughty neglect—indeed, dangerous denial—of its irreducibly material matrices. (On the other hand, conversion to a more austerely ascetic eros may be just what is needed, if the planet is to recover from the ravages of gluttonous overconsumption.) Certain refusals—of misogyny or homophobia, among others—some of us will find it necessary to articulate more sharply, in response to the particular political oppressions perpetuated by ongoing regimes of "sexuality."

Our love will not be "the same" as theirs, but it will also not be utterly discontinuous. For those who would surrender themselves to transporting flights of divine eros, now as then, binding strictures of orthodoxy must be resisted and clear-cut maps of morality abandoned. Holy love begins, then, with resistance and abandonment: but where does it lead? We cannot know. Lack is not filled but eclipsed, suffering not eradicated but surpassed in joy. The secreted physicality of pleasure and pain opens onto the expansiveness of the soul, cuts between souls, extends beyond, reaches for . . . God? reaches, then, across every limit while honoring the finitude of all existence. The fertile deserts of countereroticism are vast and trackless, haunted by ambivalence. There are, however, guides for the journey—inevitably partial and poignantly fallible. Boldly navigating the unpredictable winds of the spirit, the ancient hagiographers may continue to chart paths of possibility for saintly love.

Notes

Introduction: Hagiography and the History of Sexuality

1. Michel Foucault, *The History of Sexuality*, vol. 1, *An Introduction*, 1976, trans. Robert Hurley (New York: Vintage/Random House, 1978); vol. 2, *The Use of Pleasure*, 1984, trans. Robert Hurley (New York: Random House, 1985); vol. 3, *The Care of the Self*, 1984, trans. Robert Hurley (New York: Random House, 1986).

2. Michel Foucault, "Sexuality and Solitude," 1980, in *Religion and Culture: Michel Foucault*, ed. Jeremy R. Carrette (New York: Routledge, 1999), 184.

3. See especially the shift in agenda outlined by Foucault in the introduction to the second volume of his *History of Sexuality*, where he announces his decision to interrupt his planned history of the modern sexual subject by reorganizing "the whole study around the slow formation, in antiquity, of a hermeneutics of the self," a "long detour" that was intended to result in three subsequent volumes charting "the genealogy of desiring man, from classical antiquity through the first centuries of Christianity" (*Use of Pleasure*, 6, 7, 12). The final volume, on Christianity, remained incomplete at the time of Foucault's death in 1984. James Bernauer, *Michel Foucault's Force of Flight: Toward an Ethics for Thought*, Contemporary Studies in Philosophy and the Human Sciences (Atlantic Highlands, N.J.: Humanities Press, 1990), 161–62, offers a concise and helpful account of the evolution of Foucault's *History of Sexuality*.

4. Note that Foucault's claim that the marital morality emerging in antiquity is not a distinctly Christian product but is rather the result of broader, more complex social and political realignments taking place during the early Roman imperial period depends heavily on the work of Paul Veyne, with whom Foucault collaborated closely (*Use of Pleasure*, 8; the influence of Veyne is particularly present in the third volume, *Care of the Self*, 72–80). Kate Cooper, *The Virgin and the Bride: Idealized Womanhood in Late Antiquity* (Cambridge, Mass.: Harvard University Press, 1996), 1–5, offers a concise and incisive discussion of both Veyne and Foucault. Cooper herself resists the exclusive focus on the ascetic strains within ancient Christianity by calling attention to the persisting political investment, among pagans and Christians alike, in rhetorics of marital concord; at the same time, she emphasizes the novelty and disruptive power of ascetic discourse: "The decisive shift at the end of antiquity was not a change in the social reality of aristocratic marriage, but the introduction of a competing moral language, the Christian rhetoric of virginity" (3).

5. The latter term and its association with both ancient and contemporary practices and philosophies of eros, about which I will say more below, is borrowed

from Karmen MacKendrick, *Counterpleasures*, SUNY Series in Postmodern Culture (Binghamton: State University of New York Press, 1999). My own language of "countereroticism" is most directly influenced by MacKendrick's framing of the "counterpleasures" and by the concept of "counter-apocalypse" developed by Catherine Keller, *Apocalypse Now and Then: A Feminist Guide to the End of the World* (Boston: Beacon Press, 1996); beyond that it reflects a broader poststructuralist interest in exploring dynamics of collusive resistance that evade binary oppositions.

6. Note that Cooper dates the "introduction" of the rhetoric of virginity as late as the fourth century, challenging the tendency to identify Christianity with asceticism (see especially her "de-asceticizing" interpretation of the Apocryphal Acts of the Apostles in *The Virgin and the Bride*, 45–67). I am, however, in agreement with Elizabeth Clark that "we cannot posit the fourth century as the founding moment of asceticism," on the grounds that "Christianity in the first to the third centuries— not just in the fourth—contains many testimonies to asceticism's popularity" (*Reading Renunciation: Asceticism and Scripture in Early Christianity* [Princeton, N.J.: Princeton University Press, 1999], 23, 27). In studies of asceticism, the work of Peter Brown and Elizabeth Clark has been particularly significant. See especially Peter Brown, *The Body and Society: Men, Women, and Sexual Renunciation in Early Christianity*, Lectures on the History of Religions (New York: Columbia University Press, 1988); Elizabeth A. Clark, *Ascetic Piety and Women's Faith: Essays on Late Ancient Christianity*, Studies in Women and Religion (Lewiston, N.Y.: Edwin Mellen Press, 1986); Clark, *The Origenist Controversy: The Cultural Construction of an Early Christian Debate* (Princeton, N.J.: Princeton University Press, 1992); and Clark, *Reading Renunciation*. Monographs on Christian asceticism, too numerous to be listed here, have proliferated in the wake of the work of Brown and Clark. The breadth and intensity of interest generated may, however, be partly measured by such collections as Vincent L. Wimbush and Richard Valantasis, eds., *Asceticism* (Oxford: Oxford University Press, 1995), and Leif E. Vaage and Vincent L. Wimbush, eds., *Asceticism and the New Testament* (New York: Routledge, 1999). Pagan asceticism has also received attention, for example, James A. Francis, *Subversive Virtue: Asceticism and Authority in the Second-Century Pagan World* (University Park: Pennsylvania State University Press, 1995). Daniel Boyarin locates rabbinic Judaism primarily in the resistance to asceticism while also noting the lure of asceticism for rabbis—"married monks"—whose first love was for "Torah" (*Carnal Israel: Reading Sex in Talmudic Culture* [Berkeley: University of California Press, 1993], 134–66; cf. Michael L. Satlow, *Jewish Marriage in Antiquity* [Princeton, N.J.: Princeton University Press, 2001], 30–38); intertestamental literature, Philo, and the Dead Sea Scrolls evidence the significance of ascetic practice for prerabbinic Judaism (Steven D. Fraade, "Ascetical Aspects of Ancient Judaism," in *Jewish Spirituality: From the Bible to the Middle Ages*, ed. Arthur Green [New York: Crossroad, 1986], 253–88; cf. Satlow, *Jewish Marriage in Antiquity*, 21–24).

7. Mark D. Jordan, *The Ethics of Sex*, New Dimensions to Religious Ethics (Oxford: Blackwell, 2002), 71.

8. This line of argument reflects no disagreement with the important work of classicist David Halperin, *One Hundred Years of Homosexuality and Other Essays on Greek Love* (New York: Routledge, 1990); it does, however, constitute an alternate

strategy for appropriating Foucault's work on antiquity, as will also become clear in the discussion of Halperin's *Saint Foucault: Towards a Gay Hagiography* (New York: Oxford University Press, 1995), below. Whereas Halperin highlights the resources of pre-Christian antiquity for reconceiving a "Greek love" that clearly *precedes* "sexuality," I am interested in revisiting the complexities of a historical moment in which "sexuality" emerges, already rife with an ambivalence that contains the seeds not only of modern sexuality but also of its destabilization, disruption, and self-transgression.

9. Jordan, *Ethics of Sex*, provides a critical theological assessment, as well as a lucid historical account, of the focus on procreation that came to characterize Christian sexual ethics.

10. Michel Foucault, "About the Beginning of the Hermeneutics of the Self," 1980, in Carrette, *Religion and Culture*, 163, 168.

11. Foucault, "Hermeneutics of the Self," 170.

12. Michel Foucault, "Pastoral Power and Political Reason," 1979, in Carrette, *Religion and Culture*, 143.

13. Foucault, "Hermeneutics of the Self," 169.

14. Foucault, "Sexuality and Solitude," 186.

15. Foucault, fascinated equally by Augustine's and Cassian's confessional practices, is seemingly not preoccupied by their many differences. Peter Brown, on the other hand, stages the debate between Augustine and Cassian as the culmination of his study of ancient Christian asceticism in *The Body and Society*, 387–427. For Brown, it is Augustine who places "sexuality irremovably at the center of the human person," thereby marking a radical break with the ancient traditions of "Desert Fathers" still upheld by Cassian, for whom "sexuality was a mere epiphenomenon" (422): if Augustine is the first modern subject of sexuality, it is because he has *rejected* classical asceticism. Foucault notes his debts to the work and conversation of Brown (e.g., *Use of Pleasure*, 8) while still giving a slightly different account of the relation of asceticism to modern sexuality.

16. Foucault, *Use of Pleasure*, 20. That this trajectory should culminate in the work of a Jew—Sigmund Freud—is a paradox explored in Daniel Boyarin, *Unheroic Conduct: The Rise of Heterosexuality and the Invention of the Jewish Man*, Contraversions: Critical Studies in Jewish Literature, Culture, and Society (Berkeley: University of California Press, 1997).

17. See Jean Baudrillard, *Forget Foucault*, 1977 (New York: Semiotext(e), 1987), 9–64.

18. Judith Butler, *Gender Trouble: Feminism and the Subversion of Identity*, Thinking Gender (New York: Routledge, 1990), 93–106.

19. Arnold I. Davidson, *The Emergence of Sexuality: Historical Epistemology and the Formation of Concepts* (Cambridge, Mass.: Harvard University Press, 2001), 29.

20. Foucault, *Use of Pleasure*, 7. Extending Foucault's earlier work on historical epistemology, Davidson persuasively demonstrates the shifts in "mentalities" or "styles of reasoning" that decisively separate modern concepts of sexuality and perversion from ancient or medieval concepts: "chastity and virginity are moral categories denoting a relation between the will and the flesh; they are not categories

of sexuality," he notes; regarding "Augustine's use of the term 'perversion' and the nineteenth-century psychiatric use of this term," he insists that "lexical continuity hides radical conceptual discontinuity" (*Emergence of Sexuality*, 53, 139). However, in the later volumes of his *History of Sexuality*, Foucault himself explores the continuity as well as the discontinuity of ancient and modern discourses; thus his "essay" into the study of antiquity becomes simultaneously a "history of the present" and the performative inauguration of a different future.

21. "The culturally constructed body will then be liberated, neither to its 'natural' past, nor to its original pleasures, but to an open future of cultural possibilities" (Butler, *Gender Trouble*, 93).

22. Foucault, *Use of Pleasure*, 9, 11.

23. Michel Foucault, "On the Government of the Living," 1980, in Carrette, *Religion and Culture*, 157.

24. Daniel Boyarin and Elizabeth A. Castelli, "Introduction: Foucault's *The History of Sexuality*: The Fourth Volume, or, a Field Left Fallow for Others to Till," *Journal of the History of Sexuality* 10, nos. 3–4 (2001): 363–64, comment on the apparent inconsistency of Foucault's fragmentary "fourth volume" on Christianity, locating this inconsistency in the tension between his "genealogical" and "historical" aims: on the one hand, Foucault emphasizes Christianity's decisive break with prior ("Greek" and "Roman") epistemes; on the other hand, he acknowledges "deep continuities within cultural developments." My own interest is in a closely related (but not identical) tension, namely, the tension between Foucault's dual emphases on the continuity and discontinuity of ancient Christian sexual subjectivity and that of the modern period. While not disputing the usefulness of the distinction between genealogical and historical projects, I am also suggesting that Foucault's analysis of Christianity can be read as a genealogy of both modern sexuality and its (post)modern subversions.

25. Foucault, "Hermeneutics of the Self," 180.

26. Mark Vernon, "Postscript: 'I Am Not What I Am'—Foucault, Christian Asceticism, and a 'Way Out' of Sexuality," in Carrette, *Religion and Culture*, 203

27. Michel Foucault, "Who Are You, Professor Foucault? (Interview with P. Caruso)," 1967, in Carrette, *Religion and Culture*, 98.

28. Michel Foucault, "A Preface to Transgression," 1963, in Carrette, *Religion and Culture*, 57.

29. Foucault, "Preface to Transgression," 59.

30. Bernauer, *Foucault's Force of Flight*, 178, notes: "Foucault's negative theology is a critique not of the conceptualizations employed for God but of that modern figure of finite man whose identity was put forward as capturing the essence of human beings. Nevertheless, Foucault's critical thinking is best described as a negative theology, rather than a negative anthropology, for its flight from man is an escape from yet another conceptualization of the Absolute." More recently, Jeremy R. Carrette, *Foucault and Religion: Spiritual Corporality and Political Spirituality* (London: Routledge, 2000), xi, resists the characterization of Foucault as a "negative theologian": "The creative location of Foucault in the tradition of negative theology . . . is a secondary theological redaction (interesting and valid in its own right) which does not find internal support in his work." See also Carrette's discussion of

Foucault's framing of the "death of God" and "the death of man" in relation to the thought of Bataille, Sade, and Nietzsche (79–82).

31. Foucault, "Preface to Transgression," 61.
32. Foucault, "Preface to Transgression," 62.
33. Foucault, "Preface to Transgression," 70.
34. Georges Bataille, *Erotism: Death and Sensuality*, 1957, trans. Mary Dalwood (San Francisco: City Lights Books, 1986), 263.
35. Bataille, *Erotism*, 31.
36. Halperin, *Saint Foucault*, 6, 8.
37. Halperin, *Saint Foucault*, 130–39. The biographies of Foucault include Didier Eribon, *Michel Foucault*, 1989, trans. Betsy Wing (Cambridge, Mass.: Harvard University Press, 1991); David Macey, *The Lives of Michel Foucault* (London: Hutchinson, 1993); and James Miller, *The Passion of Michel Foucault* (New York: Simon and Schuster, 1993). The last is the subject of Halperin's particular critique.
38. Halperin, *Saint Foucault*, 62.
39. Halperin, *Saint Foucault*, 76.
40. Vernon, "Postscript," 207.
41. Jeremy R. Carrette, "Prologue to a Confession of the Flesh," in Carrette, *Religion and Culture*, 6.
42. Carrette, "Prologue," 16. Perhaps it is the threat of this "religious distortion" that partly motivates Halperin's suppression of "religion" in his own ironically "hagiographical" account. More significant, of course, is Halperin's desire to align Foucault with a "gay" erotics that may be seen clearly to predate heterosexuality, the remote origins of which coincide with the birth of Christianity, as we have seen.
43. Carrette, "Prologue," 17.
44. Halperin, *Saint Foucault*, 162–82.
45. Carrette, "Prologue," 17–32.
46. Carrette, "Prologue," 20.
47. Carrette, "Prologue," 27; see also Carrette's careful comparison of Foucault's thought to mystical theology, specifically that of Pseudo-Dionysius, in his *Foucault and Religion*, 85–108. Note that Bernauer, *Foucault's Force of Flight*, 178, writing some ten years earlier, is happy to describe Foucault's "ethics" as "the practice of an intellectual freedom that may be described as an ecstatic thinking or a worldly mysticism."
48. Carrette, "Prologue," 24–25.
49. At this point, it should perhaps be acknowledged explicitly, I am arguing both with and against Carrette, *Foucault and Religion*, who emphasizes the (subtextual) continuity of Foucault's interest in "religion," which threads through Foucault's earlier engagement with the philosophical avant-garde to intersect with his later interest in Christianity, while he at the same time insists that Foucault's reading of Christianity, for all its notable hesitations and shifts, remains thoroughgoingly critical.
50. Bataille, *Erotism*, 253, 256.
51. MacKendrick, *Counterpleasures*, 18–19.
52. MacKendrick, *Counterpleasures*, 14.
53. MacKendrick, *Counterpleasures*, 100.
54. MacKendrick, *Counterpleasures*, 69–70.

55. MacKendrick, *Counterpleasures*, 77–78.

56. MacKendrick, *Counterpleasures*, 85.

57. Geoffrey Galt Harpham, *The Ascetic Imperative in Culture and Criticism* (Chicago: University of Chicago Press, 1987), 81.

58. Harpham, *Ascetic Imperative*, 60.

59. Harpham, *Ascetic Imperative*, 88.

60. Harpham, *Ascetic Imperative*, 28.

61. Harpham, *Ascetic Imperative*, 81.

62. Harpham, *Ascetic Imperative*, 220–35.

63. Harpham, *Ascetic Imperative*, 3. Harpham repeats and broadens the point: "Most accounts of the history of Western narrative form grant a seminal position to the genre of hagiography inaugurated and epitomized by *The Life of Anthony*" (67). Cf. Patricia Cox, *Biography in Late Antiquity: A Quest for the Holy Man*, Transformation of the Classical Heritage (Berkeley: University of California Press, 1983), who discovers the seeds of hagiography in the prior Lives of Origen and Plotinus.

64. I have, however, addressed the dynamics of gender and eros in the *Life of Antony* elsewhere: see my *"Begotten, Not Made": Conceiving Manhood in Late Antiquity*, Figurae: Reading Medieval Culture (Stanford, Calif.: Stanford University Press, 2000), 68–78. Also discussed therein (but omitted from consideration in the present work) is Gregory of Nyssa's remarkably queer *Life of Moses* (123–30).

65. See Harpham, *Ascetic Imperative*, 52, 80, 221, 234–35, with reference both to his own disagreements with Bersani and to Bersani's debate with Foucault.

66. Here as elsewhere, I use the term *queer* to designate erotic practices that actively resist and/or put into question the very categories of the "normal," the "conventional," or the "natural," particularly in contexts in which resistance exposes, critiques, and subverts the violence of both *domus* and *dominus*. The "queer" overlaps at some points (but by no means at all points) with the "homoerotic," e.g., where homoerotic practices resist the conventions of either marriage or pederasty.

67. MacKendrick, *Counterpleasures*, 106, 109, 119.

68. Leo Bersani, "Is the Rectum a Grave?" in *AIDS: Cultural Analysis, Cultural Activism*, ed. Douglas Crimp (Cambridge, Mass.: MIT Press, 1988), 222.

69. For Bataille, "eroticism always entails a breaking down of . . . the patterns . . . of the regulated social order basic to our discontinuous mode of existence as defined and separate individuals" (*Erotism*, 18). In Bersani's terms, the structured "self" that is "shattered" in eroticism is the Freudian "ego." Thus, for Bersani, sexuality is inherently masochistic; furthermore, "*masochism serves life*," mediating between "the quantities of stimuli to which we are exposed and the development of ego structures capable of resisting or, in Freudian terms, of binding those stimuli" (*The Freudian Body: Psychoanalysis and Art* [New York: Columbia University Press, 1986], 38–39; emphasis in original).

70. Jean-Luc Nancy, *The Inoperative Community*, ed. Peter Connor, trans. Peter Connor, Lisa Garbus, Michael Holland, and Simona Sawhney, Theory and History of Literature 76 (Minneapolis: University of Minnesota Press, 1991), 97.

71. Elaine Scarry, *The Body in Pain: The Making and Unmaking of the World* (New York: Oxford University Press, 1985), 30.

72. Bataille, *Erotism*, 18–19.

73. See Lynda Hart, *Between the Body and the Flesh: Performing Sadomasochism*, Between Men—Between Women: Lesbian and Gay Studies (New York: Columbia University Press, 1998), 85–86, who draws upon both Luce Irigaray's and Homi Bhabha's theories of mimicry in order to highlight "the value of dis-semblance to lesbian s/m," viewed "as impersonations that are not mimesis but mimicry."

74. Nancy, *Inoperative Community*, 98.

75. My perspective differs rather sharply from Scarry's at this point. She acknowledges that pain is frequently courted in religious experience—"the self-flagellation of the religious ascetic, for example"—and that such pain is distinct from the pain inflicted in political torture, not only because the element of "consent" is present, but also because the "unmaking" of one world makes way for the (re)creation of another. Nonetheless, Scarry suppresses the potentially transformative subversiveness of what she describes as merely "a *comparatively* benign situation in which the human body hurt . . . belongs to the believer himself." She reserves her celebration for those situations in which pain and power are simply unlinked, suggesting (implausibly) that such is the case with the Christian theology of the cross: "The earlier relation between [power and suffering] is eliminated." "They are unrelated and therefore can occur together: God is both omnipotent and in pain" (*Body in Pain*, 214, 148, 214).

76. Marcella Althaus-Reid, *Indecent Theology: Theological Perversions in Sex, Gender, and Politics* (London: Routledge, 2000), 47.

77. MacKendrick, *Counterpleasures*, 119.

78. Jean Baudrillard, *Seduction*, 1979, trans. Brian Singer (New York: St. Martin's Press, 1990), 142.

79. Cf. Baudrillard, *Forget Foucault*, 75: "Metamorphosis is at the radical point in the system, at the point where there is no longer any law or symbolic order. It is a process without any subject, beyond death, beyond any desire, in which only the rules of the game of form are involved. . . . Love is no longer considered as a dependence of desire upon lack, but in the unconscious form of the transformation into the other."

80. Bataille, *Erotism*, 22–23.

81. Bataille, *Erotism*, 15–16.

82. Bataille, *Erotism*, 9.

83. Bataille, *Erotism*, 31.

84. Althaus-Reid, *Indecent Theology*, 95.

85. Althaus-Reid, *Indecent Theology*, 88.

86. See also Mark Jordan's historically-inflected theological redemption of "pleasures," which attends to the resonances of mystical prayer and ascetical narratives with the experiences and narratives of "sexual S&M" (*Ethics of Sex*, 163–72).

87. Cf. Thomas J. Heffernan, *Sacred Biography: Saints and Their Biographers in the Middle Ages* (New York: Oxford University Press, 1988), who emphasizes the drive to conformity—"what for some is such a stifling sameness" (15)—that characterizes the hagiographical genre. I am not so much directly disagreeing with this (fairly typical) view as decisively shifting the emphasis, highlighting the literary inventiveness and resistance to conformity that also crucially characterizes hagiography and indeed drives its very impulse for repetition.

88. In addition to the works already discussed, mention must also be made of Edith Wyschogrod, *Saints and Postmodernism: Revisioning Moral Philosophy*, Religion and Postmodernism (Chicago: University of Chicago Press, 1990). My own study intersects with Wyschogrod's challenging and far-ranging work at many points; nonetheless, her interest in morality, alterity, and altruism—emphasizing the saintly capacity to desire on behalf of the Other—results in a rather different (though not, I think, necessarily incompatible) trajectory of argument.

89. This characterization of the novel owes much to M. M. Bakhtin, *The Dialogic Imagination: Four Essays*, trans. Caryl Emerson and Michael Holquist (Austin: University of Texas Press, 1981).

90. Foucault, *Use of Pleasure*, 11.

Chapter 1. Fancying Hermits: Sublimation and the Arts of Romance

1. As Stefan Rebenich, *Hieronymus und sein Kreis: Prosopographische und sozialgeschichtliche Untersuchungen* (Stuttgart: Franz Steiner Verlag, 1992), 93–98, points out, Ep. 22.7 appears largely responsible for the now-traditional account of Jerome's heroic exploits in the desert of Chalcis, an account dominated by descriptions of physical suffering, solitude, and struggle against the passions (see also Ep. 125.12); other evidence, for example, Jerome's desert correspondence, hints that the two or three years he spent in Chalcis (equipped with library and copyists) may have more closely matched the conditions and comforts experienced by many contemporary academics enjoying sabbatical leaves. Of course, the desert correspondence itself consists of a carefully selected corpus of letters published around the same time as Ep. 22 and likewise implicated in Jerome's "fanciful" post-desert self-fashioning as a *literary* ascetic.

2. Thus Patricia Cox Miller, *Dreams in Late Antiquity: Studies in the Imagination of a Culture* (Princeton, N.J.: Princeton University Press, 1994), 205: "Dismissive of the passing of time, the images of Jerome's tormenting fantasies continued to operate in the inner space of his mind."

3. For a nuanced consideration of how Jerome's letter itself becomes the site of displaced desire, see Patricia Cox Miller, "The Blazing Body: Ascetic Desire in Jerome's Letter to Eustochium," *Journal of Early Christian Studies* 1, no. 1 (1993): 21–45, and her *Dreams in Late Antiquity*, 205–31.

4. The "Ethiopian" whose skin Jerome has stolen was by this time a conventional figure of ascetic paradox, representing the tension and contrast between the "inner" and the "outer man," where the "blackness" of carnality was understood to be "white-washed" by the practice of spiritual virtue. As sinners, "we are naturally black," Jerome writes at the beginning of this letter, citing Song of Songs 1.5: "I am black but comely . . . ," a passage that he seams with Numbers 12.1, "He [Christ the Bridegroom] has married an Ethiopian woman," concluding with the assurance that Christ will "miraculously change your complexion" (Ep. 22.1). Jerome's retranslation of the ambiguous Hebrew conjunction in Song of Songs 1.5—shifting from the septugintal "black and beautiful" to "black but beautiful"—is implicated in the history of this problematically racialized trope. Here in Ep. 22.7, however, it is the figural

identification of "black" *with* "beautiful" that is not only accomplished with fluid ease but is (I am arguing) crucial to Jerome's textual self-construction.

5. Miller, "Blazing Body," 27–29.

6. Jerome not infrequently represents himself as weeping, e.g., in Ep. 14.1, where he enthusiastically recalls "the lamentation and weeping with which I accompanied your [Heliodorus's] departure."

7. Note that my reading at this point differs slightly from the reading of Miller, "Blazing Body," 32–33, regarding what she describes as Jerome's "failed attempt at 'feminizing' his body."

8. E. Coleiro, "St. Jerome's Lives of the Hermits," *Vigiliae Christianae* 11 (1957): 177–78.

9. Exemplary of the tendency to place Jerome's Lives within a differentiated history of classical biographical genres and to make sharp distinctions between biography and romance is Julius Plesch, *Die Originalität und literarische Form der Mönchsbiographien des hl. Hieronymus* (Munich: Wolf and Sohn, 1910). Herbert Kech, *Hagiographie als christliche Unterhaltungsliteratur: Studien zum Phänomen des Erbaulichen anhand der Mönchsviten des hl. Hieronymus* (Göppingen: Alfred Kümmerle Verlag, 1977), 1–10, offers a critical reading of the history of scholarship predating his own work, highlighting the degree to which questions of "genre" have been shaped by modern preoccupations with historical veracity (preoccupations in turn frequently pressured by confessional apologetics).

10. Coleiro, "St. Jerome's Lives," 163–66.

11. Coleiro, "St. Jerome's Lives," 166.

12. Coleiro, "St. Jerome's Lives," 167.

13. Coleiro, "St. Jerome's Lives," 171–74.

14. Coleiro, "St. Jerome's Lives," 176.

15. Coleiro, "St. Jerome's Lives," 177–78.

16. The "double appeal to imagination and feeling" is, according to Coleiro, a defining characteristic of romantic writing ("St. Jerome's Lives," 172). I am here exploring (and exploiting) the ways in which Coleiro's clear appreciation of Jerome as a romantic author is in tension with his tendency to construct an unfavorable contrast of "entertainment" (trivialized as a spurious romantic accretion) with the historical "information" presented in Jerome's Lives (e.g., 163). Note that both Kech, *Hagiographie*, and Manfred Fuhrmann, "Die Mönchsgeschichten des Hieronymus: Formexperimente in erzählender Literatur," in *Christianisme et formes littéraires de l'antiquité tardive en occident*, ed. Manfred Fuhrmann, Entretiens sur l'Antiquité Classique (Geneva: Fondation Hardt, 1977), 41–99, in some respects go farther than Coleiro in acknowledging the generic hybridity and innovative character of Hieronymian hagiography while also emphasizing the overriding concern with "edification" or "imitation" that imbues the nascent genre with both aesthetic coherence and religious seriousness. I am not inclined to dispute either the centrality of edification or the pious sincerity of Jerome's Lives; nonetheless, there is a danger that emphasis on such aspects may lead to a virtual reinscription of the dichotomy of history/biography versus romance. For this reason, I find that Coleiro's thematized ambivalence regarding the romance in Jerome's hagiography offers a more promising starting point for readings that would effectively deconstruct such a dichotomy.

17. See Mark Vessey, "From *Cursus* to *Ductus*: Figures of Writing in Western Late Antiquity (Augustine, Jerome, Cassiodorus, Bede)," in *European Literary Careers: The Author from Antiquity to the Renaissance*, ed. Patrick Cheney and Frederick A. De Armas (Toronto: University of Toronto Press, 2002), 47–114, and Mark Vessey, "Jerome and Rufinus," in *The Cambridge History of Early Christian Literature*, ed. Frances M. Young, Andrew Louth, and Lewis Ayers (Cambridge: Cambridge University Press, forthcoming).

18. To Evagrius of Antioch is also attributed the translation of the *Life of the Blessed Antony* from Athanasius's Greek into Latin (*On Famous Men*, 125).

19. I shall refer throughout this chapter to the Athanasian *Life of Antony*; it is, however, the Evagrian Latin "translation" of this text that mediates Jerome's interpretation and shapes the competitive context of his own, self-consciously "original" Latin writing project.

20. The positioning of the Athanasian text as the "source" of Western asceticism and hagiographical literature is not only a commonplace among patristic scholars. Thus, as we have seen, Geoffrey Galt Harpham, *The Ascetic Imperative in Culture and Criticism* (Chicago: University of Chicago Press, 1987), 3, begins: "The master text of Western asceticism is *The Life of Anthony*..." (3).

21. Cf. Ep. 22.36: "Huius vitae auctor Paulus, inlustrator Antonius et, ut ad superiora conscendam, princeps Iohannes baptista fuit." Jerome, like Paul, is the *auctor*.

22. Note that by surfacing and intensifying Jerome's claims for priority I am not only repeating but also exceeding the more common literary-historiographic representation of Jerome as the father of *Latin* hagiography. Thus Fuhrmann, "Die Mönchsgeschichten des Hieronymus," 82: "The last decades of the fourth century were a time of extreme love of experimentation: the Christian Latin writers attempted then to empower themselves with almost all forms of the ancient literary tradition and to reinscribe them with the meaning of the new religion. Jerome contributed to this process among others his three monks' histories—they are no small contribution, when one considers that with them Latin hagiography was founded.... The overlapping contexts [of Christian and pagan Greek literary practices on which Jerome's hagiographies draw] are patterned in turn on the romance and the biography, in their methods and forms." More recently, William Robins has explored the "remarkable period of experimentation in hagiographic writing" in the century after Constantine, commenting that "a generation of Latin writers in the late fourth and early fifth centuries reevaluated the narrative models available to the spiritual imagination, and among these models was the mode of romance" ("Romance and Renunciation at the Turn of the Fifth Century," *Journal of Early Christian Studies* 8, no. 4 [2000]: 531).

23. Attempts have, of course, been made. See, for example, the responses of Yves-Marie Duval and Jacques Fontaine to Fuhrmann's essay (Fuhrmann, "Die Mönchsgeschichten des Hieronymus," 94–96), which project a clean trajectory leading from Jerome's rhetorically excessive and self-consciously artful hagiographical juvenalia (Ep. 1 as well as the *Life of Paul*) to his more mature Lives, reflecting an overall increase in stylistic decorum, religious depth, and seriousness of historical purpose, and progressing steadily from the more modest essay into historiographic

writing represented by *On the Captive Monk* to the more ambitious *Life of Hilarion*, Jerome's culminating effort to put Palestinian and Syrian monasticism on the map for Western readers. Such developmental accounts are plausible but not, I am suggesting, inevitable or necessary; indeed, they impose extremely strong readings of the texts that suppress both complexity and difference at many points.

24. In what sense "queering"? Jerome's hagiographies resist both the generic conventions of romance and the social conventions of marriage and civic life. Implicit in the juxtaposition of ancient and contemporary texts and contexts—conveyed, for example, in the "anachronistic" depiction of ancient ascetic figures as "homosexual," "bisexual," or "just friends"—is an argument not only for the similarity or comparability of late (or post-) antiquity and late (or post-) modernity but also for a historical relation between the two, as I have argued in the Introduction.

25. Translations of the *Life of Paul* follow Paul B. Harvey, "Jerome, 'Life of Paul, the First Hermit,'" in *Ascetic Behavior in Greco-Roman Antiquity: A Sourcebook*, ed. Vincent L. Wimbush (Minneapolis: Fortress Press, 1990), 357–69. Latin texts for Jerome's hagiographies: W. Oldfather et al., *Studies in the Text Traditions of St. Jerome's Vitae Patrum* (Urbana: University of Illinois Press, 1943).

26. A parallel passage in Apuleius, *Metamorphoses* 8.22, may, however, allow us to hazard a guess: "Then he had the man stripped, smeared all over with honey, and bound fast to a fig-tree, where a countless horde of ants (hurrying trickles of quick-life) had built their nests in the rotten trunk. As soon as the ants smelt the honey sweating out of the man's body, they swarmed upon him; and with tiny multitudinous nips they shred by shred pincered out all his flesh and entrails. The man hung on this cross of slow torture till he was picked quite clean."

27. We should not miss the skill with which Jerome has turned a potential embarrassment—Paul's flight from martyrdom—into an advantage. As Pierre Leclerc, "Antoine et Paul: Métamorphose d'un héros," in *Jérôme entre l'occident et l'orient*, ed. Yves-Marie Duval (Paris: Études Augustiniennes, 1988), 260, points out, whereas the *Life of Antony* positions asceticism as a compensatory substitute for the still-much-desired martyrdom of blood, Jerome's *Life of Paul* more aggressively displaces martyrdom by inscribing asceticism as Paul's active choice. I would also suggest that Jerome's withholding of death from his "martyrs" already begins to effect their conversion to asceticism, thereby anticipating the appearance of Paul.

28. Pierre Leclerc, "Antoine et Paul," gives a nuanced account of the literary techniques by which Jerome's *Life of Paul* "metamorphoses" the image of the hermit by repeatedly demoting the Antony of the Athanasian Life to the place of second-best, in relation to Jerome's distinctly "Roman" (as well as romantic) hero Paul.

29. For example, J. N. D. Kelly, *Jerome: His Life, Writings and Controversies* (London: Duckworth, 1975), 61, who finds the second martyr's tale "quite unnecessarily introduced" into the *Life of Paul*, suggesting that its presence is accounted for by Jerome's "obsession with sex"—an "obsession" that Kelly is seemingly able to distinguish clearly from "the ecstatic nature of his piety" evidenced in other parts of the text.

30. Kech, *Hagiographie*, 33, refers to this pervasive narrative technique as the "Hang zur Vereinzelung," that is, the tendency to isolation or fragmentation, characterized by "concentration, selection, concretization and objectification," aiming for an effect of "urgent immediacy."

31. Fuhrmann, "Die Mönchsgeschichten des Hieronymus," 72, n. 1, notes that an account of the tyrant-resisting, tongue-biting woman is also preserved in Iamblichus, *Life of Pythagoras* 194, and Brent D. Shaw, "Body/Power/Identity: Passions of the Martyrs," *Journal of Early Christian Studies* 4, no. 3 (1996): 276, n. 19, records the parallel case of Leaena the *meretrix* in Pliny, *Natural History* 7.23.87. See also Tertullian, *Apology* 50.7–8, and Ambrose, *On Virgins* 1.4.17, where the woman is identified as a Pythagorean.

32. Philomela, it will be recalled, was raped by her sister's husband, Tereus, who severed her tongue to prevent her telling of his deed; she wove a tapestry depicting the rape (and thereby brought about Tereus's discovery and punishment) and was later transformed into either a swallow or a nightingale.

33. This is not to say that male tongue biters are altogether absent from ancient texts. Diogenes Laertius records the cases of Zeno and Anaxarchus, who bit off their tongues and spat them in the faces of tyrants (*Lives of the Philosophers* 9.27, 59). In addition, there is no lack of parallel accounts of men resisting the unwanted sexual advances of women, e.g., in the *Testament of Joseph*, discussed by Shaw, "Body/Power/Identity," 280, and the *Acts of John*, discussed by T. Adamik, "The Influence of the Apocryphal Acts on Jerome's Lives of Saints," in *The Apocryphal Acts of John*, ed. Jan Bremmer (Kampen, The Netherlands: Kok Pharos, 1995), 177. I am suggesting, however, that both tongue biting and defense against sexual aggression are culturally "feminine" stances and more often associated with female figures.

34. See J. N. Adams, *The Latin Sexual Vocabulary* (Baltimore: Johns Hopkins University Press, 1982), 69–70, on the term's association with castration.

35. Cf. Kech, *Hagiographie*, 35: "For the information concerning the condition of the tools as well as the dating to Cleopatra's time must be evaluated as an understandable attempt on the part of the author to anchor the idyll in the realm of the real with characteristic embellishments." "Realism" itself—although crucial to Jerome's generic disruptions as well as his competitive claims for Paul—cannot, I think, adequately account for all the queer particularities of this passage.

36. Aeneas and Dido—another couple in a cave—may also be invoked. Antony will quote Virgil to Paul later in this text.

37. Patricia Cox Miller, "Jerome's Centaur: A Hyper-Icon of the Desert," *Journal of Early Christian Studies* 4, no. 2 (1996): 227, borrowing the language of W. J. T. Mitchell.

38. Miller, "Jerome's Centaur," 217.

39. Miller, "Jerome's Centaur," 218.

40. As Kech, *Hagiographie*, 24, points out, the phrase also serves to diffuse the contradiction between Jerome's repeated insistence on historical veracity, on the one hand, and his introduction of recognizably "poetic" figures, on the other. This reading does not, however, go far enough, failing to acknowledge either Jerome's interest in actively problematizing "the real" or the disruptive effects of his refusal to clarify the status of the centaur.

41. Jerome's desert exceeds the dimensions of its Athanasian prototype in large part by gorging itself on other literary bodies, both classical and biblical; see the fine study by Paul B. Harvey, "Saints and Satyrs: Jerome the Scholar at Work," *Estratto da Athenaeum: Studi di Letteratura e Storia dell'Antichità* 86, no. 1 (1998): 35–56.

42. Miller, "Jerome's Centaur," 222–23.

43. "Paul is at his window and, below, Antony plays the role of the transfixed lover" (Leclerc, "Antoine et Paul," 263). The phrase "a little more ridiculous" actually occurs in Leclerc's description of Antony's noisy stumbling in the cave (262). Jerome's own address to Heliodorus in Ep. 14.1–2 (contemporaneous with the *Life of Paul*) is perhaps more conventional in its erotic tropes. He represents himself (less ridiculously?) as the active pursuer of an appropriately hesitant "younger" man: "With the pretty ways of a child you then softened your refusal by soothing words, and I, being off my guard, knew not what to do. . . . I could not conceal my eagerness by a show of indifference." Continuing to represent Heliodorus as youthful, he remonstrates: "What keeps you, effeminate soldier, in your father's house?" Jerome's lover's appeal to Rufinus in Ep. 3 (also contemporaneous) is somewhat more complex, turning on his own passively eroticized immobility and his desire to lure Rufinus into the role of pursuer: "Oh if only the Lord Jesus Christ would suddenly transport me to you . . . , with what a close embrace would I clasp your neck, how fondly would I press kisses upon that mouth. . . . But as I am unworthy (not that you should so come to me but) that I should so come to you . . . , I send this letter to meet you instead of coming myself, in the hope that it may bring you hither to me caught in the meshes of love's net." By the end of the letter, the two men are represented in the more egalitarian terms of "friendship": "Love is not to be purchased, and affection has no price. The friendship which can cease has never been real."

44. The immediate reference is to Matthew 7.7/Luke 11.9. However, Song of Songs 5.2—"Hark! my beloved is knocking"—and Revelation 30.20—"Behold, I stand at the door and knock; if any man hear my voice and open the door, I will come in to him, and will sup with him, and he with me"—also hover in the background.

45. Harpham's reading of the play between the human body and the "natural setting" in Sasetta's painting surfaces the eroticism in this encounter: "Life in a cave also represents a renunciation of natural desire, the very type of which is anal intercourse. The cave—or anus—is the natural and human site of gender conversion or transformation" (Geoffrey Galt Harpham, "Asceticism and the Compensations of Art," in *Asceticism*, ed. Vincent L. Wimbush and Richard Valantasis [New York: Oxford University Press, 1995], 364).

46. Miller, "Jerome's Centaur," 229.

47. Kech, *Hagiographie*, 40–46, provides a nuanced reading of the complex power dynamics at work in Jerome's presentation of the encounter between Antony and Paul. If Paul's superiority is repeatedly asserted, Jerome's poetics effectively exonerate his polemics: the stylized speech, the disruptive, episodic mode of narration, and the idyllic scenography diffuse—without actually undoing—the hierarchically structured relationship of the two ascetics. By no means contesting but perhaps further complicating this reading, I might ask whether the highly charged and problematized (as well as fragmented) presentation of the inferior Antony in the conventionally superior role of the active lover, in relation to a (more or less) receptive Paul, does not partly destabilize the hierarchical positioning of the two men.

48. Cf. *Life of Antony*, 91, where the cloak is returned to Athanasius at Antony's death. Jerome is here quite pointedly redirecting the transmission of the Athanasian mantle of authority.

49. The second-century *Acts of Paul and Thecla*, for example, includes two episodes involving friendly lions; Dennis Ronald MacDonald, *The Legend and the Apostle: The Battle for Paul in Story and Canon* (Philadelphia: Westminster Press, 1983), 21–23, 35–36, discusses these in relation to the tale of Androclus and the lion, with attention to their folkloristic origins.

50. Interestingly, erotic interest is not among those "romantic" features of the text acknowledged by Coleiro—although he does mention the "sense of seduction [that] pervades the beauties of the garden of P.3," in the context of his discussion of Jerome's skill in imbuing "situations" and "scenes" with "feeling" (Coleiro, "St. Jerome's Lives," 177). Episodes in the *Life of Paul* that I have read as erotic tend to be categorized by Coleiro as instances of a general, nonerotic "romantic" tendency to "present the reader continually with unexpected situations"—for example, Paul's initial refusal to admit Antony into his cave, the two men's bickering over the breaking of the bread, Antony's encounter with Paul's praying corpse, and the miraculous arrival of the pair of leonine gravediggers. Concerning all these, Coleiro remarks tellingly, "The behaviour of characters is often too deep to be easily understood and they act in a wholly unexpected way" (173–74). Among recent studies focusing specifically on the *Life of Paul*, Harvey, "Saints and Satyrs," 39–40, suggests that Jerome adds "romantic coloring . . . to a didactic work to render it attractive to a broad audience," highlighting Jerome's mining of sources both classical and biblical and locating his self-consciously "scholarly" endeavors as a hagiographer in the context of his larger, innovative project "to create a Christian literature." Jerome's *Life of Paul* is, however, innovative not least *as a romance*, I am arguing; it is, adapting Leo Bersani's term, a counterpastoral (and thus a countererotic) romance (Leo Bersani, "Is the Rectum a Grave?" in *AIDS: Cultural Analysis, Cultural Activism*, ed. Douglas Crimp [Cambridge, Mass.: MIT Press, 1988], 215, 221). Note that Miller, "Jerome's Centaur," 216, resists the "romanticizing" interpretation not in order to reinscribe the historicity of the *Life of Paul* with Coleiro but rather to affirm its mythopoetic seriousness and complexity, an impulse with which I am in full sympathy.

51. Ever open to desire's corruption, Jerome represents his own body as "shattered" by his beloved Rufinus's departure—swiftly augmenting this representation with accounts of other loves found and lost in the Syrian desert (Ep. 3.1, 3).

52. Leo Bersani, *The Freudian Body: Psychoanalysis and Art* (New York: Columbia University Press, 1986), 102.

53. Bersani, *Freudian Body*, 110; see also 115–16, regarding "Freud's failure to develop a theory of sublimation." Jean-Luc Nancy, *The Inoperative Community*, 1986, ed. Peter Connor, trans. Peter Connor, Lisa Garbus, Michael Holland, and Simona Sawhney, Theory and History of Literature 76 (Minneapolis: University of Minnesota Press, 1991), 90, takes a different tack in making a similar point: "There is no sublimation of the heart, nor of love. Love is what it is, identical and plural, in all its registers or in all its explosions, and it does not sublimate itself, even when it is 'sublime.' It is always the beating of an exposed heart."

54. See Fuhrmann, "Die Mönchsgeschichten des Hieronymus," 64, and Robins, "Romance and Renunciation," 534.

55. "Syneisaktism, we think, offered to men and women a unique opportunity for friendships which involved a high degree of emotional and spiritual intimacy," notes Elizabeth Clark. "It is of interest in this regard that both Chrysostom and Jerome, outspoken critics of spiritual marriage, had longstanding relationships with women" (*Ascetic Piety and Women's Faith: Essays on Late Ancient Christianity*, Studies in Women and Religion [Lewiston, N.Y.: Edwin Mellen Press, 1986], 279).

56. Translations of the *Life of Malchus* are based on *St. Jerome: Letters and Select Works*, trans. W. H. Fremantle, Nicene and Post-Nicene Fathers, 2nd ser. 6 (reprint Grand Rapids, Mich.: Eerdmans, 1989), 315–18; I also had the benefit of consulting an unpublished translation by Paul Harvey.

57. Kech, *Hagiographie*, 162–63, understands the prolongation of the romance in terms of a "classical" three-stage narration of ascent—fall—re-ascent, in which Malchus may also serve as a "type" of the church.

58. Fuhrmann, "Die Mönchsgeschichten des Hieronymus," 66, notes parallels in romance literature. The tales of Christian virgin martyrs are perhaps a still closer parallel: see my "Reading Agnes: The Rhetoric of Gender in Ambrose and Prudentius," *Journal of Early Christian Studies* 3, no. 1 (1995): 25–46.

59. See Fuhrmann, "Die Mönchsgeschichten des Hieronymus," 63.

60. Indeed, as Paul Harvey points out, it most likely has a quite specific apologetic occasion, namely, the defense of his "romance" with Paula.

61. Kech, *Hagiographie*, 159–61, notes the allusion to the "curiosity" that evokes the first-person narrative in Apuleius's *Metamorphoses*.

62. Fuhrmann, "Die Mönchsgeschichten des Hieronymus," 63, n. 1.

63. Translations of the *Life of Hilarion* are based on Fremantle, *St. Jerome: Letters and Select Works*, 303–15.

64. Fuhrmann, "Die Mönchsgeschichten des Hieronymus," 48.

65. As Derek Krueger reminds me, this is not quite true: *Life of Antony* 14, depicting Antony's emergence from the fortress, virtually fetishizes the holy man's body. Yet it remains the case that the only visual detail provided is rather abstract, namely, that Antony was neither fat nor thin.

66. Compare Jerome's self-descriptions, for example, in Epp. 3, 22.

67. Antony, of course, has done time in a tomb (*Life of Antony* 8).

68. Cf. *Life of Antony* 14, where Antony emerges dramatically into public view after almost twenty years of solitude.

69. Fuhrmann, "Die Mönchsgeschichten des Hieronymus," 43.

70. A threat acknowledged by Kech, *Hagiographie*, 62, who refers to Jerome's need to counteract the fragmentation and lack of coherence of "a series of miracles that perhaps grows boring."

71. Fuhrmann, "Die Mönchsgeschichten des Hieronymus," 44.

72. Fuhrmann, "Die Mönchsgeschichten des Hieronymus," 50–54, suggests that Jerome competes successfully with the Athanasian *Life* in part by dipping more deeply into traditional (non-Christian) biographical representations of holy men as miracle workers. But see also Kech's analysis of the numerous biblical allusions woven into the fabric of Jerome's representation of the holy man as miracle worker (*Hagiographie*, 74–78).

73. And also by prior traditions of representing miracle workers; see Fuhrmann, "Die Mönchsgeschichten des Hieronymus," 49.

74. Kech, *Hagiographie*, 85, comments: "If one looks more closely at this place (ch. 43) and compares it with the Antonine mountain in Egypt, one makes an astonishing identification: the place where Hilarion ends his ascetic existence resembles that described in ch. 31 to such a degree that one glimpses in it a copy of the Antonine mountain; this not without irony, since Hilarion communicated to his disciple Hesychius his intention to leave Cyprus again and choose as the resting place of his old age one of the regions in Egypt inhabited by barbarians." See also 90–95. For Kech it is pilgrimage and the cult of the saints that link these two idyllic "places" with the themes of both wandering and miracle working.

75. Note references to Hilarion's "smiling" at 18, 20, 26, 41. See Kech, *Hagiographie*, 108–12, for a more soberly "edifying" reading of Hilarion's "laugh" or "smiling."

76. Fuhrmann, "Die Mönchsgeschichten des Hieronymus," 48, n. 1, notes: "With the temple Jerome may have thought of a Venus-shrine, as then with the words *Paphum urbem Cypri nobilem carminibus poetarum* (ch. 42) he presumably had in mind first of all Hor. *Carm.* I.30, 1–2; III 28, 13–15, and Verg. *Aen.* I 415."

77. Hélène Cixous, "Coming to Writing," in *"Coming to Writing" and Other Essays*, ed. Deborah Jenson (Cambridge, Mass.: Harvard University Press, 1991), 41.

78. Bersani, *Freudian Body*, 47. Translation of Mallarmé, "Afternoon of a Faun" reprinted by permission of Columbia University Press.

79. Bersani, *Freudian Body*, 48.

80. Bersani, *Freudian Body*, 49.

81. Bersani, *Freudian Body*, 49.

82. Bersani, *Freudian Body*, 49.

83. Bersani, *Freudian Body*, 50.

84. See Luce Irigaray, *This Sex Which Is Not One*, 1977, trans. Catherine Porter and Carolyn Burke (Ithaca, N.Y.: Cornell University Press, 1985), 171, with reference not to male "homosexuality" per se but rather to the masculinist (and indeed paradigmatically heterosexist) economy in which "the production of women, signs, and commodities is always referred back to men . . . , and they always pass from one man to another, from one group of men to another."

85. Bersani, "Is the Rectum a Grave?" 222.

86. Lynda Hart, *Between the Body and the Flesh: Performing Sadomasochism*, Between Men—Between Women: Lesbian and Gay Studies (New York: Columbia University Press, 1998), 87–90, offers a critical discussion of both Bersani's tendency to masculinize sexuality itself and his biological/anatomical essentialism.

87. Cf. my *"Begotten, Not Made": Conceiving Manhood in Late Antiquity*, Figurae: Reading Medieval Culture (Stanford, Calif.: Stanford University Press, 2000), 68–78, on the masculinization of the desert "city" in the Athanasian Life.

88. "Whose 'self' is shattered?" queries Lynda Hart, in response to Bersani. She goes on to suggest that performative s/m is less an attempt to "shatter" the ego than to "lose (self)-consciousness." "Paradoxically, people who are self-conscious are not really focusing on themselves but, rather, on the mirrors of the others who are watching them. . . . Thus self-consciousness is precisely what one has to lose in order to focus on oneself. It is a 'truism' that women are more inclined to this form of self-consciousness than men" (*Between the Body and the Flesh*, 99, 116).

Chapter 2. Dying for a Life: Martyrdom, Masochism, and Female (Auto)Biography

1. Ambrose compares Agnes favorably with a Pythagorean tongue biter; see also the reference to Agnes in Jerome, Ep. 130.5.

2. This comment occurs in the recorded discussion of Manfred Fuhrmann, "Die Mönchsgeschichten des Hieronymus: Formexperimente in erzählender Literatur," in *Christianisme et formes littéraires de l'antiquité tardive en occident*, ed. Manfred Fuhrmann, Entretiens sur l'Antiquité Classique (Geneva: Fondation Hardt, 1977), 94. Duval is not, it should be acknowledged, here addressing the issue of gender.

3. In Fuhrmann, "Die Mönchsgeschichten des Hieronymus," 96.

4. On eroticized representations of virgin martyrs, see my "Reading Agnes: The Rhetoric of Gender in Ambrose and Prudentius," *Journal of Early Christian Studies* 3, no. 1 (1995): 25–46.

5. This would not surprise many in the contemporary s/m community: "Usually it's the top that's burdened; usually it's the master who says [groan] 'Oh, I gotta whip her *again*.'... A *real* masochist never gets enough; they want it to go on 24 hours a day" (Bob Flanagan, as cited by Karmen MacKendrick, *Counterpleasures*, SUNY Series in Postmodern Culture [Binghamton: State University of New York Press, 1999], 131).

6. Brent D. Shaw, "Body/Power/Identity: Passions of the Martyrs," *Journal of Early Christian Studies* 4, no. 3 (1996): 274, n. 14.

7. Cf. the accounts of political torture analyzed by Elaine Scarry, *The Body in Pain: The Making and Unmaking of the World* (New York: Oxford University Press, 1985). Scarry explains the success of torture; texts of martyrdom perform its failure. As Judith Perkins puts it, with reference to Scarry's work: "Traditionally injuring other people, killing them, provided a method of establishing dominance.... But Christian discourse reverses this equation and thus redefines some of the most basic signifiers in any culture—the body, pain, and death" (*The Suffering Self: Pain and Narrative Representation in the Early Christian Era* [London: Routledge, 1995], 115).

8. For a discussion of the resurrections (or seeming resurrections) of the heroines in the novels of Chariton, Xenophon of Ephesus, and Achilles Tatius, among others, see G. W. Bowersock, *Fiction As History: Nero to Julian*, Sather Classical Lectures (Berkeley: University of California Press, 1994), 99–119.

9. J. H. D. Scourfield, *Consoling Heliodorus: A Commentary on Jerome, Letter 60* (Oxford: Clarendon Press, 1993), 27.

10. Lynda Coon, for example, names Ep. 108 Jerome's "*Vita Paulae*," though she also notes carefully that "Jerome's narrative of Paula's life employs the classical genres of funeral elegy, panegyric, and biography" (*Sacred Fictions: Holy Women and Hagiography in Late Antiquity*, Middle Ages Series [Philadelphia: University of Pennsylvania Press, 1997], 104, 103). Elizabeth Clark distinguishes between the "full blown *Vitae* (*Lives*), such as those of Melania the Younger, of Olympias, of Macrina, and of Syncletica" and "shorter accounts, such as Palladius's description of Melania the Elder in his *Lausiac History*, and Jerome's depiction of his friends (and patrons) Paula in Epistle 108 and Marcella in Epistle 127" ("The Lady Vanishes: Dilemmas of a Feminist Historian After 'the Linguistic Turn,'" *Church History* 67, no. 1 [1998]: 15).

11. For example, Pierre Maraval, "La Vie de sainte Macrine de Grégoire de Nysse: continuité et nouveauté d'un genre littéraire," in *Du héros païen au saint chrétien*, ed. Gérard Freyburger and Laurent Pernot (Paris: Institut d'Études Augustiniennes, 1997), 138: "c'est la première biographie chrétienne consacrée à une femme."

12. Derek Krueger, "Writing and the Liturgy of Memory in Gregory of Nyssa's Life of Macrina," *Journal of Early Christian Studies* 8, no. 4 (2000): 493, proposes that Gregory uses the peculiar phrase συγγραφική μακρηγορία not only to call attention to the complicated relation between writing and speech but also to pun on the name Macrina: "Thus, Gregory calls his composition a 'written Macrina-speech,' its own genre, a history masquerading as a letter, written words imaging oral words." This observation is made in the context of a larger argument regarding the innovativeness and generic indeterminacy of Gregory's hagiographical composition.

13. Note that Gregory is in effect defamiliarizing and problematizing an ambiguity that is virtually inherent to literary biography. As Tomas Hägg and Philip Rousseau observe, biography, lacking the performative context of the panegyric speech or funeral oration, "to find a corresponding natural home, sometimes masqueraded as a letter" ("Introduction: Biography and Panegyric," in *Greek Biography and Panegyric in Late Antiquity*, ed. Tomas Hägg and Philip Rousseau [Berkeley: University of California Press, 2000], 2). See also Krueger, "Writing and the Liturgy of Memory," 492: "It is worth recalling that at the time Gregory was writing, Christian biography had not yet developed into a generic tradition. Athanasius's *Life of Antony*, written in 357, also presents itself as a letter. Other contemporary Christian biographical narratives took the form of encomia . . . or funeral orations."

14. Pierre Maraval, *Grégoire de Nyssa: Vie de Sainte Macrine*, Sources Chrétiennes (Paris: Éditions du Cerf, 1971), 21–34. On the importance of the representation of Macrina as a martyr, see also Monique Alexandre, "Les nouveaux martyrs: Motifs martyrologiques dans la vie des saints et thèmes hagiographiques dans l'éloge des martyrs chez Grégoire de Nysse," in *The Biographical Works of Gregory of Nyssa*, ed. Andreas Spira (Philadelphia: Philadelphia Patristic Foundation, 1984), 33–42.

15. Anthony Meredith, "A Comparison Between the Vita Sanctae Macrinae of Gregory of Nyssa, the Vita Plotini of Porphyry, and the De Vita Pythagorica of Iamblichus," in Spira, *Biographical Works of Gregory of Nyssa*, 190.

16. Elena Giannarelli, "La biografia femminile: Temi e problemi," in *La donna nel pensiero cristiano antico*, ed. Umberto Mattioli (Genoa: Marietti, 1992), 240.

17. Hers is of course not the only alluring corpse. As Arnaldo Momigliano observes: "Macrina had decided to remain faithful to her dead fiancé and never to marry. On her deathbed the love for the young boy is transfigured into love for the celestial bridegroom—for Jesus himself. . . . The transformation of the love for the earthly fiancé into love for the celestial bridegroom is inseparable from Macrina's Socratic role in leading Gregory towards the contemplation of the world of immortality and resurrection. Between these two moments there is the stark and uncompromising *contemplatio mortis* with its explicit details" ("The Life of St. Macrina by Gregory of Nyssa," in *On Pagans, Jews, and Christians* [Middletown, Conn.: Wesleyan University Press, 1987], 343).

18. Elizabeth Clark critically interrogates the influence of the romance on

female hagiography, in the face of the overwhelming maleness of the biographical genre: "Although the *Vitae* of early Christian women stress their overcoming of femaleness and subsequent incorporation into a world of 'maleness,' it is still dubious whether the classical *bioi* furnished any fitting models for these *Lives*. And if they did not, did any other form of ancient literature, more focused on women, suggest itself as a more suitable model? Might not the Hellenistic romance, with its concentration on lively heroines, provide a better paradigm for a Vita like Melania's?" (*The Life of Melania the Younger: Introduction, Translation, and Commentary*, Studies in Women and Religion [Lewiston, N.Y.: Edwin Mellen Press, 1984], 155). Returning to the question more recently, Clark reaffirms that "the Vitae of early Christian women saints share many features with the relatively new genre of novels or romances popular in this period rather than with classical biography that focused on the public activity of statesmen and generals: women did not operate in a public, political sphere." She also notes, however, the influence of the philosophical biography, as measured by the fact that all ancient female hagiographical subjects are represented as teachers and purveyors of wisdom (Clark, "Lady Vanishes," 16, 22).

19. See Giannarelli, "Biografia femminile," 231–35, and "Women and Miracles in Christian Biography (IVth–Vth Centuries)," *Studia Patristica* 25 (1993): 377. As Momigliano points out, Gregory of Nyssa, even when composing a funeral oration on his brother Basil, elides rather than emphasizes his close relationship to his male subject: "While Macrina is brought near by a biography, Basil is made distant by a panegyric" ("Life of St. Macrina," 339). David Konstan, "How to Praise a Friend: St. Gregory of Nazianzus's Funeral Oration for St. Basil the Great," in Hägg and Rousseau, *Greek Biography and Panegyric*, 164–66, 173–74, similarly emphasizes Gregory's careful distancing of Basil, noting his willingness, however, "to incorporate references to himself in describing the magnanimity of his deceased sister."

20. As Nicole Loraux argues, the classical Greek funeral oration is not only a distinctly masculine form of discourse, suppressing the "feminine" element of lament in favor of praise; it is also directed toward the praise of the public deeds and virtues of elite *men* (*The Invention of Athens: The Funeral Oration in the Classical City*, trans. Alan Sheridan [Cambridge, Mass.: Harvard University Press, 1986], 42–56). Martin Heinzelmann's study of the relation of hagiography to the funeral oration in the Latin tradition also strongly emphasizes the public, male context of both panegyric speeches and the related literary genre of biography ("Neue Aspeckte der biographischen und hagiographischen Literatur in der lateinischen Welt [1.-6. Jahrhundert]," *Francia* 1 [1973]: 27–44).

21. Moreover, as noted by Hägg and Rousseau, "it is precisely the transgression of the boundaries between" biography and panegyric, "their interaction and coalescence, that is most in evidence" in late antiquity ("Introduction: Biography and Panegyric," 1).

22. Although two of Gregory of Nazianzus's other funeral orations also honor family members (and a third his intimate friend Basil), it is only in the oration for his sister that he rhetorically problematizes the act of praising a close relative, explicitly marking his speech as in need of justification (3). The "Life" of Gorgonia is notable not only for its apologetic tone but also for its distinctly martyrial and ascetic representation of a matron who seems to have died peacefully. Gorgonia's

suffering is thematized via vivid representations of a carriage accident that left her "crushed and mangled internally and externally in bone and limb" (15) and a mysterious illness that rendered her periodically fevered and paralyzed (17). Her death itself is described at some length, represented as the culmination of her desire "to be purely joined with her fair One and embrace her Beloved completely, and I will even add, her Lover" (19), an event taking on "the semblance of a sacred ceremony" (22). As for her husband, Gregory comments dismissively, "If you wish me to describe him briefly, let me say that he was her husband, for I know not what further need be added" (20).

23. Susan Ashbrook Harvey, "Sacred Bonding: Mothers and Daughters in Early Syriac Hagiography," *Journal of Early Christian Studies* 4, no. 1 (1996): 27–56, remarks upon the surprising incidence of portraits of mothers and daughters in ancient hagiographical texts, surprising for at least two reasons—namely, the scant attention given to the mother-daughter relationship in ancient literature more generally and the tendency of ascetic literature to undermine biological kinship in favor of the family of faith.

24. I am here distinguishing my reading from the typological approach best represented by Elena Giannarelli, *La tipologia femminile nella biografia e nell'autobiografia cristiana del IVo secolo* (Rome: Instituto Storico Italiano per il Medio Evo, 1980).

25. MacKendrick, *Counterpleasures*, 102.

26. The English translation of Ep. 108 follows *St. Jerome: Letters and Select Works*, trans. W. H. Fremantle, Nicene and Post-Nicene Fathers, 2nd ser. 6 (reprint Grand Rapids, Mich.: Eerdmans, 1989), 195–212. Latin text: I. Hilberg, *Sancti Eusebii Hieronymi Epistulae*, Corpus Scriptorum Ecclesiasticorum Latinorum 55 (Vindobonae: Verlag der österreichischen Akademie der Wissenschaften, 1996), 306–51.

27. See the fine discussion of Paula's "eyes of faith" in Georgia Frank, *The Memory of the Eyes: Pilgrims to Living Saints in Christian Late Antiquity*, Transformation of the Classical Heritage (Berkeley: University of California Press, 2000), 104–14.

28. I hope this question does not seem facile. Although scholarly study of ancient Christian pilgrimage has proliferated in recent years (see, e.g., the recent work of Frank, *Memory of the Eyes*), there is still a widespread tendency to assume the figure of the pilgrim as a "given" when studying texts like Jerome's Ep. 108. In fact, Jerome's "Life of Paula," like his *Life of Hilarion*, participates heavily in the imaginative construction of pilgrimage. More work remains to be done on the remarkably consistent privileging of *female* figures in the earliest literature of pilgrimage.

29. Thus, in this case at least, I would resist Frank's notion that pilgrimage to places (as opposed to holy people) is linear or goal-directed (*Memory of the Eyes*, 8–9).

30. Coon, *Sacred Fictions*, 108.

31. For Steven D. Driver, "The Development of Jerome's Views on the Ascetic Life," *Recherches de théologie ancienne et médiévale* 62 (1995): 68, Jerome's ongoing revision of the ascetic ideal in the direction of greater "moderation" is the primary interpretive context for his "criticism of Paula."

32. Cf. Clark, "Lady Vanishes," 31.

33. Thus MacKendrick, *Counterpleasures*, 126: "In the everyday (nonecstatic) economy of investment, expenditure is loss (and desire is lack, founded upon the

need to fill what is empty, replace what is lost). This is precisely the economy of productivity, the teleological economy found in the security of the center.... Within the economy of joy, power seeks expenditure; materially, as force, the body expends itself. But in expenditure is its increase; the more it expends itself (its energy, its vitality, its strength) the more powerful it becomes."

34. I borrowed the title of this section from Krueger, "Writing and the Liturgy of Memory," 485. The English translation of the *Life of Macrina* follows Gregory of Nyssa, *Ascetical Works*, trans. Virginia Woods Callahan, Fathers of the Church 46 (Washington, D.C.: Catholic University of America Press, 1967), 163–91. Greek text: Maraval, *Grégoire de Nyssa: Vie de Sainte Macrine*.

35. My reading of the *Life of Macrina* is greatly indebted to the exploration of its Homeric allusions by Georgia Frank, "Macrina's Scar: Homeric Allusion and Heroic Identity in Gregory of Nyssa's *Life of Macrina*," *Journal of Early Christian Studies* 8, no. 4 (2000): 522.

36. On the prehistory of the (Pauline) athletic metaphor in martyrial literature—where it is frequently applied to women—see Elena Giannarelli, *La vita di S. Macrina: Introduzione, traduzione, e note* (Milan: Figlie di S. Paolo, 1988), 42–48.

37. Teresa M. Shaw, *The Burden of the Flesh: Fasting and Sexuality in Early Christianity* (Minneapolis: Fortress Press, 1998), 239, notes the contrast between Jerome and the more Origenistic writers of the east. Whereas Gregory and others represent the ascetic woman as "masculine," Jerome avoids this image: "Jerome's virgin never forgets for a minute that she is burdened by female flesh."

38. Krueger, "Writing and the Liturgy of Memory."

39. MacKendrick, *Counterpleasures*, 108.

40. Patricia Cox Miller, *Dreams in Late Antiquity: Studies in the Imagination of a Culture* (Princeton, N.J.: Princeton University Press, 1994), 237.

41. As Krueger, "Writing and the Liturgy of Memory," 492, remarks, Gregory here represents Macrina's speech as a kind of writing, whereas he has previously presented his own writing as a (Macrinan) speech.

42. See Clark, "Lady Vanishes," 24, on the possible influence of Wisdom traditions on the portrait of Macrina as philosophic teacher.

43. The maternal representation of the virginal Macrina is strong and consistent. See, e.g., the discussion of Giannarelli, *Vita di S. Macrina*, 49–56.

44. Frank, "Macrina's Scar," 516–25.

45. Frank, "Macrina's Scar," 528–29.

46. See Miller, *Dreams in Late Antiquity*, 239–40: "Despite all his metaphors of light, Gregory seems reluctant to let Macrina's body disappear in a blaze of glory.... The body is still there as a sign.... Her body was thus a formal analogue to Gregory's dream.... Indeed, Macrina's body and Gregory's dream can hardly be separated, because it was the dream that had given him 'eyes to see' the truth of his sister's body."

47. Miller, *Dreams in Late Antiquity*, 237.

48. Frank, "Macrina's Scar," 529.

49. See my *"Begotten, Not Made": Conceiving Manhood in Late Antiquity*, Figurae: Reading Medieval Culture (Stanford, Calif.: Stanford University Press, 2000), 112–22.

50. Shoshana Felman, *What Does a Woman Want? Reading and Sexual Difference* (Baltimore: Johns Hopkins University Press, 1993), 54–55.

51. "Diving into the Wreck," cited by Felman, *What Does a Woman Want?* 137.

52. The English translation of *Confessions* follows Augustine, *Confessions*, trans. R. S. Pine-Coffin (London: Penguin Books, 1961). Latin text: P. Knoll, ed., *Sancti Aureli Augustini. Confessionum Libri Tredecim*, Corpus Scriptorum Ecclesiasticorum Latinorum 33 (Vindobonae: F. Tempsky, 1896).

53. I am not simply opposing—though I am strongly glossing—the insightful remarks of Francoise Lionnet, *Autobiographical Voices: Race, Gender, Self-Portraiture* (Ithaca, N.Y.: Cornell University Press, 1989), 63: "Just as the universe was created out of nothingness, Augustine re-creates himself, the plenitude of his being, out of an experience of emptiness. This re-creation is mediated through the process of reading, which allows him to absorb in his human, historical, linear dimension the timelessness of eternal substance. The result of that re-creation is his own book, the *Confessions*."

54. I presuppose Elizabeth Clark's critique of the positivistic trend in scholarship on Monica. Monica, as we encounter her in Augustine's *Confessions*, is always already a creature of text (as is her son, for that matter). See Elizabeth A. Clark, "Rewriting Early Christian History," in *Theology and the New Histories*, ed. Gary Macy (Maryknoll, N.Y.: Orbis Books, 1998), 89–111.

55. Book 8's conversion seems all the more *conclusive* in that it supplements and apparently perfects an earlier vision that followed his reading not of Scripture but of "some of the books of the Platonists" (7.9, 10)—a transient illumination of intellect that proves after all no match for daily drag of habit (7.17). But cf. Lionnet, *Autobiographical Voices*, 56: "It is through the death of the mother's body that Augustine can be resuscitated in spirit: the death of the mother is the culmination of his narrative of a life of sin and marks his liberation from earthly and bodily connections."

56. Augustine notes elsewhere Pelagius's dismay upon reading *Confessions* 10, where he repeatedly addresses God: "Give what you command, and command what you will." In the same place Augustine recalls his emphasis in the *Confessions* on the role of "the faithful and daily tears of my mother" in securing his salvation, seeming to link divine and maternal grace very closely indeed (*On the Gift of Perseverance* 20.53).

57. This seems to be the opinion of Margaret R. Miles, *Desire and Delight: A New Reading of Augustine's Confessions* (New York: Crossroad, 1992), 129, who argues that in books 10–13 (in contrast to 1–9), "author's pleasure and reader's pleasure do not coincide." "Longing for peace, he is pleasured by finding its trustworthy source.... Yet the *Confessions* does not reproduce Augustine's pleasure in his reader."

58. Danuta Shanzer, "Latent Narrative Patterns, Allegorical Choices, and Literary Unity in Augustine's Confessions," *Vigiliae Christianae* 46, no. 1 (1992): 45.

59. Cf. Francoise Lionnet's framing of the "unity" of the *Confessions*: "For Augustine, the project of narrating his own life is doomed to a dead end and must be redeemed by his reading of the sacred texts. This reading is a mode of revelation or illumination quite different from the experience of ecstasy (that is, the vision at Ostia or the unsuccessful attempts at atemporal contemplation of the "One" in book

7, which momentarily abolish time and give him a taste of eternity)" (*Autobiographical Voices*, 39).

60. Shanzer, "Latent Narrative Patterns," 53.

61. John J. Winkler, *Auctor and Actor: A Narratological Reading of Apuleius's The Golden Ass* (Berkeley: University of California Press, 1985), 273.

62. Winkler, *Auctor and Actor*, 179, 124.

63. Hans Joachim Mette, "Curiositas," in *Festschrift Bruno Snell zum 60. Geburtstag* (Munich: Beck, 1956), 228, proposes that the first ten books of Augustine's *Confessions* correspond to, and are intended to recall, the first ten books of Apuleius's *Golden Ass*—itself a crucial mediator of a negativized conception of "curiosity." Pierre Courcelle, *Les Confessions de Saint Augustin dans la tradition littéraire* (Paris: Études Augustiniennes, 1963), 103–07, extends the comparison of the treatment of curiosity and conversion in the two works without, however, considering similarities in the texts' endings, in the use of female figures, or in the development of hermeneutical ambivalence—the aspects of primary interest to me.

64. Victor Schmidt, "Reaktionen auf das Christentum in den Metamorphosen des Apuleius," *Vigiliae Christianae* 51, no. 1 (1997): 51–71.

65. In the following passage Augustine simultaneously identifies *The Golden Ass* as autobiographical composition, by assuming the identity of the narrator Lucius and the author Apuleius, and insinuates doubts about its veracity: "This is what Apuleius, in the work bearing the title *The Golden Ass*, describes as his experience, that after taking a magic potion he became an ass, while retaining his human mind. But this may be either fact or fiction" (*City of God* 18.18). Modern scholars have hotly debated the question of whether *Augustine*'s autobiography is "fact" or "fiction." (For one summary, see Colin Starnes, *Augustine's Conversion: A Guide to the Argument of Confessions I–IX* [Waterloo, Ontario: Wilfrid Laurier University Press, 1990], 277–89). Shanzer rightly questions the assumption underlying the sharp framing of alternatives—namely, that to invoke a literary topos is to engage in "falsehood": "We should not rule out the possibility that life may imitate literature" ("Latent Narrative Patterns," 43). One might further question her own easy distinction between "literature" and "life."

66. The links with the Apuleian Venus are strengthened by the links with the Virgilian Venus, as argued persuasively by Eric J. Ziolkowski, "St. Augustine: Aeneas' Antitype, Monica's Boy," *Literature and Theology* 9, no. 1 (1995): 11–23 (though I cannot agree with his idealizing reading of Augustine's portrait of Monica in book 9).

67. Derrida's reinscription of Augustine's text may be less disruptive than he indicates: "not that I dare link what he says about confession with the deaths of our respective mothers, ... for my mother was not a saint" ("Circumfession," in *Jacques Derrida*, Geoffrey Bennington and Jacques Derrida [Chicago: University of Chicago Press, 1993], 18–19). Of course, my claim that Augustine's text (like Derrida's) sustains an ambivalent portrayal of the maternal figure is by no means identical with the claim—simultaneously positivistic and misogynistic—that Monica was a bad mother, as reflected, e.g., in Rodolph Yanney, "The Sins of Saint Monica," *Coptic Church Review* 19, no. 3 (1998): 75–82.

68. Peter Brown, *Augustine of Hippo: A Biography* (Berkeley: University of California Press, 1967), 164.

69. As pointed out by Sabine MacCormack, *The Shadows of Poetry: Vergil in the Mind of Augustine*, Transformation of the Classical Heritage (Berkeley: University of California Press, 1998), 97–99, Augustine's close paralleling of the Virgilian account of Aeneas's departure from Carthage highlights both similarities and differences, "for whereas Dido had been ensnared and then deserted by treacherous gods, Monica's prayers were heard and fulfilled beyond her most cherished hopes by the Christian God."

70. Augustine here not only disrupts the "Dido narrative" but also implicitly compares Monica to another Virgilian figure, namely, the mother of the hero Euryalus, who also followed her son "across land and sea" (*Aeneid* 9.42), as noted by MacCormack, *Shadows of Poetry*, 130.

71. Kevin Coyle's revival of the suggestion that it is only Monica who should be understood to achieve mystical heights at Ostia—a suggestion based in part on the improbability of "l'extase à deux"—is not without merit (J. Kevin Coyle, "In Praise of Monica: A Note on the Ostia Experience of Confessions IX," *Augustinian Studies* 13 [1982]: 87–96). At the same time, the charged intimacy of the scene seems particularly well described by the phrase "l'extase à deux."

72. Book 11 of Apuleius's "goddess novel" ends, perplexingly, with a brief vision of the *god* Osiris. While describing his quest for Wisdom, Augustine is of course addressing himself to his "Lord God" throughout the *Confessions*. At the same time, the second-person address of the *Confessions* renders the divine addressee effectively gender-ambiguous.

73. Lynda Hart, *Between the Body and the Flesh: Performing Sadomasochism*, Between Men—Between Women: Lesbian and Gay Studies (New York: Columbia University Press, 1998), 6.

74. Maurice Blanchot, *The Instant of My Death*, trans. Elizabeth Rottenberg (Stanford, Calif.: Stanford University Press, 2000), 11.

75. Jacques Derrida, *Demeure: Fiction and Testimony*, trans. Elizabeth Rottenberg (Stanford, Calif.: Stanford University Press, 2000), 16.

76. Derrida, *Demeure*, 46–47.

77. Derrida, *Demeure*, 27–28.

78. Derrida, *Demeure*, 97.

79. Felman, *What Does a Woman Want?* 15.

80. Felman, *What Does a Woman Want?* 17.

81. Derrida, *Demeure*, 16.

82. MacKendrick, *Counterpleasures*, 155.

Chapter 3. Hybrid Desire: Empire, Sadism, and the Soldier Saint

1. As Clare Stancliffe, *St. Martin and His Hagiographer: History and Miracle in Sulpicius Severus* (Oxford: Clarendon Press, 1983), 79, puts it, "the *Vita* is anything but the work of a *disengagé* author."

2. E.-Ch. Babut, *Saint Martin de Tours* (Paris: Librairie Ancienne H. Champion, 1912).

3. Jacques Fontaine, *Sulpice Sévère. Vie de Saint Martin: Introduction, texte,*

traduction, et commentaire, 3 vols., Sources Chrétiennes 133–35 (Paris: Éditions du Cerf, 1967–69), 1: 97–134

4. Fontaine, *Sulpice Sévère*, 1: 210.

5. Stancliffe, *St. Martin and His Hagiographer*, 9.

6. This is Hart's (re)framing of the complex Lacanian concept of the real, "which is not only that brute, inscrutable core or essence, but also the incredible, non-ontological phantasm." Hart shifts from Lacan's notion of the real as what is *excluded* by the symbolic order to an understanding of the real "as that which *evades* the frame of representation and its (en)closures" (*Between the Body and the Flesh: Performing Sadomasochism*, Between Men—Between Women: Lesbian and Gay Studies [New York: Columbia University Press, 1998], 67). See also Judith Butler's critique of Slavoj Žižek's appropriation of the Lacanian real. Resisting the absolutizing of the (excluded) real, she queries: "How might these ostensibly constitutive exclusions be rendered less permanent, more dynamic?" (*Bodies That Matter: On the Discursive Limits of "Sex"* [New York: Routledge, 1993], 189).

7. See Hart, *Between the Body and the Flesh*, 161: "The future anterior is the grammar of the Real." See also Derrida, *Demeure: Fiction and Testimony*, trans. Elizabeth Rottenberg (Stanford, Calif.: Stanford University Press, 2000), 49, citing Blanchot: "'The imminence of what has always already taken place': this is an unbelievable tense. . . . Imminence, the instance of what will already have taken place, will be in question." Finally, see Stephen May, *Stardust and Ashes: Science Fiction in Christian Perspective* (London: Society for Promoting Christian Knowledge, 1998), 16: "What we are offered is a world conclusively different to the familiar one, even if what is presented can be argued . . . to be a plausible development of present tendencies, readily visible now to those with eyes to see. In so far as this is the case, science fiction claims to be prophetic literature, pointing out what is to happen before it happens."

8. The apocalypticism evident in Sulpicius's Martinian writings (see Stancliffe, *St. Martin and His Hagiographer*, 238, 248) is still more explicit in his *Chronicles* (in which Martin plays a minor but by no means insignificant role). On the importance of the eschatological intertext of 2 Timothy 3 for the *Chronicles*, see my *Making of a Heretic: Gender, Authority, and the Priscillianist Controversy*, Transformation of the Classical Heritage (Berkeley: University of California Press, 1995), 134–38.

9. In contemporary science fiction, the queering of sex/gender and also the emergence of distinctly feminist science fiction is associated with the controversial "New Wave" and the rise of cyberpunk sf. For helpful overviews of the convergence of feminism and science fiction, see Robin Roberts, *A New Species: Gender and Science in Science Fiction* (Urbana: University of Illinois Press, 1993), 1–14, and Jenny Wolmark, *Aliens and Others: Science Fiction, Feminism, and Postmodernism* (Iowa City: University of Iowa Press, 1994), 1–26. A focus on sexuality is sustained in the essays collected in Donald Palumbo, *Erotic Universe: Sexuality and Fantastic Literature* (New York: Greenwood Press, 1986).

10. Donna J. Haraway, *Modest_Witness@Second_Millennium.FemaleMan_Meets_OncoMouse: Feminism and Technoscience* (New York: Routledge, 1997), 14. Science fiction more generally centers around the efforts (frequently violent) of humanity to control nature; see, e.g., May, *Stardust and Ashes*, 23–24.

11. Stancliffe, *St. Martin and His Hagiographer*, 93, emphasizes the lack of a conversion as a point of contrast with the Lives of Antony and Hilarion. Raymond Van Dam, *Leadership and Community in Late Antique Gaul* (Berkeley: University of California Press, 1985), 124, likewise emphasizes Martin's militant interpretation of Christianity: "Martin remained a soldier throughout his life, . . . and his background was particularly evident in the identification of his version of monastic Christianity with the Christian army."

12. Hart, *Between the Body and the Flesh*, 123, with reference to "lesbian dicks."

13. In exceeding convention it participates, however, in the establishment of a new convention. Derek Krueger, "Hagiography As Ascetic Practice in the Early Christian East," *Journal of Religion* 79 (1999): 216–32, offers a careful analysis of the significance of tropes of authorial humility, which are nearly ubiquitous in hagiographical literature: "Rather than a rhetoric of false modesty, it might be more accurate to speak of a rhetoric of longed-for humility" (221).

14. Here Sulpicius implicitly compares himself to the "apostolic" gospel writers. At the same time, references to the low style of the text—the voluntary humiliation of the word—have christological resonance; see Krueger, "Hagiography As Ascetic Practice," 230.

15. English translations of Sulpicius's works follow *The Works of Sulpicius Severus*, trans. Alexander Roberts, Nicene and Post-Nicene Fathers, 2nd ser. 11 (reprint, Grand Rapids, Michigan: Wm. B. Eerdmans, 1991). Latin editions: Fontaine, *Sulpice Sévère*, and Karl Halm, *Sulpicii Severi Libri Qui Supersunt*, Corpus Scriptorum Ecclesiasticorum Latinorum 1 (Vindobonae: C. Geroldi Filium Bibliopolam Academiae, 1866).

16. Fontaine, *Sulpice Sévère*, 2: 479.

17. Fontaine, *Sulpice Sévère*, 2: 508.

18. Stancliffe, *St. Martin and His Hagiographer*, 141–48. See also the more general discussion of the Life as part of a broader linking of "militarism and martyrdom" in Mathew Kuefler, *The Manly Eunuch: Masculinity, Gender Ambiguity, and Christian Ideology in Late Antiquity*, Chicago Series on Sexuality, History, and Society (Chicago: University of Chicago Press, 2001), 111–17.

19. Stancliffe, *St. Martin and His Hagiographer*, 93–95.

20. Van Dam, *Leadership and Community*, 48. Van Dam's discussion of the Bagaudae emphasizes "the fuzziness of the distinction between legitimate and illegitimate authority at a local level" (19); he associates (the historical) Martin with figures like the Bagaudae—or the Emperor Julian (119–28). I am here highlighting resonance between the social situation that Van Dam describes and the textual dynamics of the *Life of Martin*, in which the distinctions between demon and angel, emperor and bandit, bandit and bishop, are simultaneously invoked and transgressed. Cf. the discussion of the figure of the bandit in earlier novelistic texts in Keith Hopwood, "'All That May Become a Man': The Bandit in the Ancient Novel," in *When Men Were Men: Masculinity, Power, and Identity in Classical Antiquity*, ed. Lin Foxhall and John Salmon (London: Routledge, 1998), 195–204. Hopwood notes (but does not exploit the implications of) the interchangeability of the figures of the soldier and the bandit: if bandits are "just like real soldiers, but in parodic imitation," real soldiers may also appear in disguise as bandits (197). Fontaine, *Sulpice Sévère*, 2: 560–65, affirms the historical realism of the dramatic scenario of capture

by bandits while also noting its novelistic overtones, especially evident in comparison with the central books of Apuleius's *Metaphorphoses* (4–6), as well as its resonance with earlier Christian literary traditions of banditry and conversion, not least the figures of the "bandits" crucified alongside Jesus. The Talmudic figure of Resh Lakish constitutes an intriguing (and perhaps roughly contemporaneous) parallel instance of the narrative of conversion from brigandry; see Daniel Boyarin, *Unheroic Conduct: The Rise of Heterosexuality and the Invention of the Jewish Man*, Contraversions: Critical Studies in Jewish Literature, Culture, and Society (Berkeley: University of California Press, 1997), 127–38.

21. Fontaine, *Sulpice Sévère*, 2: 613–16.

22. Fontaine offers a dense reading of the intertextual echoes in this passage, noting the resonance with Matthew 9.23–26 as well as with 2 Kings 4.32–37, while also highlighting Sulpicius's subtle departures from such scripts, for example, the hyperbolic and incongruous reference to "bolting the doors" and the reversed sequencing of acts of thaumaturgy and prayer, which emphasize the bold initiative of the militant holy man (*Sulpice Sévère*, 2: 618–23). Here as elsewhere Sulpicius employs a familiar method of typological exegesis that is arguably definitive of hagiographical literature as postbiblical composition, as Derek Krueger has suggested. Cf. Krueger's claim that Theodoret's use of biblical typology "asserted the biblical character of his own day," interpreting "the stories he tells within the text as reenactments of biblical narrative" while at the same time positioning his own text as "a reenactment, a mimesis of biblical narrative" ("Typological Figuration in Theodoret of Cyrrhus's Religious History and the Art of Postbiblical Narrative," *Journal of Early Christian Studies* 5, no. 3 [1997]: 412–13).

23. See Fontaine, *Sulpice Sévère*, 2: 705–6.

24. Fontaine, *Sulpice Sévère*, 2: 720.

25. As pointed out by Fontaine, who notes further that this links the incident closely with the prior account of the misrecognized funeral procession, in which Fontaine also detects hints of Cybelan association (*Sulpice Sévère*, 2: 721–25, 741–42).

26. Fontaine, *Sulpice Sévère*, 2: 760.

27. Paulinus, Ep. 11.11, describes the *Vita* as Sulpicius's "fleece"; in return for Sulpicius's own textual gift, Christ will clothe the author with his own wool. See Stancliffe, *St. Martin and His Hagiographer*, 76.

28. A frequently replayed scene that Fontaine, *Sulpice Sévère*, 3: 1054–56, suggests, attains a virtually liturgical status in monastic circles.

29. Fontaine discusses the intertextual significance of the story of the "rich young man" (Matt.19.16–22) for the exemplary role of Paulinus in Martin's "sermon" (*Sulpice Sévère*, 3:1056–66). With Jerome's *Life of Paula* in mind, one might recall also the greater extravagance of the widow's renunciation.

30. See the fine discussion of Sulpicius's subtle rewriting of Petrine failure as triumph over nature in Fontaine, *Sulpice Sévère*, 3: 1136–37.

31. This insistence that Paul is not "less" but "greater" hints audaciously at the apostle's superiority not only to Peter (thus, Fontaine, *Sulpice Sévère*, 3: 1139) but also to Christ himself, who in the Matthean passage traversed not the depths but the surface of the depths. If Paul's three days and nights in the sea (blatantly borrowed from Jonah and only tenuously anchored in the text of 2 Cor. 11) displace Christ's three

days in the tomb (cf. Matt. 12.39–41), so does Martin (as "Paul") displace Christ in Sulpicius's text, which, like most early Lives of men, is marked by the suppression of overt christological interest, or rather by the saint's displacement of Christ. (Cf. *Dialogues* 3.10, where Sulpicius names Martin the rival of the Savior in miracle working). See Krueger's discussion in "Typological Figuration" of hagiography's tendency to extend typological exegesis in such a way that biblical figures—even, I am suggesting, the figure of Christ—are understood to refer (and thus also to defer) to the saints.

32. Reference to shipwreck at sea is in 2 Cor. 11.25, to robbers in 11.26, to hunger and exposure in 11.27.

33. See the discussion of the intricate intertextuality of Sulpicius's subtle "romanizing" of the vision of Rev. 1.12–19, with special reference to the "Dream of Scipio," in Fontaine, *Sulpice Sévère*, 3: 1190–96.

34. Fontaine, *Sulpice Sévère*, 3: 1298.

35. Stancliffe, *St. Martin and His Hagiographer*, 105–7.

36. Cf. M. M. Bakhtin, *The Dialogic Imagination: Four Essays*, 1975, trans. Caryl Emerson and Michael Holquist (Austin: University of Texas Press, 1981), 24–26, on the Socratic dialogues and the birth of the novel.

37. Stancliffe, *St. Martin and His Hagiographer*, 81–82.

38. Cf. the remarks of Fontaine, *Sulpice Sévère*, 3: 1291, comparing the "Egyptian" animal miracles related by Postumianus, with their emphasis on the reconciliation of humanity with nature, to Martin's exercise of power over the animals (e.g., *Dialogues* 2.9, 3.3).

39. Cf. my *Making of a Heretic*, 145–48, where I earlier explored Sulpicius's extreme privatization of women in the *Dialogues* from a more social-historical perspective, with reference to his own interest in distinguishing himself from ascetic men like Priscillian (or Jerome), who were critiqued for their free relations with ascetic women; I also hinted at the paradoxical privileging of the female virgin as the idealized role model for ascetic men, who were effectively opting for a "feminized" role by withdrawing from public life. Considered from the perspective of Sulpicius's erotics, the text now seems to me even more complex in its gendered dynamics: the hyperbolic patriarchalism expressed in the voice of the Gaul exceeds mere apologetic concerns and occupies, as I shall continue to argue, an unstable position in the text, simultaneously embraced and disavowed; furthermore, it must be interpreted in relation to the strong homoerotic dynamics of the *Dialogues* and the Martinian corpus more generally.

40. Anne McClintock, *Imperial Leather: Race, Gender, and Sexuality in the Colonial Contest* (New York: Routledge, 1995), 138. 1995 was a good year for the publication of studies of modern colonialism and sexuality. See also Christopher Lane, *The Ruling Passion: British Colonial Allegory and the Paradox of Homosexual Desire* (Durham, N.C.: Duke University Press, 1995), Ann Laura Stoler, *Race and the Education of Desire: Foucault's History of Sexuality and the Colonial Order of Things* (Durham, N.C.: Duke University Press, 1995), and Robert J. C. Young, *Colonial Desire: Hybridity in Theory, Culture, and Race* (London: Routledge, 1995). For my purposes, Lane's work is particularly suggestive, given its exploration of the complex play of male homoerotic desire in literary texts in which military figures frequently loom large.

41. McClintock, *Imperial Leather*, 202, 143.

42. Cf. the concept of "contact zone" as "the space of colonial encounters . . . in which peoples geographically and historically separated come into contact with each other and establish ongoing relations, usually involving conditions of coercion, radical inequality, and intractable conflict," developed by Mary Louise Pratt, *Imperial Eyes: Travel Writing and Transculturation* (London: Routledge, 1992), 6–7. As Young, *Colonial Desire*, 5, notes, earlier postcolonial criticism has tended to construct "two antithetical groups, the colonizer and colonized, self and Other"; "it is only recently that cultural critics have begun to develop accounts of the commerce between cultures that map and shadow the complexities of its generative and destructive processes."

43. Homi K. Bhabha, *The Location of Culture* (London: Routledge, 1994), 44–45.

44. Cf. Pratt, *Imperial Eyes*.

45. In an analysis of the earlier period of Roman imperial domination, Simon Swain details the process by which "Greekness" was reinvented through the grammatical and narrative cultural projects of provincial elites who thereby subtly resisted their subjection to imperial authority while at the same time assimilating in such a way as to effectively subject "Rome" to the terms of "the Greek." In emphasizing the sheer resilience and aristocratic conservatism of Hellenism, Swain perhaps underplays the menace to Roman imperialism represented by this subversively mimetic act of cultural countercolonization; he also suppresses the remarkable multiplication and diversity of hybrid positionalities mobilized by an ethnic "Greekness" not only denaturalized in the service of cultural transcendence but also itself internally subverted in rhetorical and literary performances that glory in (frequently highly ironic) acts of temporal and spatial displacement (Simon Swain, *Hellenism and Empire: Language, Classicism, and Power in the Greek World, AD 50–250* [Oxford: Clarendon Press, 1996]). A finer attunement to the subversive complexity of constructions of Greekness is exhibited by Simon Goldhill, "Introduction. Setting an Agenda: 'Everything Is Greek to the Wise,'" in *Being Greek Under Rome*, ed. Simon Goldhill (Cambridge: Cambridge University Press, 2001), 1–25; see also the other essays in this volume.

46. Cf. the contrast drawn between western and eastern (or "Greek") patterns of romanization by Greg Woolf, "Becoming Roman, Staying Greek: Culture, Identity and the Civilizing Process in the Roman East," *Proceedings of the Cambridge Philological Society* 40 (1994): 116–43: "The desire to demonstrate a complete rejection of past savagery made the cultural transformation of the west much less selective than in the east" (128). The more complete adoption of Roman identity in (some parts of) Spain and Gaul, for example, entailed appropriation of the "notion that Greeks were over-civilized, and that Romans were balanced between barbarism and decadence" (121).

47. Note the closely parallel "postcolonial" reading of asceticism, demonology, sexuality, and ethnicity in David Brakke, "Ethiopian Demons: Male Sexuality, the Black-Skinned Other, and the Monastic Self," *Journal of the History of Sexuality* 10, nos. 3–4 (2001): 501–35.

48. McClintock, *Imperial Leather*, 149.

49. Hart, *Between the Body and the Flesh*, 85–86, 91.
50. Hart, *Between the Body and the Flesh*, 160.
51. Cf. Wolmark, *Aliens and Others*, 117–21, regarding cyberpunk's reinscription of a masculinist transcendence.
52. Wolmark, *Aliens and Others*, 6–16, provides a critical analysis of the pessimistic readings of recent science fiction by apocalyptic theorists of the "postmodern" Frederic Jameson and Jean Baudrillard.
53. Haraway, *Modest Witness*, 8, 269.
54. See Donna J. Haraway, *Simians, Cyborgs, and Women: The Reinvention of Nature* (New York: Routledge, 1991), 149, 151.
55. Haraway, *Modest Witness*, 267.

Chapter 4. Secrets of Seduction: The Lives of Holy Harlots

1. Sebastian P. Brock and Susan Ashbrook Harvey, *Holy Women of the Syrian Orient*, 1987, 2nd ed. (Berkeley: University of California Press, 1998), 27.
2. Brock and Harvey, *Holy Women of the Syrian Orient*, 40–41.
3. Maria Kouli, "Life of St. Mary of Egypt," in *Holy Women of Byzantium: Ten Saints' Lives in English Translation*, ed. Alice-Mary Talbot (Washington, D.C.: Dumbarton Oaks Research Library and Collection, 1996), 66. In his paper "Mary the Egyptian: Sources and Purpose," Paul B. Harvey makes a plausible case for Sophronian authorship (or redaction), suggesting that the Greek Life "aimed at affirming the significance of the Feast of the Exaltation of the Cross at the Holy Sepulcher church in Jerusalem within the context of the iconoclastic controversy as that conflict occurred in a Judaean ambiance."
4. Lynda L. Coon, *Sacred Fictions: Holy Women and Hagiography in Late Antiquity*, Middle Ages Series (Philadelphia: University of Pennsylvania Press, 1997), 84.
5. As Patricia Cox Miller points out, Pelagia and Mary of Egypt are not "presented as prostitutes in Roman legal, social, and economic terms, despite the presence of the term *meretrix* in the titles of their stories." She elaborates: "Neither is attached to a *leno*, a pimp, or indeed to any man, unlike most prostitutes who had very little control over their bodies and were subject to legal regulation and disabilities. In fact neither Mary nor Pelagia takes money in exchange for sex." "Is There a Harlot in This Text? Asceticism and the Grotesque," *Journal of Medieval and Early Modern Studies* 33, 3 (2003). For a detailed account of legal regulations and disabilities, see Thomas A. J. McGinn, *Prostitution, Sexuality, and the Law in Ancient Rome* (New York: Oxford University Press, 1998).
6. For example, the tales of Thais, Paesia, and two anonymous women, translated by Benedicta Ward, *Harlots of the Desert: A Study of Repentance in Early Monastic Sources* (Kalamazoo, Mich.: Cistercian Publications, 1978), 76–84.
7. Ward, *Harlots of the Desert*, 1–25.
8. Coon, *Sacred Fictions*, 94.
9. Coon, *Sacred Fictions*, 27.
10. Coon, *Sacred Fictions*, 80–81. On Syriac interpretations of the "sinful woman" (which, notably, do not identify her with Mary Magdalene), see Susan

Ashbrook Harvey, "Why the Perfume Mattered: The Sinful Woman in Syriac Exegetical Tradition," in *In Dominico Eloquio/In Lordly Eloquence: Essays on Patristic Exegesis in Honor of Robert Louis Wilken*, ed. Paul M. Blowers, Angela Russel Christman, David G. Hunter, and Robin Darling Young (Grand Rapids, Mich.: Eerdmans, 2002), 69–89.

11. Coon, *Sacred Fictions*, 77. As Ward, *Harlots of the Desert*, 7, notes, the "sinful" woman who repents is not only Eve but also the unfaithful Israel, frequently chastised for her "harlotry" in the prophetic texts of the Hebrew Bible.

12. Coon, *Sacred Fictions*, 74.

13. Brock and Harvey, *Holy Women of the Syrian Orient*, 20–21, 25.

14. Cf. Chapter 2 above, regarding the de-eroticizing tendency in readings of earlier women's Lives.

15. An exception is Miller, "Is There a Harlot?"

16. Jane Miller, *Seductions: Studies in Reading and Culture* (Cambridge, Mass.: Harvard University Press, 1991), 22–23.

17. Jean Baudrillard, *Seduction*, 1979, trans. Brian Singer (New York: St. Martin's Press, 1990), 14.

18. References are to the English translation of the Syriac life in Brock and Harvey, *Holy Women of the Syrian Orient*, 27–39. The Latin Life is the basis of the English translations of Helen Waddell, *The Desert Fathers* (Ann Arbor: University of Michigan Press, 1936), 189–201, and Ward, *Harlots of the Desert*, 85–101.

19. Miller, *Seductions*, 21.

20. Cf. the stark account of Paesia, contained in the sayings tradition regarding John the Dwarf: "The parents of a young girl died and she was left an orphan.... She decided to make her house a hospice for the use of the fathers of Scetis.... Some wicked men came to see her and turned her aside from her aim. She began to live an evil life to the point of becoming a prostitute" (Ward, *Harlots of the Desert*, 77).

21. See also the closely parallel Talmudic account of Rabbi Meʿir, who dressed as a soldier to visit a virgin in a brothel, a passage discussed (with reference to the trickster role played not only by the rabbi but also by the virgin) by Daniel Boyarin, *Dying for God: Martyrdom and the Making of Christianity and Judaism* (Stanford, Calif.: Stanford University Press, 1999), 72.

22. Here again the narrative parallels the account of Paesia and John the Dwarf; see Ward, *Harlots of the Desert*, 77–78.

23. Brock and Harvey, *Holy Women of the Syrian Orient*, 28.

24. Derek Krueger, *Symeon the Holy Fool: Leontius's Life and the Late Antique City*, Transformation of the Classical Heritage (Berkeley: University of California Press, 1996).

25. Note also that Leontius's *Life of John the Almsgiver* relates a parallel story of a monk who solicits prostitutes, as discussed by Krueger, *Symeon the Holy Fool*, 67.

26. On "hysteria" and the (seduced) "feminine," see, for example, Luce Irigaray, *Speculum of the Other Woman*, 1974, trans. Gillian C. Gill (Ithaca, N.Y.: Cornell University Press, 1985), 37–39, and Irigaray, *This Sex Which Is Not One*, 1977, trans. Catherine Porter and Carolyn Burke (Ithaca, N.Y.: Cornell University Press, 1985), 136–39.

27. Jane Gallop, *The Daughter's Seduction: Feminism and Psychoanalysis* (Ithaca, N.Y.: Cornell University Press, 1982), 79.

28. Zoja Pavloskis, "The Life of St. Pelagia the Harlot: Hagiographic Adaptation of Pagan Romance," *Classical Folia* 30 (1976): 142.

29. Miller, "Is There a Harlot?"

30. Cf. Pavloskis, "Life of St. Pelagia," 143, regarding Pelagia's apparent "nakedness."

31. References are to the English translation of the Syriac Life in Brock and Harvey, *Holy Women of the Syrian Orient*, 40–62. The Latin text is the basis of the English translations of Ward, *Harlots of the Desert*, 57–75, and Waddell, *Desert Fathers*, 173–88.

32. Ward, *Harlots of the Desert*, 63. See also resonances with similar scenes in pagan novels, as noted by Pavloskis, "Life of St. Pelagia," 141.

33. Pavloskis, "Life of St. Pelagia," 144, points out that Nonnos here makes the deacon his confidant, "much like the stock figure of the hero's friend in romance— a person who provides an opportunity for the lover to voice his passion."

34. Ward, *Harlots of the Desert*, 64.

35. Joyce Salisbury, *Church Fathers, Independent Virgins* (London: Verso, 1991), 100.

36. Pavloskis, "Life of St. Pelagia," 145.

37. Susanna Elm, "Marking the Self in Late Antiquity: Inscriptions, Baptism and the Conversion of Mimes," in *Stigmata-Koerperinschriften*, ed. B. Vinken and B. Menken (Weimar, 2003) emphasizes the Life's emphasis on the religio-magical power of baptism (and behind that, the power of bishop and emperor) to "reinscribe" or "transcribe" social identity. Late antique "conversion," she argues, was less a matter of an "interior" transformation or of the emergence of a newly "interiorized" sense of self than of the enactment of a decisive shift in social role. This argument highlights the power of the Life of an actress to convey an account of social conversion—not only because of the dramatic character of the social relocation involved but also because of the power of tropes of performativity to communicate changes in social roles.

38. Miller, "Is There a Harlot?"

39. As noted by Evelyne Patlagean, "L'histoire de la femme déguisée en moine et l'évolution de la sainteté féminine à Byzance," *Studi medievali* 17 (1976): 606: "The eunuch participates in spiritual virility without being subjected to a sexual category; he transcends the distinction of the sexes, from which he is liberated. The appearance of a eunuch thus signifies at once more and less for a woman than the use of men's clothing condemned by the Council of Gangra." More recently, Stephen J. Davis, "Crossed Texts, Crossed Sex: Intertextuality and Gender in Early Christian Legends of Holy Women Disguised as Men," *Journal of Early Christian Studies* 10, no. 1 (2002): 22, also remarks on the conjunction of the figures of female transvestite and eunuch: "Given the ancient perception of eunuchs as liminal figures, it is significant that, in their legends, transvestite female saints are often mistaken for eunuchs during their lives as monks." For a more extended discussion of the significance of the disturbingly ambiguous figure of the eunuch in late ancient Christian discourses of masculinity, see Mathew Kuefler, *The Manly Eunuch: Masculinity,*

Gender Ambiguity, and Christian Ideology in Late Antiquity, Chicago Series on Sexuality, History, and Society (Chicago: University of Chicago Press, 2001).

40. Cf. the careful exploration of the theme of the grotesque in Miller, "Is There a Harlot?"

41. Brock and Harvey, *Holy Women of the Syrian Orient*, 21, 24.

42. For example, Ward, *Harlots of the Desert*, 62–63; Caroline Walker Bynum, *Holy Feast and Holy Fast: The Religious Significance of Food to Medieval Women* (Berkeley: University of California Press, 1987), 291; Salisbury, *Church Fathers, Independent Virgins*, 110; Gillian Cloke, *"This Female Man of God": Women and Spiritual Power in the Patristic Age, AD 350–450* (London: Routledge, 1995), 196; Coon, *Sacred Fictions*, 80. On female transvestite saints and travel, see Stephen J. Davis, *The Cult of Saint Thecla: A Tradition of Women's Piety in Late Antiquity*, Oxford Early Christian Studies (Oxford: Oxford University Press, 2001), 31–35, 141–48. John Anson, "The Female Transvestite in Early Monasticism: The Origin and Development of a Motif," *Viator: Medieval and Renaissance Studies* 5 (1974): 30, does not participate in this consensus, suggesting rather that the disguise of the transvestite saints serves the psychological purpose of masking the desire of their male authors: "Thus, quite simply, the secret longing for a woman in a monastery is brilliantly concealed by disguising the woman as a man and making her appear guilty of the very temptation to which the monks are most subject; finally, after she has been punished for their desires, their guilt is compensated by turning her into a saint with universal remorse and sanctimonious worship." Pursuing an analysis informed less by psychology than by cultural anthropology, Patlagean, "L'histoire de la femme," also focuses on the function of the figure for male authors and readers, arguing that the transgressive sanctity of the female transvestite signifies the liberation of the (masculinized) ascetic subject from the (feminized) realm of flesh, marriage, and sexual difference itself.

43. Marjorie Garber, *Vested Interests: Cross-Dressing and Cultural Anxiety* (1992; reprint New York: HarperCollins, 1993), 69–70. See also her specific discussion of transvestite female saints, including Pelagia, 213–17.

44. Miller, "Is There a Harlot?"

45. Davis, "Crossed Texts, Crossed Sex,." analyzes the "fragmentation and defeminization" of the transvestite saint's body (28). He does not intend "defeminization" to signify either gender neutrality or simple masculinization; his emphasis is rather on "the polyphony of gender discourses in the texts [of early Christian transvestite saint legends]—a fugal chorus of competing voices that echo in the ear of the reader" (36).

46. Miller, "Is There a Harlot?"

47. Note that some commentators have preferred to credit Nonnos with cowardice. Thus, Ward, *Harlots of the Desert*, 64, speculates that Pelagia and Nonnos plot her departure from Antioch because they fear the power of their own desire: "It was a love purified and strengthened by parting." The more delicate reading of Waddell, *Desert Fathers*, 176, likewise hints at the denial and renunciation that haunt this great love between bishop and harlot. Neither the Syriac nor the Latin text, however, clearly supports this interpretation. The audacity of desire claimed by both Nonnos and Pelagia is never, it seems to me, denied or renounced. Nor is their

"intense, erotic passion" a mere surface effect that masks the deeper truth of an authorial "intention" that is "clearly theological, not sexual," as Coon, *Sacred Fictions*, 81, suggests. The *Life of Pelagia*, it should by now be clear, consistently locates spiritual depth *within* the surface of seductive display and persistently resists the sharp distinction between the "theological" and the "sexual," the "sacred" and the "erotic."

48. References are to the English translation of the Greek by Kouli, "Life of St. Mary of Egypt," 65–93. Greek text: J. P. Migne, *Patrologia Graeca*, 87: 3697–726. The Latin version is the basis of the translation in Ward, *Harlots of the Desert*, 26–56.

49. Coon, *Sacred Fictions*, 86, points out that "the hagiographer intends his audience to view this initial contact between male confessor and female penitent as an allusion to Jesus' first encounter with the devil in the desert (Matt. 4.13)." That "encounter" is, however, significantly reinterpreted. Harvey, "Mary the Egyptian," notes the probable allusion to Jerome's *Life of Paul*, which offers a closer parallel: there Antony similarly encounters creatures—centaur and faun—which he first assumes (incorrectly, in at least the second case) to be demonic illusions.

50. Coon, *Sacred Fictions*, 85, 93.

51. Miller, "Is There a Harlot?"

52. As Coon, *Sacred Fictions*, 87, points out, Mary's distaff makes a mockery of this classical symbol of matronal chastity.

53. Derek Krueger pointed out to me that the thirty years of perfection may be an allusion to Christ's lifespan—thirty years, according to eastern traditions.

54. Coon, *Sacred Fictions*, 88.

55. Susan Harvey called my attention to the complexity of the intertextual resonances at this point in the text: Mary not only walks on water like Jesus (and with considerably more success than Peter; cf. Matt. 14.25–31) but also baptizes herself like Thecla (*Acts of Paul and Thecla* 34).

56. Cf. Coon, *Sacred Fictions*, 88.

57. Harvey, "Mary the Egyptian," directs attention to a previously unnoticed intertext that may help explain the transformation of Jerome's two lions into Sophronius's one—namely, the account of the Piancenzan pilgrim Antoninus, which records a visit to a Palestinian community of ascetic women who kept a pet lion and whose patroness was an anchorite named Mary (34). Harvey also suggests a possible logic of "sexism" operating, where a man requires two lions for burial, but a woman only one. I am proposing instead that the twin lions of Jerome's text reinforce the "coupling" of Paul and Antony, whereas the single lion of Sophronius's text emphasizes Mary's resistance to even a queerly asceticized marriage.

58. Coon, *Sacred Fictions*, 94.

59. Coon, *Sacred Fictions*, 91.

60. In her discussion of prostitute/porn star/performance artist Annie Sprinkle, whose words are quoted above, Linda Williams notes the now-familiar bind of a feminist theory that, in an attempt to protect the purity of female agency, paradoxically erases the agency of many women: "For sex workers have all too often been regarded by feminists as objectified victims of an aggressive, sadistic, masculine sexuality rather than as sexual agents themselves" ("A Provoking Agent: The

Pornography and Performance Art of Annie Sprinkle," in *Dirty Looks: Women, Pornography, Power*, ed. Pamela Church Gibson and Roma Gibson [London: British Film Institute, 1993], 178). Like Williams, I want to consider the possibility of a feminist agency arising out of the embrace (rather than the refusal) of patriarchy's sexual saturation of "woman." I by no means intend to deny that sex workers are *also* collective "victims of an aggressive, sadistic, masculine sexuality."

61. Baudrillard, *Seduction*, 7.
62. Baudrillard, *Seduction*, 9.
63. Baudrillard, *Seduction*, 6.
64. Baudrillard, *Seduction*, 10.
65. Baudrillard, *Seduction*, 12, 17, 79.
66. Baudrillard, *Seduction*, 81.
67. Sadie Plant, "Baudrillard's Woman: The Eve of Seduction," in *Forget Baudrillard?* ed. Chris Rojek and Bryan S. Turner (London: Routledge, 1993), 94.
68. Irigaray, *This Sex*, 150; emphasis in the original. Cf. the nuanced discussion of Irigaray's ambivalent "seduction" by Father Freud in Gallop, *Daughter's Seduction*, 56–79.
69. Irigaray reflects explicitly on the technique of mimicry that pervades her *Speculum*, in *This Sex*, 76–77.
70. Baudrillard, *Seduction*, 9.
71. See especially her essay "Any Theory of the 'Subject' Has Always Been Appropriated by the 'Masculine,'" in *Speculum*, 133–46.
72. Irigaray, *This Sex*, 152, 76, 77.
73. Irigaray, *Speculum*, 143–44.
74. Irigaray, *This Sex*, 29.
75. Irigaray, *This Sex*, 28–29.
76. Plant, "Baudrillard's Woman," 105. Cf. Jane Gallop, "French Theory and the Seduction of Feminism," in *Men in Feminism*, ed. Alice Jardine and Paul Smith (New York: Routledge, 1987), 114: "Baudrillard cannot seduce feminism with his truth, because he protects his truth from being seduced by feminism." Note that while I sympathize with the general aims of the "feminist reading" of Baudrillard offered by Victoria Grace, *Baudrillard's Challenge: A Feminist Reading* (London: Routledge, 2000), I do not find her apologetic rejection of the feminist critique of Baudrillard compelling; her claim, for example, that Plant's (to my mind, subtle) reading of Baudrillard's *Seduction* is merely tendentious seems itself notably tendentious (159–61), and the same could be said of her treatment of Irigaray's 1980 review of *Seduction*, which appeared in *Histoires d'Elles* 21 (161–62).
77. Baudrillard, *Seduction*, 81.
78. Baudrillard, *Seduction*, 22.
79. Georges Bataille, *Erotism: Death and Sensuality*, 1957, trans. Mary Dalwood (San Francisco: City Lights Books, 1986), 269.
80. Baudrillard, *Seduction*, 142.

Bibliography

Ancient Hagiographical Works

Augustine. *Confessions*. English translation R. S. Pine-Coffin. London: Penguin Books, 1961. Latin edition P. Knoll, *Sancti Aureli Augustini. Confessionum Libri Tredecim*. Corpus Scriptorum Ecclesiasticorum Latinorum 33. Vindobonae: F. Tempsky, 1896.

Gregory of Nyssa. *Life of Macrina*. English translation Virginia Woods Callahan, *Gregory of Nyssa: Ascetical Works*, 163–91. Fathers of the Church 46. Washington, D.C.: Catholic University of America Press, 1967. Greek edition Pierre Maraval. *Grégoire de Nyssa: Vie de Sainte Macrine*. Sources Chrétiennes 178. Paris: Éditions du Cerf, 1971.

Jerome. *Epistle* 108. English translation W. H. Fremantle, *St. Jerome: Letters and Select Works*, 195–212. Nicene and Post-Nicene Fathers, ser. 2, vol. 6. Grand Rapids, Mich.: Eerdmans, 1989. Latin edition I. Hilberg, *Sancti Eusebii Hieronymi Epistulae*, 306–51. Corpus Scriptorum Ecclesiasticorum Latinorum 55. Vindobonae: Verlag der österreichischen Akademie der Wissenschaften, 1996.

———. *Life of Hilarion*. English translation W. H. Fremantle, *St. Jerome: Letters and Select Works*, 303–15. Nicene and Post-Nicene Fathers ser. 2, vol. 6. Grand Rapids, Mich.: Eerdmans, 1989. Latin edition W. Oldfather et al., *Studies in the Text Traditions of St. Jerome's Vitae Patrum*, 42–59. Urbana: University of Illinois Press, 1943.

———. *Life of Paul*. English translation Paul B. Harvey, in *Ascetic Behavior in Greco-Roman Antiquity: A Sourcebook*, ed. Vincent L. Wimbush, 357–69. Minneapolis: Fortress Press, 1990. Latin edition W. Oldfather et al., *Studies in the Text Traditions of St. Jerome's Vitae Patrum*, 36–42. Urbana: University of Illinois Press, 1943.

———. *On Malchus, the Captive Monk*. English translation W. H. Fremantle, *St. Jerome: Letters and Select Works*, 315–18. Nicene and Post-Nicene Fathers, ser. 2, vol. 6. Grand Rapids, Mich.: Eerdmans, 1989. Latin edition W. Oldfather et al., *Studies in the Text Traditions of St. Jerome's Vitae Patrum*, 60–64. Urbana: University of Illinois Press, 1943.

Life of Mary, Niece of Abraham. English translation Sebastian P. Brock and Susan Ashbrook Harvey, in *Holy Women of the Syrian Orient*, 29–36. 1987; 2nd ed. Berkeley: University of California Press, 1998. Syriac edition T. J. Lamy, *Sancti Ephraem Syri Hymni et Sermones*, vol. 4, cols. 1–84. Malines, 1902.

Life of Mary of Egypt. English translation Maria Kouli, "Life of St. Mary of Egypt," in *Holy Women of Byzantium: Ten Saints' Lives in English Translation*, ed.

Alice-Mary Talbot, 65–93. Washington, D.C.: Dumbarton Oaks Research Library and Collection, 1996. Greek edition *Patrologia Graeca*, ed. J. P. Migne, vol. 87, cols. 3697–3726.

Life of Pelagia. English translation Sebastian P. Brock and Susan Ashbrook Harvey, in *Holy Women of the Syrian Orient*, 41–62. 1987; 2nd ed. Berkeley: University of California Press, 1998. Syriac edition J. Gildemeister, *Acta sanctae Pelagiae syriace*. Bonn, 1879.

Sulpicius Severus. *Dialogues*. English translation Alexander Roberts, *The Works of Sulpitius Severus*, 24–54. Nicene and Post-Nicene Fathers, ser. 2, vol. 11. Grand Rapids, Mich.: Eerdmans, 1991. Latin edition Karl Halm, *Sulpicii Severi Libri Qui Supersunt*, 152–216. Corpus Scriptorum Ecclesiasticorum Latinorum 1. Vindobonae: C. Geroldi Filium Bibliopolam Academiae, 1866.

———. *Life of Martin* and *Letters* 1–3. English translation Alexander Roberts, *The Works of Sulpitius Severus*, 3–23. Nicene and Post-Nicene Fathers, 2nd ser., vol. 11. Grand Rapids, Mich.: Eerdmans, 1991. Latin edition Jacques Fontaine, *Sulpice Sévère. Vie de Saint Martin: Introduction, texte, traduction, et commentaire*. Sources Chrétiennes 133–35. Paris: Éditions du Cerf, 1967–69.

Modern Works

Adamik, T. "The Influence of the Apocryphal Acts on Jerome's Lives of Saints." In *The Apocryphal Acts of John*, ed. Jan Bremmer, 171–82. Kampen, The Netherlands: Kok Pharos Publishing House, 1995.

Adams, J. N. *The Latin Sexual Vocabulary*. Baltimore: Johns Hopkins University Press, 1982.

Alexandre, Monique. "Les nouveaux martyrs: Motifs martyrologiques dans la vie des saints et thèmes hagiographiques dans l'éloge des martyrs chez Grégoire de Nysse." In *The Biographical Works of Gregory of Nyssa*, ed. Andreas Spira, 33–70. Philadelphia: Philadelphia Patristic Foundation, 1984.

Althaus-Reid, Marcella. *Indecent Theology: Theological Perversions in Sex, Gender, and Politics*. London: Routledge, 2000.

Anson, John. "The Female Transvestite in Early Monasticism: The Origin and Development of a Motif." *Viator: Medieval and Renaissance Studies* 5 (1974): 1–32.

Babut, E.-Ch. *Saint Martin de Tours*. Paris: Librairie Ancienne H. Champion, 1912.

Bakhtin, Mikhail M. *The Dialogic Imagination: Four Essays*. 1975. Trans. Caryl Emerson and Michael Holquist. Austin: University of Texas Press, 1981.

Bataille, Georges. *Erotism: Death and Sensuality*. 1957. Trans. Mary Dalwood. San Francisco: City Lights Books, 1986.

Baudrillard, Jean. *Forget Foucault*. 1977. New York: Semiotext(e), 1987.

———. *Seduction*. 1979. Trans. Brian Singer. New York: St. Martin's Press, 1990.

Bernauer, James. *Michel Foucault's Force of Flight: Toward an Ethics for Thought*. Contemporary Studies in Philosophy and the Human Sciences. Atlantic Highlands, N.J.: Humanities Press, 1990.

Bersani, Leo. *The Freudian Body: Psychoanalysis and Art*. New York: Columbia University Press, 1986.

———. "Is the Rectum a Grave?" In *AIDS: Cultural Analysis, Cultural Activism*, ed. Douglas Crimp, 197–222. Cambridge, Mass.: MIT Press, 1988.

Bhabha, Homi K. *The Location of Culture*. London: Routledge, 1994.

Blanchot, Maurice. *The Instant of My Death*. Trans. Elizabeth Rottenberg. Stanford, Calif.: Stanford University Press, 2000.

Bowersock, G. W. *Fiction as History: Nero to Julian*. Sather Classical Lectures. Berkeley: University of California Press, 1994.

Boyarin, Daniel. *Carnal Israel: Reading Sex in Talmudic Culture*. The New Historicism: Studies in Cultural Poetics 25. Berkeley: University of California Press, 1993.

———. *Dying for God: Martyrdom and the Making of Christianity and Judaism*. Figure: Reading Medieval Culture. Stanford, Calif.: Stanford University Press, 1999.

———. *Unheroic Conduct: The Rise of Heterosexuality and the Invention of the Jewish Man*. Contraversions: Critical Studies in Jewish Literature, Culture, and Society. Berkeley: University of California Press, 1997.

Boyarin, Daniel and Elizabeth A. Castelli. "Introduction: Foucault's *The History of Sexuality*: The Fourth Volume, or, a Field Left Fallow for Others to Till." *Journal of the History of Sexuality* 10, nos. 3–4 (2001): 357–74.

Brakke, David. "Ethiopian Demons: Male Sexuality, the Black-Skinned Other, and the Monastic Self." *Journal of the History of Sexuality* 10, nos. 3–4 (2001): 501–35.

Brock, Sebastian P. and Susan Ashbrook Harvey. *Holy Women of the Syrian Orient*. 1987. 2nd ed. Berkeley: University of California Press, 1998.

Brown, Peter. *Augustine of Hippo: A Biography*. Berkeley: University of California Press, 1967.

———. *The Body and Society: Men, Women, and Sexual Renunciation in Early Christianity*. Lectures on the History of Religions. New York: Columbia University Press, 1988.

Burrus, Virginia. *"Begotten, Not Made": Conceiving Manhood in Late Antiquity*. Figurae: Reading Medieval Culture. Stanford, Calif.: Stanford University Press, 2000.

———. *The Making of a Heretic: Gender, Authority, and the Priscillianist Controversy*. Transformation of the Classical Heritage. Berkeley: University of California Press, 1995.

———. "Reading Agnes: The Rhetoric of Gender in Ambrose and Prudentius." *Journal of Early Christian Studies* 3, no. 1 (1995): 25–46.

Burrus, Virginia and Catherine Keller. "Confessing Monica." In *Feminist Interpretations of Augustine*, ed. Judith Chelius Stark. Re-Reading the Canon. University Park: Pennsylvania State University Press, forthcoming.

Butler, Judith. *Bodies That Matter: On the Discursive Limits of "Sex"*. New York: Routledge, 1993.

———. *Gender Trouble: Feminism and the Subversion of Identity*. Thinking Gender. New York: Routledge, 1990.

Bynum, Caroline Walker. *Holy Feast and Holy Fast: The Religious Significance of Food to Medieval Women*. Berkeley: University of California Press, 1987.

Carrette, Jeremy R. *Foucault and Religion: Spiritual Corporality and Political Spirituality*. London: Routledge, 2000.

———. "Prologue to a Confession of the Flesh." In *Religion and Culture: Michel Foucault*, ed. Jeremy R. Carrette, 1–47. New York: Routledge, 1999.
Cixous, Hélène. "Coming to Writing." In *"Coming to Writing" and Other Essays*, ed. Deborah Jenson, 1–58. Cambridge, Mass.: Harvard University Press, 1991.
Clark, Elizabeth A. *Ascetic Piety and Women's Faith: Essays on Late Ancient Christianity*. Studies in Women and Religion. Lewiston, N.Y.: Edwin Mellen Press, 1986.
———. "The Lady Vanishes: Dilemmas of a Feminist Historian After 'the Linguistic Turn.'" *Church History* 67, no. 1 (1998): 1–31.
———. *The Life of Melania the Younger: Introduction, Translation, and Commentary*. Studies in Women and Religion. New York: Edwin Mellen Press, 1984.
———. *The Origenist Controversy: The Cultural Construction of an Early Christian Debate*. Princeton, N.J.: Princeton University Press, 1992.
———. *Reading Renunciation: Asceticism and Scripture in Early Christianity*. Princeton, N.J.: Princeton University Press, 1999.
———. "Rewriting Early Christian History." In *Theology and the New Histories*, ed. Gary Macy, 89–111. Maryknoll, N.Y.: Orbis Books, 1998.
Cloke, Gillian. *"This Female Man of God": Women and Spiritual Power in the Patristic Age, AD 350–450*. London: Routledge, 1995.
Coleiro, E. "St. Jerome's Lives of the Hermits." *Vigiliae Christianae* 11 (1957): 161–78.
Coon, Lynda L. *Sacred Fictions: Holy Women and Hagiography in Late Antiquity*. Middle Ages Series. Philadelphia: University of Pennsylvania Press, 1997.
Cooper, Kate. *The Virgin and the Bride: Idealized Womanhood in Late Antiquity*. Cambridge, Mass.: Harvard University Press, 1996.
Courcelle, Pierre. *Les Confessions de Saint Augustin dans la tradition littéraire*. Paris: Études Augustiniennes, 1963.
Cox, Patricia. *Biography in Late Antiquity: A Quest for the Holy Man*. Transformation of the Classical Heritage. Berkeley: University of California Press, 1983.
Coyle, J. Kevin. "In Praise of Monica: A Note on the Ostia Experience of *Confessions* IX." *Augustinian Studies* 13 (1982): 87–96.
Davidson, Arnold I. *The Emergence of Sexuality: Historical Epistemology and the Formation of Concepts*. Cambridge, Mass.: Harvard University Press, 2001.
Davis, Stephen J. "Crossed Texts, Crossed Sex: Intertextuality and Gender in Early Christian Legends of Holy Women Disguised as Men." *Journal of Early Christian Studies* 10, no. 1 (2002): 1–36.
———. *The Cult of Saint Thecla: A Tradition of Women's Piety in Late Antiquity*. Oxford Early Christian Studies. Oxford: Oxford University Press, 2001.
Derrida, Jacques. "Circumfession." In Geoffrey Bennington and Jacques Derrida, *Jacques Derrida*, 3–315. Chicago: University of Chicago Press, 1993.
———. *Demeure: Fiction and Testimony*. Trans. Elizabeth Rottenberg. Stanford, Calif.: Stanford University Press, 2000.
Driver, Steven D. "The Development of Jerome's Views on the Ascetic Life." *Recherches de théologie ancienne et médiévale* 62 (1995): 44–70.
Elm, Susanna. "Marking the Self in Late Antiquity: Inscriptions, Baptism and the Conversion of Mimes." In *Stigmata-Koerperinschriften*, ed. Barbara Vinken and B. Menken. Weimar, 2003.

Eribon, Didier. *Michel Foucault.* 1989. Trans. Betsy Wing. Cambridge, Mass.: Harvard University Press, 1991.
Felman, Shoshana. *What Does a Woman Want? Reading and Sexual Difference.* Baltimore: Johns Hopkins University Press, 1993.
Fontaine, Jacques. *Sulpice Sévère. Vie de Saint Martin: Introduction, texte, traduction, et commentaire.* 3 vols. Sources Chrétiennes 133–35. Paris: Éditions du Cerf, 1967–69.
Foucault, Michel. "About the Beginning of the Hermeneutics of the Self." 1980. In *Religion and Culture: Michel Foucault,* ed. Jeremy R. Carrette, 158–81. New York: Routledge, 1999.
———. "On the Government of the Living." 1980. In *Religion and Culture: Michel Foucault,* ed. Jeremy R. Carrette, 154–57. New York: Routledge, 1999.
———. *The History of Sexuality.* Vol. 1, *An Introduction.* 1976. Trans. Robert Hurley. New York: Vintage/Random House, 1978.
———. *The History of Sexuality.* Vol. 2, *The Use of Pleasure.* 1984. Trans. Robert Hurley. New York: Random House, 1985.
———. *The History of Sexuality.* Vol. 3, *The Care of the Self.* 1984. Trans. Robert Hurley. New York: Random House, 1986.
———. "Pastoral Power and Political Reason." 1979. In *Religion and Culture: Michel Foucault,* ed. Jeremy R. Carrette, 135–52. New York: Routledge, 1999.
———. "A Preface to Transgression." 1963. In *Religion and Culture: Michel Foucault,* ed. Jeremy R. Carrette, 57–71. New York: Routledge, 1999.
———. "Sexuality and Solitude." 1980. In *Religion and Culture: Michel Foucault,* ed. Jeremy R. Carrette, 182–87. New York: Routledge, 1999.
———. "Who Are You, Professor Foucault? (Interview with P. Caruso)." 1967. In *Religion and Culture: Michel Foucault,* ed. Jeremy R. Carrette, 87–103. New York: Routledge, 1999.
Fraade, Steven D. "Ascetical Aspects of Ancient Judaism." In *Jewish Spirituality: From the Bible to the Middle Ages,* ed. Arthur Green, 253–88. New York: Crossroad, 1986.
Francis, James A. *Subversive Virtue: Asceticism and Authority in the Second-Century Pagan World.* University Park: Pennsylvania State University Press, 1995.
Frank, Georgia. "Macrina's Scar: Homeric Allusion and Heroic Identity in Gregory of Nyssa's *Life of Macrina.*" *Journal of Early Christian Studies* 8, no. 4 (2000): 511–30.
———. *The Memory of the Eyes: Pilgrims to Living Saints in Christian Late Antiquity.* Transformation of the Classical Heritage, Berkeley: University of California Press, 2000.
Fuhrmann, Manfred. "Die Mönchsgeschichten des Hieronymus: Formexperimente in erzählender Literatur." In *Christianisme et formes littéraires de l'antiquité tardive en occident,* ed. Manfred Fuhrmann, 41–99. Entretiens sur l'Antiquité Classique. Geneva: Fondation Hardt, 1977.
Gallop, Jane. *The Daughter's Seduction: Feminism and Psychoanalysis.* Ithaca, N.Y.: Cornell University Press, 1982.
———. "French Theory and the Seduction of Feminism." In *Men in Feminism,* ed. Alice Jardine and Paul Smith, 111–15. New York: Routledge, 1987.
Gane, Mike, ed. *Baudrillard Live: Selected Interviews.* London: Routledge, 1993.

Garber, Marjorie. "Bisexuality and Celebrity." In *The Seductions of Biography*, ed. Mary Rhiel and David Suchoff, 13–30. New York: Routledge, 1996.

———. *Vested Interests: Cross-Dressing and Cultural Anxiety*. 1992. New York: HarperCollins, 1993.

Giannarelli, Elena. "La biografia femminile: temi e problemi." In *La donna nel pensiero cristiano antico*, ed. Umberto Mattioli, 223–45. Genova: Marietti, 1992.

———. *La tipologia femminile nella biografia e nell'autobiografia cristiana del IVo secolo*. Rome: Instituto Storico Italiano per il Medio Evo, 1980.

———. *La vita di S. Macrina: introduzione, traduzione e note*. Milan: Figlie di S. Paolo, 1988.

———. "Women and Miracles in Christian Biography (IVth–Vth Centuries)." *Studia Patristica* 25 (1993): 376–80.

Goldhill, Simon. "Introduction. Setting an Agenda: 'Everything Is Greek to the Wise.'" In *Being Greek Under Rome*, ed. Simon Goldhill, 1–25. Cambridge: Cambridge University Press, 2001.

Grace, Victoria. *Baudrillard's Challenge: A Feminist Reading*. London: Routledge, 2000.

Hägg, Tomas and Philip Rousseau. "Introduction: Biography and Panegyric." In *Greek Biography and Panegyric in Late Antiquity*, ed. Tomas Hägg and Philip Rousseau, 1–28. Berkeley: University of California Press, 2000.

Halperin, David. *One Hundred Years of Homosexuality and Other Essays on Greek Love*. New York: Routledge, 1990.

———. *Saint Foucault: Towards a Gay Hagiography*. New York: Oxford University Press, 1995.

Haraway, Donna J. *Modest Witness@Second_Millennium.FemaleMan_Meets_OncoMouse: Feminism and Technoscience*. New York: Routledge, 1997.

———. *Simians, Cyborgs, and Women: The Reinvention of Nature*. New York: Routledge, 1991.

Harpham, Geoffrey Galt. *The Ascetic Imperative in Culture and Criticism*. Chicago: University of Chicago Press, 1987.

———. "Asceticism and the Compensations of Art." In *Asceticism*, ed. Vincent L. Wimbush and Richard Valantasis, 357–68. New York: Oxford University Press, 1995.

Hart, Lynda. *Between the Body and the Flesh: Performing Sadomasochism*. Between Men—Between Women: Lesbian and Gay Studies. New York: Columbia University Press, 1998.

Harvey, Paul B. "Mary the Egyptian: Sources and Purpose." Unpublished paper.

———. "Saints and Satyrs: Jerome the Scholar at Work." *Estratto da Athenaeum: Studi di Letteratura e Storia dell'Antichità* 86, no. 1 (1998): 35–56.

Harvey, Susan Ashbrook. "Sacred Bonding: Mothers and Daughters in Early Syriac Hagiography." *Journal of Early Christian Studies* 4, no. 1 (1996): 27–56.

———. "Why the Perfume Mattered: The Sinful Woman in Syriac Exegetical Tradition." In *In Dominico Eloquio/In Lordly Eloquence: Essays on Patristic Exegesis in Honor of Robert Louis Wilken*, ed. Paul M. Blowers, Angela Russel Christman, David G. Hunter, and Robin Darling Young, 69–89. Grand Rapids, Mich.: Eerdmans, 2002.

Heffernan, Thomas J. *Sacred Biography: Saints and Their Biographers in the Middle Ages.* New York: Oxford University Press, 1988.
Heinzelmann, Martin. "Neue Aspeckte der biographischen und hagiographischen Literatur in der lateinischen Welt (1.-6. Jahrhundert)." *Francia* 1 (1973): 27–44.
Hopwood, Keith. "'All That May Become a Man': The Bandit in the Ancient Novel." In *When Men Were Men: Masculinity, Power, and Identity in Classical Antiquity,* ed. Lin Foxhall and John Salmon, 195–204. London: Routledge, 1998.
Irigaray, Luce. *Speculum of the Other Woman.* 1974. Trans. Gillian C. Gill. Ithaca, N.Y.: Cornell University Press, 1985.
———. *This Sex Which Is Not One.* 1977. Trans. Catherine Porter and Carolyn Burke. Ithaca: Cornell University Press, 1985.
Jordan, Mark D. *The Ethics of Sex.* New Dimensions to Religious Ethics. Oxford: Blackwell Publishers, 2002.
Kech, Herbert. *Hagiographie als christliche Unterhaltungsliteratur: Studien zum Phänomen des Erbaulichen anhand der Mönchsviten des hl. Hieronymus.* Göppingen: Verlag Alfred Kümmerle, 1977.
Keller, Catherine. *Apocalypse Now and Then: A Feminist Guide to the End of the World.* Boston: Beacon Press, 1996.
Kelly, J. N. D. *Jerome: His Life, Writings and Controversies.* London: Duckworth, 1975.
Konstan, David. "How to Praise a Friend: St. Gregory of Nazianzus's Funeral Oration for St. Basil the Great." In *Greek Biography and Panegyric in Late Antiquity,* ed. Tomas Hägg and Philip Rousseau, 160–79. Berkeley: University of California Press, 2000.
Kouli, Maria. "Life of St. Mary of Egypt." In *Holy Women of Byzantium: Ten Saints' Lives in English Translation,* ed. Alice-Mary Talbot, 65–93. Washington, D.C.: Dumbarton Oaks Research Library and Collection, 1996.
Krueger, Derek. "Hagiography as Ascetic Practice in the Early Christian East." *Journal of Religion* 79 (1999): 216–32.
———. *Symeon the Holy Fool: Leontius's Life and the Late Antique City.* Transformation of the Classical Heritage. Berkeley: University of California Press, 1996.
———. "Typological Figuration in Theodoret of Cyrrhus's *Religious History* and the Art of Postbiblical Narrative." *Journal of Early Christian Studies* 5, no. 3 (1997): 393–419.
———. "Writing and the Liturgy of Memory in Gregory of Nyssa's *Life of Macrina.*" *Journal of Early Christian Studies* 8, no. 4 (2000): 483–510.
Kuefler, Mathew. *The Manly Eunuch: Masculinity, Gender Ambiguity, and Christian Ideology in Late Antiquity.* Chicago Series on Sexuality, History, and Society. Chicago: University of Chicago Press, 2001.
Lane, Christopher. *The Ruling Passion: British Colonial Allegory and the Paradox of Homosexual Desire.* Durham, N.C.: Duke University Press, 1995.
Leclerc, Pierre. "Antoine et Paul: Métamorphose d'un héros." In *Jérôme entre l'occident et l'orient,* ed. Yves-Marie Duval, 257–65. Paris: Études Augustiniennes, 1988.
Lionnet, Francoise. *Autobiographical Voices: Race, Gender, Self-Portraiture.* Ithaca, N.Y.: Cornell University Press, 1989.

Loraux, Nicole. *The Invention of Athens: The Funeral Oration in the Classical City.* Trans. Alan Sheridan. Cambridge, Mass.: Harvard University Press, 1986.

Lorde, Audre. *Our Dead Behind Us.* New York: Norton, 1986.

Luftig, Victor. *Seeing Together: Friendship Between the Sexes in English Writing, from Mill to Woolf.* Stanford, Calif.: Stanford University Press, 1993.

MacCormack, Sabine. *The Shadows of Poetry: Vergil in the Mind of Augustine.* Transformation of the Classical Heritage. Berkeley: University of California Press, 1998.

MacDonald, Dennis Ronald. *The Legend and the Apostle: The Battle for Paul in Story and Canon.* Philadelphia: Westminster Press, 1983.

Macey, David. *The Lives of Michel Foucault.* London: Hutchinson, 1993.

MacKendrick, Karmen. *Counterpleasures.* SUNY Series in Postmodern Culture. Albany: State University of New York Press, 1999.

Maraval, Pierre. *Grégoire de Nyssa: Vie de Sainte Macrine.* Sources Chrétiennes 178. Paris: Éditions du Cerf, 1971.

———. "La *Vie de sainte Macrine* de Grégoire de Nysse: continuité et nouveauté d'un genre littéraire." In *Du héros païen au saint chrétien,* ed. Gérard Freyburger and Laurent Pernot, 133–38. Paris: Institut d'Études Augustiniennes, 1997.

May, Stephen. *Stardust and Ashes: Science Fiction in Christian Perspective.* London: Society for Promoting Christian Knowledge, 1998.

McClintock, Anne. *Imperial Leather: Race, Gender, and Sexuality in the Colonial Contest.* New York: Routledge, 1995.

McGinn, Thomas A. J. *Prostitution, Sexuality, and the Law in Ancient Rome.* New York: Oxford University Press, 1998.

Meredith, Anthony. "A Comparison Between the *Vita Sanctae Macrinae* of Gregory of Nyssa, the *Vita Plotini* of Porphyry, and the *De Vita Pythagorica* of Iamblichus." In *The Biographical Works of Gregory of Nyssa,* ed. Andreas Spira, 181–95. Philadelphia: Philadelphia Patristic Foundation, 1984.

Mette, Hans Joachim. "Curiositas." In *Festschrift Bruno Snell zum 60. Geburtstag,* 227–35. Munich: Beck, 1956.

Miles, Margaret R. *Desire and Delight: A New Reading of Augustine's Confessions.* New York: Crossroad, 1992.

Miller, James. *The Passion of Michel Foucault.* New York: Simon and Schuster, 1993.

Miller, Jane. *Seductions: Studies in Reading and Culture.* Cambridge, Mass.: Harvard University Press, 1991.

Miller, Patricia Cox. "The Blazing Body: Ascetic Desire in Jerome's Letter to Eustochium." *Journal of Early Christian Studies* 1, no. 1 (1993): 21–45.

———. *Dreams in Late Antiquity: Studies in the Imagination of a Culture.* Princeton, N.J.: Princeton University Press, 1994.

———. "Is There a Harlot in This Text? Asceticism and the Grotesque." *Journal of Medieval and Early Modern Studies* 33, no. 3 (2003).

———. "Jerome's Centaur: A Hyper-Icon of the Desert." *Journal of Early Christian Studies* 4, no. 2 (1996): 209–33.

Momigliano, Arnaldo. "The *Life of St. Macrina* by Gregory of Nyssa." In *On Pagans, Jews, and Christians,* 333–47. Middletown, Conn.: Wesleyan University Press, 1987.

Nancy, Jean-Luc. *The Inoperative Community.* Ed. Peter Connor, trans. Peter Connor, Lisa Garbus, Michael Holland, and Simona Sawhney. Theory and History of Literature 76. Minneapolis: University of Minnesota Press, 1991.
Palumbo, Donald. *Erotic Universe: Sexuality and Fantastic Literature.* New York: Greenwood Press, 1986.
Patlagean, Evelyne. "L'histoire de la femme déguisée en moine et l'évolution de la sainteté féminine à Byzance." *Studi medievali* 17 (1976): 597–623.
Pavloskis, Zoja. "The *Life of St. Pelagia the Harlot*: Hagiographic Adaptation of Pagan Romance." *Classical Folia* 30 (1976): 138–49.
Perkins, Judith. *The Suffering Self: Pain and Narrative Representation in the Early Christian Era.* London: Routledge, 1995.
Plant, Sadie. "Baudrillard's Woman: The Eve of Seduction." In *Forget Baudrillard?* ed. Chris Rojek and Bryan S. Turner, 88–106. London: Routledge, 1993.
Plesch, Julius. *Die Originalität und literarische Form der Mönchsbiographien des hl. Hieronymus.* Munich: Wolf and Sohn, 1910.
Pratt, Mary Louise. *Imperial Eyes: Travel Writing and Transculturation.* London: Routledge, 1992.
Rebenich, Stefan. *Hieronymus und sein Kreis: Prosopographische und sozialgeschichtliche Untersuchungen.* Stuttgart: Franz Steiner Verlag, 1992.
Rich, Adrienne. *Diving into the Wreck: Poems 1971–1972.* New York: Norton, 1973.
Roberts, Robin. *A New Species: Gender and Science in Science Fiction.* Urbana: University of Illinois Press, 1993.
Robins, William. "Romance and Renunciation at the Turn of the Fifth Century." *Journal of Early Christian Studies* 8, no. 4 (2000): 531–57.
Salisbury, Joyce E. *Church Fathers, Independent Virgins.* London: Verso, 1991.
Satlow, Michael L. *Jewish Marriage in Antiquity.* Princeton, N.J.: Princeton University Press, 2001.
Scarry, Elaine. *The Body in Pain: The Making and Unmaking of the World.* New York: Oxford University Press, 1985.
Schmidt, Victor. "Reaktionen auf das Christentum in den Metamorphosen des Apuleius." *Vigiliae Christianae* 51, no. 1 (1997): 51–71.
Scourfield, J. H. D. *Consoling Heliodorus: A Commentary on Jerome, Letter 60.* Oxford: Clarendon Press, 1993.
Shanzer, Danuta. "Latent Narrative Patterns, Allegorical Choices, and Literary Unity in Augustine's *Confessions.*" *Vigiliae Christianae* 46, no. 1 (1992): 40–56.
Shaw, Brent D. "Body/Power/Identity: Passions of the Martyrs." *Journal of Early Christian Studies* 4, no. 3 (1996): 269–312.
Shaw, Teresa M. *The Burden of the Flesh: Fasting and Sexuality in Early Christianity.* Minneapolis: Fortress Press, 1998.
Stancliffe, Clare. *St. Martin and His Hagiographer: History and Miracle in Sulpicius Severus.* Oxford: Clarendon Press, 1983.
Starnes, Colin. *Augustine's Conversion: A Guide to the Argument of Confessions I–IX.* Waterloo, Ontario: Wilfrid Laurier University Press, 1990.
Stoler, Ann Laura. *Race and the Education of Desire: Foucault's History of Sexuality and the Colonial Order of Things.* Durham, N.C.: Duke University Press, 1995.

Swain, Simon. *Hellenism and Empire: Language, Classicism, and Power in the Greek World, AD 50–250*. Oxford: Clarendon Press, 1996.
Vaage, Leif E. and Vincent L. Wimbush, eds. *Asceticism and the New Testament*. New York: Routledge, 1999.
Van Dam, Raymond. *Leadership and Community in Late Antique Gaul*. Berkeley: University of California Press, 1985.
Vernon, Mark. "Postscript: 'I Am Not What I Am'—Foucault, Christian Asceticism, and a 'Way Out' of Sexuality." In *Religion and Culture: Michel Foucault*, ed. Jeremy R. Carrette, 199–209. New York: Routledge, 1999.
Vessey, Mark. "From *Cursus* to *Ductus*: Figures of Writing in Western Late Antiquity (Augustine, Jerome, Cassiodorus, Bede)." In *European Literary Careers: The Author from Antiquity to the Renaissance*, ed. Patrick Cheney and Frederick A. De Armas, 47–114. Toronto: University of Toronto Press, 2002.
———. "Jerome and Rufinus." In *Cambridge History of Early Christian Literature*, ed. Frances M. Young, Andrew Louth, and Lewis Ayers. Cambridge: Cambridge University Press, forthcoming.
Waddell, Helen. *The Desert Fathers*. Ann Arbor: University of Michigan Press, 1936.
Ward, Benedicta. *Harlots of the Desert: A Study of Repentance in Early Monastic Sources*. Kalamazoo, Mich.: Cistercian Publications, 1978.
Williams, Linda. "A Provoking Agent: The Pornography and Performance Art of Annie Sprinkle." In *Dirty Looks: Women, Pornography, Power*, ed. Pamela Church Gibson and Roma Gibson, 176–91. London: British Film Institute, 1993.
Wimbush, Vincent L. and Richard Valantasis, eds. *Asceticism*. Oxford: Oxford University Press, 1995.
Winkler, John J. *Auctor and Actor: A Narratological Reading of Apuleius's The Golden Ass*. Berkeley: University of California Press, 1985.
Wolmark, Jenny. *Aliens and Others: Science Fiction, Feminism, and Postmodernism*. Iowa City: University of Iowa Press, 1994.
Woolf, Greg. "Becoming Roman, Staying Greek: Culture, Identity and the Civilizing Process in the Roman East." *Proceedings of the Cambridge Philological Society* 40 (1994): 116–43.
Wyschogrod, Edith. *Saints and Postmodernism: Revisioning Moral Philosophy*. Religion and Postmodernism. Chicago: University of Chicago Press, 1990.
Yanney, Rodolph. "The Sins of Saint Monica." *Coptic Church Review* 19, no. 3 (1998): 75–82.
Young, Robert J. C. *Colonial Desire: Hybridity in Theory, Culture, and Race*. London: Routledge, 1995.
Ziolkowski, Eric J. "St. Augustine: Aeneas' Antitype, Monica's Boy." *Literature & Theology* 9, no. 1 (1995): 11–23.

Index

Adamik, T., 174n33
Adams, J. N., 174n34
Alexandre, Monique, 180n14
Althaus-Reid, Marcella, 15, 17, 169n76, 84–85
Ambrose. See *On Virgins* (Ambrose)
Anson, John, 195n42
Antony: in Augustine's *Confessions*, 84; in Jerome's *Life of Hilarion*, 40–44, 63; in Jerome's *Life of Paul*, 24, 28–32, 51, 106, 147, 149, 153. See also *Life of Antony* (Athanasius)
Apuleius. See *Golden Ass* (Apuleius)
Athanasius, 22–23, 31, 39. See also *Life of Antony* (Athanasius)
Augustine, 4, 87, 89–90, 165n15, 165–66n20. See also *Confessions* (Augustine)
Autobiography: and female biography, 13, 60; and the (im)possibility of female autobiography, 86–91; in Augustine's *Confessions*, 77–81; in Gregory of Nyssa's *Life of Macrina*, 70–71; in Jerome's Epistle 22, 19, 170n1; in Jerome's Epistle 108, 69; in Sulpicius Severus's *Life of Martin*, 107

Babut, E.-Ch., 92, 186n2
Bakhtin, Mikhail, 109, 170n89, 190n36
Bataille, Georges, 1, 6–9, 15–16, 159, 167nn34–35, 50, 168nn69, 72, 169nn80–83, 197n79
Baudrillard, Jean, 4, 13, 15–16, 128, 131, 147, 156–59, 165n17, 169nn78–79, 193n17, 197nn61–66, 70, 76–78, 80
Bernauer, James, 163n3, 166–67n30, 167n47
Bersani, Leo, 12, 14, 19, 33, 46–47, 50, 168nn68–69, 176nn50, 52–53, 178nn78–83, 85–86, 88
Bhabha, Homi, 13, 122–26, 169n73, 191n43
Bisexuality, 39
Blaesilla, 61, 88–89
Blanchot, Maurice, 6, 87, 186n74, 187n6
Bowersock, G. W., 179n8

Boyarin, Daniel, 164n6, 165n17, 166n24, 188–89n20, 193n21
Brakke, David, 191n47
Brides of Christ: as contrasted with holy harlots, 158; as female saints, 59; as virgin martyrs, 53–54; in Augustine's *Confessions*, 85–86; in Gregory of Nyssa's *Life of Macrina*, 72–75; in Jerome's Epistle 108, 64, 67; in *Life of Pelagia*, 142–43
Brock, Sebastian, 130, 135, 192nn1–2, 193nn13, 23, 195n41
Brown, Peter, 83, 164n6, 165n15, 185n68
Burrus, Virginia, 168n64, 177n58, 178n87, 179n4, 183n49, 187n8, 190n39
Butler, Judith, 4–5, 165n18, 166n21, 187n6
Bynum, Caroline Walker, 195n42

Carrette, Jeremy, 8–9, 166–67n30, 167nn41–43, 45–49
Castelli, Elizabeth, 166n24
Cixous, Hélène, 60, 76, 178n77
Clark, Elizabeth, 164n6, 177n55, 179n10, 180–81n18, 182n32, 183n42, 184n54
Cloaks, 2, 31–32, 40, 44, 51, 75, 96–98, 102, 116, 122, 143, 149, 154, 175n48
Cloke, Gillian, 195n42
Coleiro, E., 20–21, 171nn8, 10–16, 176n50
Confessions (Augustine), 10, 12, 76–86, 96, 129
Coon, Lynda, 64, 129–30, 155, 179n10, 182n30, 192nn4, 8–9, 192–93n10, 193nn11–12, 195n42, 195–96n47, 196nn49–50, 52, 54, 56, 58, 59
Cooper, Kate, 163n4, 164n6
Countereroticism, 3, 13–14, 16, 160–62, 163–64n5
Counterpleasures, 3, 9, 10, 11, 163–64n5
Courtesans. *See* Harlots
Coyle, Kevin, 186n71

Davidson, Arnold, 4, 165n19, 165–66n20
Davis, Stephen, 194–95n39, 195nn42, 45

Index

Death: and ascetic practice, 4; and seduction, 158; and testimonial literature, 13, 86–88; and women's Lives, 12–13, 53–60; of God, 6; of Hilarion, 44–45, 52; of language, 7; of Macrina, 71–76; of Martin, 91, 103, 105–9, 121; of Mary of Egypt, 153–54; of Monica, 77, 82, 85; of Paul the Hermit, 30–32, 51; of Paula, 67–68; of Pelagia, 144–46; of the subject, 14–15. *See also* Martyrdom; Sacrifice

Derrida, Jacques, 13, 86–88, 103, 185n67, 186nn75–78, 81, 187n6

Dialogues (Sulpicius Severus), 92, 109–22

Dreams, 28, 71–72, 75, 90, 96, 106, 109, 134, 140

Driver, Steven, 182n31

Duval, Yves-Marie, 54, 56, 172–73n23, 179n2

Elm, Susanna, 194n37

Epistle 1 (Jerome), 54–56, 58–59

Epistles 1–3 (Sulpicius Severus), 92, 103–9, 115–16

Epistle 22 (Jerome), 19–20, 170n1, 172n21

Epistle 108 (Jerome), 12, 53, 54, 57, 60–70, 73, 106, 179n10

Eribon, Didier, 167n37

Eunuchs, 137, 143–46, 194–95n39

Eustochium, 19–20, 22, 53, 57, 60, 64, 67–68, 73

Evagrius, Latin translator of the *Life of Antony*, 12, 54, 172nn18–19

Felman, Shoshana, 13, 76, 86–87, 184nn50–51, 186nn79–80

Feminine subjectivity, 4, 12–13, 56–60, 130–32, 161; and autobiography, 13, 86–90; and hyperfemininity, 13, 131, 146, 155; and martyrdom, 12, 53–56; and seduction, 155–59; and virilization, 58–59, 70, 131, 138, 143–46, 149, 183n37; in Augustine's *Confessions*, 76–86; in Gregory of Nyssa's *Life of Macrina*, 69–76; in Jerome's Epistle 108, 60–69; in Jerome's Lives of men, 27, 49–52; in *Life of Mary, Niece of Abraham*, 132–37; in *Life of Pelagia*, 137–46; in Sophronius's *Life of Mary of Egypt*, 147–55. *See also* Gender; Women

Fontaine, Jacques, 54, 92, 96, 108, 172–73n23, 179n3, 186–87n3, 187n4, 188nn16–17, 188–89n20, 189nn21–26, 28–30, 189–90n31, 190nn33–34, 38

Foucault, Michel, 2–9, 11, 12, 13, 18, 162, 163nn1–4, 8, 165nn10–16, 165–66n20, 166nn22–25, 27–29, 166–67n30, 167nn31–33, 42, 47, 49, 170n90

Fraade, Steven, 164n6

Francis, James, 164n6

Frank, Georgia, 74, 76, 182nn27–29, 183nn35, 44–45, 48

Fuhrman, Manfred, 38, 171n16, 172n22, 174n31, 176n54, 177nn58–59, 62, 64, 69, 71–72, 178nn73, 76

Gallop, Jane, 132, 194n27, 197n76

Garber, Marjorie, 39, 137, 145–46, 195n43

Gender, 13, 59–60, 130, 161; colonized, 118, 125, 130; queered, 7, 9, 14; reversible, 13, 27, 76; transgressed, 144–46, 155. *See also* Feminine subjectivity; Masculine subjectivity

Giannarelli, Elena, 58–59, 180n16, 181n19, 182n24, 183nn36, 43

Golden Ass (Apuleius), 79–82, 84, 173n26, 188–89n20

Goldhill, Simon, 191n45

Gorgonia, 59, 181–82n22

Grace, Victoria, 197n76

Gregory of Nazianzus, 59, 181–82n22

Gregory of Nyssa, 12, 82, 87. See also *Life of Macrina* (Gregory of Nyssa)

Hägg, Tomas, 180n13, 181n21

Halperin, David, 7–8, 164–65n8, 167nn36–39, 42, 44

Haraway, Donna, 91, 126–27, 187n10, 192nn53–55

Harlots, 13, 25–28, 30, 128–59

Harpham, Geoffrey Galt, 10–11, 12, 24–25, 168nn57–63, 65, 172n20, 175n45

Hart, Lynda, 12, 53, 87, 93, 94, 125–26, 169n73, 178nn86, 88, 186n73, 187nn6–7, 188n12, 192nn49–50

Harvey, Paul, 173n25, 174n41, 176n50, 177nn56, 60, 192n3, 196n57

Harvey, Susan Ashbrook, 130, 135, 182n23, 192nn1–2, 192–93n10, 193nn13, 23, 195n41, 196n55

Heffernan, Thomas, 169n87

Heinzelmann, Martin, 181n20

Heterosexuality, 3, 6, 17

Hilarion. See *Life of Hilarion* (Jerome)

History of sexuality, 1–12, 18, 163n3
Holy fools, 135–37
Homoeroticism, male, 30–32, 81, 93, 102–3, 106–7, 111–12, 118, 125, 161, 175n45. See also Queer
Homosexuality, 6, 50
Hopwood, Keith, 188–89n20

Irigaray, Luce, 49, 125, 132, 156–58, 169n73, 178n84, 193n26, 197nn68–69, 71–76

Jerome, 11–12, 13, 19–70, 82, 87–88, 91, 106, 113–14, 119, 126, 144, 161. See also Epistle 1; Epistle 22; Epistle 108; Life of Hilarion; Life of Paul; On Famous Men (Jerome); On the Captive Monk
Jordan, Mark, 3, 164n7, 165n9, 169n86

Kech, 171nn9, 16, 173n30, 174nn35, 40, 175n47, 177nn57, 61, 72, 178nn74–75
Keller, Catherine, 163–64n5
Kelly, J. N. D., 173n29
Konstan, David, 181n19
Kouli, Maria, 192n3
Krueger, Derek, 71, 136, 177n65, 180nn12–13, 183nn34, 38, 41, 188nn13–14, 189n22, 189–90n31, 193nn24–25, 196n53
Kuefler, Mathew, 188n18, 194–95n39

Lane, Christopher, 190n40
Leclerc, Pierre, 173nn27–28, 175n43
Life of Antony (Athanasius), 10, 11, 22–23, 26, 37, 40–41, 43, 54, 91, 168n63
Life of Hilarion (Jerome), 12, 20, 22–23, 39–45, 47–49, 52, 54, 62–63, 91, 114
Life of Macrina (Gregory of Nyssa), 12, 57–60, 69–76
Life of Martin (Sulpicius Severus), 13, 91–103, 106, 115–16
Life of Mary, Niece of Abraham, 13, 128, 132–37, 155
Life of Mary of Egypt (Sophronius), 13, 128, 132, 147–56
Life of Paul (Jerome), 11, 13, 20, 22–33, 37, 40, 42, 47–51, 53, 54, 56, 91, 106, 114, 149–50, 153–55
Life of Pelagia, 13, 128, 132, 137–46, 155–56
Lionnet, Francoise, 184nn53, 55, 184–85n59
Lions, 32, 37, 47, 51, 114, 154–55, 176n49
Loraux, Nicole, 181n20

Lorde, Audre, 69
Luftig, Victor, 33

MacCormack, Sabine, 186nn69–70
MacDonald, Dennis, 176n49
Macey, David, 167n37
MacKendrick, Karmen, 9–10, 12, 14–15, 53, 163–64n5, 167nn51–54, 168nn55–56, 67, 169n77, 179n5, 182n25, 182–83n33, 183n39, 186n82
Macrina, 89, 108–9. See also Life of Macrina
Malchus. See On the Captive Monk (Jerome)
Mallarmé, Stéphane, 46–47
Maraval, Pierre, 58, 180nn11, 14
Marriage, 2–3, 31–39, 48, 83–84, 155, 163n4, 177n55. See also Bride of Christ
Martin of Tours. See Dialogues; Epistles 1–3; Life of Martin (Sulpicius Severus)
Martyrdom: and female hagiography, 56–60, 68, 71–75, 87, 90, 158; and male hagiography, 25–29, 35–36, 39, 53, 92, 99–100, 103–4, 106, 173n27; and sadomasochism, 8; virgin martyrs, 35–36, 53–56, 179n7. See also Brides of Christ; Death; Martyrology; Masochism; Sacrifice
Martyrology, 12, 18, 22, 56–57. See also Martyrdom
Mary, Niece of Abraham, 129–30, 140, 147, 156. See also Life of Mary, Niece of Abraham
Mary of Egypt, 129, 156. See also Life of Mary of Egypt (Sophronius)
Masculine subjectivity, 11–13, 161; and autobiography, 86–88, 107; and feminization, 11, 19–20, 26–27, 31–32, 68, 73, 91; and hypermasculinity, 13, 28–29, 91, 93, 125–26, 131; and martyrdom, 25–27, 55–56; in Jerome's male Lives, 24–45; in Lives of women, 59–60, 68–69, 73, 75–76, 85–86; in Sulpicius Severus's Martinian writings, 94–122. See also Gender
Masochism, 9, 11–12, 53, 60, 168n69, 179n5. See also Martyrdom; Sacrifice; Sadomasochism
May, Stephen, 91, 187nn7, 10
McClintock, Anne, 13, 122–25, 190n40, 191nn41, 48
McGinn, Thomas, 192n5
Meredith, Anthony, 58, 180n15
Metamorphoses. See Golden Ass (Apuleius)
Mette, Hans Joachim, 185n63

Index

Miles, Margaret, 184n57
Miller, James, 8, 167n37
Miller, Jane, 128, 131, 133, 193nn16, 19
Miller, Patricia Cox, 28–30, 72, 144–46, 149, 168n63, 170nn2–3, 171nn5, 7, 174nn37–39, 175nn42, 46, 176n50, 183nn40, 46–47, 192n5, 193n15, 194nn29, 38, 195nn40, 44, 46, 196n51
Momigliano, Arnaldo, 180n17, 181n19
Monica, 12, 89–90. See also *Confessions*
Mysticism, 6, 8, 16

Nancy, Jean-Luc, 14–15, 168n70, 169n74, 176n53
Negative theology, 6, 16
Novel. See Romance

On Famous Men (Jerome), 21–23
On the Captive Monk (Jerome), 12, 20, 22–23, 33–39, 48, 49, 51–52, 54
On the Soul and Resurrection (Gregory of Nyssa), 72, 76
On Virgins (Ambrose), 53, 134, 174n31
Origenism, 65–66, 68, 113, 183n37

Palumbo, Donald, 187n9
Patlagean, Evelyne, 194–95n39, 195n42
Paul the Hermit, 39, 147. See also *Life of Paul* (Jerome)
Paula, 12, 22, 34, 89, 106, 109, 144, 177n60. See also Epistle 108 (Jerome)
Pavloskis, Zoja, 194nn28, 30, 32–33, 36
Pederasty, 30, 161, 175n43
Pelagia of Antioch, 129–30, 147, 149, 156. See also *Life of Pelagia*
Perkins, Judith, 179n7
Pilgrimage, 63, 147, 151, 155, 182n28
Plant, Sadie, 157, 197nn67, 76
Plesch, Julius, 171n9
Postcolonial theory, 18, 110, 122–26
Pratt, Mary Louise, 191nn42, 44
Prostitutes. See Harlots

Queer: definitions, 168n66, 173n24; genres, 18, 24, 91, 154; pleasures, 9; marriages, 36, 38–39; subjectivities and sexualities, 7, 12–14, 32, 50, 70, 93, 125. See also Gender; Homoeroticism.

Rebenich, Stefan, 170n1
Rich, Adrienne, 76

Roberts, Robin, 187n9
Robins, William, 172n22, 176n54
Romance, 18; and Jerome's male Lives, 12, 20–24, 32, 34, 38–39, 48, 93, 154, 171nn9, 16, 176n50; and Lives of women, 54, 56, 59, 70, 138, 141, 154, 180–81n18
Rousseau, Philip, 180n13, 181n21

Sacrifice, 5, 7, 14–18, 60, 147, 155
Sade, Marquis de, 6, 8
Sadomasochism (S/M), 8–10, 13, 17, 117, 123, 125–26, 169n86, 179n5. See also Masochism
Salisbury, Joyce, 194n35, 195n42
Satlow, Michael, 164n6
Scars, 58, 59, 68, 74, 76, 89
Scarry, Elaine, 14–15, 168n71, 169n75, 179n7
Schmidt, Victor, 185n64
Scourfield, J. H. D., 57, 179n9
Scripture, 20, 78–79, 96, 98–99, 104–5, 129–30, 138, 149, 153
Seduction, 9–10, 13, 15–16, 128, 131–37, 139–42, 146, 150–51, 155–60
Shanzer, Danuta, 78–79, 184n58, 185nn60, 65
Shaw, Brent, 55, 174nn31, 33, 179n6
Shaw, Teresa, 183n37
Sophronius. See *Life of Mary of Egypt*
Sprinkle, Annie, 155
Stancliffe, Clare, 92, 97, 186n1, 187nn5, 8, 188nn11, 18, 19, 189n27, 190nn35, 37
Starnes, Colin, 185n65
Stoler, Ann Laura, 190n40
Sublimation, 12, 17, 19–20, 24, 33–34, 46–49, 53–54, 176n53
Sulpicius Severus, 13, 161. See also *Dialogues*; Epistles 1–3; *Life of Martin* (Sulpicius Severus)
Swain, Simon, 191n45

Tongue biters, 25–27, 53, 174nn31–33, 179n1
Transvestites, 16, 17, 131, 137, 144–46, 156

Vaage, Leif, 164n6
Valantasis, Richard, 164n6
Van Dam, Raymond, 188n11, 188–89n20
Vernon, Mark, 8, 166n26, 167n40
Vessey, Mark, 172n17

Waddell, Helen, 195–96n47
Ward, Benedicta, 129, 139, 192nn6–7, 193nn18, 20, 22, 194nn32, 34, 195n42, 195–96n47

Williams, Linda, 196–97n60
Wimbush, Vincent, 164n6
Winkler, John, 80–81, 185nn61–62
Wisdom, 73, 75, 78–80, 82, 85–86
Wolmark, Jenny, 187n9, 192nn51–52
Women: in Jerome's *Life of Hilarion*, 44–45, 49–52; in Jerome's *On the Captive Monk*, 34–39, 48, 51–52; in Sulpicius Severus's Epistle 3 and *Dialogues*, 107–8, 117–20, 125. *See also* Feminine subjectivity; Blaesilla; Eustochium; Gorgonia; Macrina; Mary, niece of Abraham; Mary of Egypt; Monica; Paula; Pelagia
Woolf, Greg, 191n46
Wychogrod, Edith, 170n88

Yanney, Rodolph, 185n67
Young, Robert, 190n40, 191n42

Ziolkowski, Eric, 185n66

Acknowledgments

I am deeply grateful to Dean Maxine Beach, my colleagues in the Theological School and Caspersen School of Graduate Studies of Drew University, and the Association of Theological Schools Lilly Theological Research Grant: their combined assistance enabled me to take a break from teaching and committee duties during fall 2001 in order to complete a draft of this book. I thank Elizabeth Clark, Rebecca Lyman, Patricia Cox Miller, and Philip Rousseau for their support of my project during the process of grant applications, and Michael Nausner and Nicole Roskos for their willingness to stand in for me in the classroom and for the dedication and expertise they brought to the pedagogical task.

I also owe much to my students. Every fall I teach a required course in ancient and medieval church history for (primarily but not exclusively Protestant) Master of Divinity students; their consistent enthusiasm for hagiographical writings has surprised and delighted me year after year and is in no small part responsible for my own continued fascination with such texts. The members of my hagiography seminar in spring 1999 helped me focus the agenda for this book and taught me much about how to read for sex in the Lives of Saints. Also crucial was an earlier interdisciplinary seminar team-taught with Dorothy Austin on "Writing Gay and Lesbian Lives." Repeated guest lectures in Otto Maduro's "Gay and Lesbian Liberation Theologies" seminars have provided opportunities for me to work through my thoughts regarding the implications of Foucault's *History of Sexuality* for the study of ancient Christian eroticism. Invitations to speak at Theological and Religious Studies graduate colloquia allowed me further to test the formulation of my arguments.

I was able to present material from the first two chapters at the American Society of Church History, the North American Patristics Society, Princeton University, Syracuse University, the Graduate Theological Union, and the University of California at Berkeley. In each case, I profited from the responses of careful listeners. A slightly earlier draft of Chapter 1 appeared as "Queer Lives of Saints: Jerome's Hagiography," *Journal of the History of Sexuality* 10 (2001) 442–479. Reprinted by permission of the University of

Texas Press. The section "Confessing Monica," in Chapter 2, was originally drafted as part of an essay by the same name, coauthored with Catherine Keller, in *Feminist Interpretations of Augustine*, edited by Judith Chelius Stark, Rereading the Canon (University Park: Pennsylvania State University Press, forthcoming).

This text was initially submitted for publication with Stanford University Press, and I benefited greatly from the helpfully incisive critique of an anonymous reader for that press, as well as from the expert guidance and generous—indeed courageous—support of my editor, Helen Tartar. I am very pleased indeed to be working now with the University of Pennsylvania Press and am particularly grateful to my "new" editor, Jerry Singerman, whose energy, enthusiasm, and insight have graced both this book and the "Divinations" series in which it is lodged with the hope of new beginnings.

Scholarly writing is for me an intensely pleasurable, as well as a painfully difficult, practice. The sensual joy—*jouissance*—that has lured and sustained me through the writing of this book has derived not only from the excitement of my encounter with the hagiographical texts but also from the stimulation of a number of extraordinarily rich intellectual friendships. Sharon Betcher and Karen Torjesen have always been willing to lend a sympathetic ear to even my most inarticulate mutterings. David Brakke, Elizabeth Castelli, Marion Grau, Robert Gregg, Paul Harvey, Susan Ashbrook Harvey, Derek Krueger, Patricia Cox Miller, and Eric Thurman have offered insightful readings of portions (or in some cases all) of the text. In particular, Daniel Boyarin, Catherine Keller, Karmen MacKendrick, and Stephen Moore have challenged, encouraged, and improved my thinking and writing immeasurably. Their generosity as both scholars and friends has taught me much about saintly love.